75 Scrambles in
WASHINGTON

classic routes to the summits

75 Scrambles in
WASHINGTON

classic routes to the summits

PEGGY GOLDMAN

THE
MOUNTAINEERS
BOOKS

Published by
The Mountaineers Books
1001 SW Klickitat Way, Suite 201
Seattle, WA 98134

© 2001 by Peggy Goldman

First printing 2001, second printing 2003, third printing 2005

Published simultaneously in Great Britain by Cordee, 3a DeMontfort Street, Leicester, England, LE1 7HD

Manufactured in the United States of America

Project Editor: Julie Van Pelt
Editor: Erin Moore
Cover and Book Designer: Kristy L. Welch
Layout Artist: Kristy L. Welch
Mapmaker: Ben Pease
Photographers: John Roper, Cliff Leight, Mike Torok, Chris Weidner, Susan Alford, Jason Griffith, Dale Flynn

Cover photograph: *Ascending summit snow ridge of Mount Daniel* (Photo by Cliff Leight)
Frontispiece: *Alpine scrambler on Mount Daniel* (Photo by Cliff Leight)

Library of Congress Cataloging-in-Publication Data

Goldman, Peggy, 1949-
    75 scrambles in Washington : classic routes to the summits / Peggy Goldman.— 1st ed.
       p.   cm.
    Includes index.
    ISBN 0-89886-761-4 (pbk.)
    1. Alpine scrambling—Washington (State)—Guidebooks. 2. Washington (State—Guidebooks. I. Title: Seventy-five scrambles in Washington.
II. Title.
  GV199.42.W2 G65 2001
  917.9704'44—dc21
                            00-013069

Table of Contents

Preface   10
Acknowledgments   12
Introduction   13

NORTH CASCADES
1. Church Mountain   45
2. Yellow Aster Butte   47
3. Hannegan Peak   49
4. Hadley Peak   51
5. Ruby Mountain   53
6. North Gardner Mountain and Gardner Mountain   56
7. Hock Mountain   58
8. Snowking Mountain   61

PASAYTEN WILDERNESS
9. Osceola Peak, Mount Lago, and Mount Carru   64
10. Ptarmigan Peak   68
11. Remmel Mountain   71
12. Big Craggy Peak and West Craggy Peak   73
13. Pass Butte and Lost Peak   76
14. Monument Peak and Lake Mountain   79
15. Robinson Mountain   82

LAKE CHELAN–SAWTOOTH WILDERNESS
16. Gilbert Mountain   84
17. Abernathy Peak   87
18. Hoodoo Peak   89
19. Sawtooth Ridge   91

GLACIER PEAK WILDERNESS
20. Fortress Mountain and Buck Mountain   97
21. Chiwawa Mountain   101
22. Mount Maude and Seven Fingered Jack   104
23. Entiat Crest   107
24. Carne Mountain   112

STEVENS PASS
25. Mount Index   115
26. Baring Mountain   117
27. Labyrinth Mountain   119
28. Mount Mastiff and Mount Howard   121
29. Dirtyface Peak   123

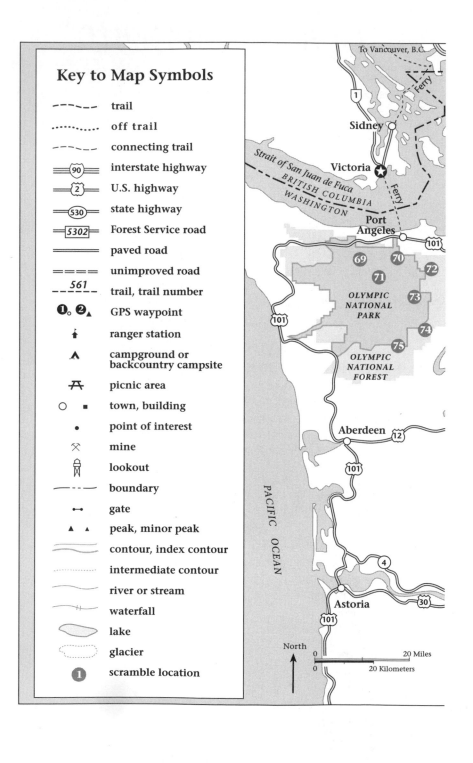

Key to Map Symbols

- – – – – – – trail
- ⋯⋯⋯⋯ off trail
- – – – – – connecting trail
- ═(90)═ interstate highway
- ═(2)═ U.S. highway
- ═(530)═ state highway
- ═5302═ Forest Service road
- ═══ paved road
- ════ unimproved road
- _561_ trail, trail number
- ❶○ ❷▲ GPS waypoint
- ⸸ ranger station
- ⋏ campground or backcountry campsite
- ⊼ picnic area
- ○ ▪ town, building
- • point of interest
- ⤬ mine
- ⌸ lookout
- —–·· — boundary
- ↦ gate
- ▲ ▲ peak, minor peak
- ⩰ contour, index contour
- ⋯⋯ intermediate contour
- ⌇ river or stream
- ⊢⊣ waterfall
- ⬯ lake
- ⬭ glacier
- ❶ scramble location

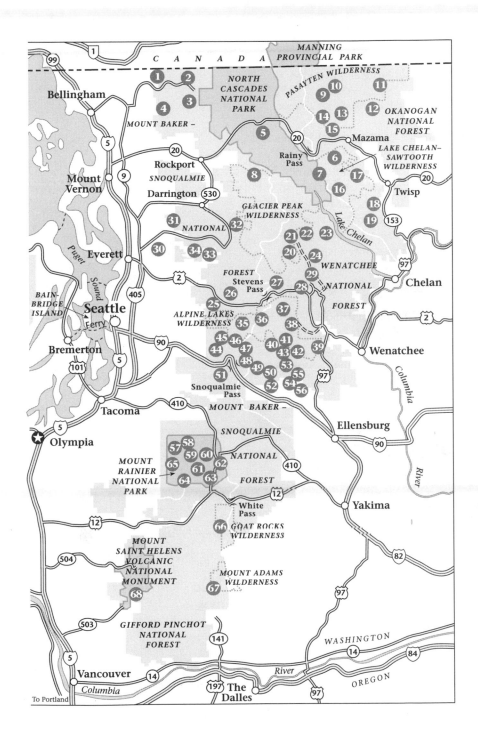

MONTE CRISTO
30. Mount Pilchuck   126
31. Three Fingers South Peak   128
32. Mount Pugh   130
33. Del Campo Peak   132
34. Sperry Peak and Vesper Peak   135

ALPINE LAKES WILDERNESS
35. Mount Daniel   138
36. Granite Mountain and Trico Mountain   140
37. Grindstone Mountain   143
38. Cashmere Mountain   145
39. Wedge Mountain   147
40. Colchuck Peak   150
41. Dragontail Peak   153
42. Enchantment Peak   156
43. Little Annapurna   158

SNOQUALMIE PASS
44. Kaleetan Peak   162
45. Mount Roosevelt   165
46. Snoqualmie Mountain and Guye Peak   167
47. Red Mountain   170
48. Kendall Peak   172
49. Alta Mountain   174
50. Hibox Mountain   176
51. Silver Peak   178

TEANAWAY
52. Mount Skookum and Jolly Mountain   181
53. Ingalls South Peak   183
54. Esmeralda Peaks   186
55. Bill Peak, Bean Peak, and Volcanic Neck   188
56. Koppen Mountain and Iron Peak   191

MOUNT RAINIER
57. First Mother Mountain and Castle Peak   193
58. Fay Peak, Mount Pleasant, and Hessong Rock   195
59. Echo Rock and Observation Rock   198
60. The Palisades and Marcus Peak   201
61. Goat Island Mountain   203
62. Naches Peak and Yakima Peak   205
63. Governors Ridge and Barrier Peak   207
64. Tatoosh Range Traverse   209
65. Mount Wow   212

SOUTH CASCADES

66. Mount Curtis Gilbert 214
67. Mount Adams 216
68. Mount Saint Helens 219

OLYMPIC MOUNTAINS

69. Boulder Peak, Everett Peak, and Mount Appleton 222
70. Mount Angeles 224
71. Bailey Range Traverse 227
72. Mount Townsend 231
73. Mount Elk Lick and Mount LaCrosse 234
74. The Brothers 237
75. Mount Ellinor 240

Appendix A: Scramble Statistics 242
Appendix B: Scramble by Season 245
Appendix C: Equipment Lists 246
Appendix D: Contact Information 247
Index 250

Preface

An enormous variety and diversity of terrain is the hallmark of the state of Washington and is what distinguishes the Cascade Range and the Olympic Mountains from other mountains in the United States. Mountaineering experiences range from a simple hike in old-growth rain forest to a highly technical and demanding climb over glaciers and vertical rock and ice. In between is a rank of mountaineering that has a special niche—it is called scrambling.

In contrast to hiking, scrambling involves off-trail travel, and navigation and routefinding skills, as well as the ability to move over moderate rock and snow. In contrast to climbing, scrambling occurs over easier terrain and generally lacks the need for ropes or the use of hardware for protection from a serious fall. Though exposed to the objective hazards of the mountain milieu, the scrambler is generally safer than the technical climber, and does not need to carry as much heavy equipment. Consequently, scrambling is a pursuit that can be executed by the average person with ordinary talent, skill, and courage.

Of the profusion of guidebooks covering the state of Washington, none specifically targets the realm of scrambles. The purpose of this book is to help fill that niche. Whether easy or strenuous, short or multiday, all the scrambles described here have a common theme: travel on foot with a goal of visiting a high point in mountainous country, and an objective of a visually appealing summit. This book is intended to help the reader decide where to go and which route to choose. *75 Scrambles in Washington* is not meant to be a comprehensive list of the "best" scramble peaks available: a subjective and impossible task. Instead, the selections present a potpourri of choices—something for everyone. Each scramble differs by location, type of terrain, and difficulty of travel. Enough options are supplied so that with forethought, a beginner can progress along the ranks to proficiency while developing skills and self-reliance. *75 Scrambles in Washington* is a book for people of all abilities with desire and motivation.

I have been constantly inspired by the fact that gender and age are irrelevant when it comes to scrambling. The first scrambling leader I had the great fortune to travel with was in his eighties and about as spry as anyone going up the mountain, as well as quicker to jump into a glissade on the descent. Women are excellent scramblers because of their endurance and ability to pace themselves and for the companionship and conversation they generally bring to the group. I first began scrambling when I reached my mid-forties, and I look forward to many decades of outings to come. Scrambling is an excellent aerobic pursuit that enhances endurance and strength. Not only does scrambling keep you young, it also improves your balance, mood, and perspective on life. You can't get any better than that!

As a physician, I am committed to the premise that scrambling is a healthy

Having fun on Monument Peak (Photo by John Roper)

and wholesome way to promote fitness and to ameliorate the aging process. Scrambling provides a sense of adventure, a freedom from the usual restrictions of the civilized world, a sense of accomplishment, a release of endorphins, and camaraderie. It satisfies the most basic human needs for contact with nature and spiritual renewal. However, the gift of journeying through the exquisite natural and wild realm of Washington is a gift that is also a responsibility. We must be accountable for sharing this realm considerately and with regard for others as well as for future generations.

When I first proposed writing this book nearly a decade ago, there was great opposition to dissemination of the information. Even today some members of the scrambling community believe that writing such a book will be detrimental to the lands themselves. In spite of that, it is clear that in this age of wilderness and world overpopulation that there is no keeping a secret. In the age of the computer and the Internet, it is impossible to turn back the clock and keep the public ignorant. The only reasonable approach is not to try to hide the places we love, but to manage the impact of use by educating people and by changing attitudes. The paradox is that to save the wilderness, it must be used. It is clear that, even though Washington enjoys a vibrant culture of preserving our alpine environment, the job is not done. We need to create a larger constituency and a stronger voice to protect the wildlands that we cherish from extinction. We need wilderness to nourish our souls, but we must also be responsible stewards and share our pursuit with others to sustain the health and well being of our community. We need to work together so that others too may join in the conservation of our local treasures.

Acknowledgments

I want to thank all those who contributed to this project information, photographs, reviews, suggestions, and advice. Writing this book has been a fascinating learning experience. To all who furnished information over the years, written or verbal, I thank you very much, especially my fellow scramblers in The Mountaineers. I got my start in the Alpine Scrambles Course of The Mountaineers, and I will always be extremely grateful for the kind guidance and support that I received while learning the skills and aspects of traveling safely in the mountains off the trail. The Mountaineers is an organization of volunteers who give to others. I sincerely hope that in a positive way this book will give something back to them from me.

I would like to specifically thank all those people who provided a special effort in producing this book. I wish especially to thank John Roper, who opened to me his extensive file of decades of photographing the peaks in Washington State. I also thank others who have shared some of their images: Cliff Leight, Mike Torok, Jason Griffith, Chris Weidner, Susan Alford, Dale Flynn, Steve Fellstrom, and Don Paulson. I thank the reviewers, Ron Chase, Mike Torok, and Steve Fellstrom, for their suggestions and comments. Laurence Smith volunteered for the lengthy job of proofreading. I particularly acknowledge Dale Flynn, who has contributed valuable technical advice and was a good person to bounce ideas against. I also am indebted to all the land management personnel who reviewed the draft and gave valuable comments. Last, I thank my husband, Jim Quade. His support and encouragement were essential in getting this project done.

A special acknowledgment is due to the Scrambling instructors, leaders and committee members of The Mountaineers. The Scrambling Committee pioneered the use of written route descriptions in their teaching program. I am deeply indebted to the instructors and leaders for their information as well as for corrections and comments. In some instances, I have drawn directly from route descriptions authored by my fellow Mountaineers scramble leaders. I express my own appreciation, and that of the scramblers who will follow in their footsteps, for their gracious willingness to more widely share their insights and information. In future editions, we will try to individually thank these trailblazers.

To those who find errors in this book, please let me know. Inaccuracies are bound to occur as conditions change. Moreover, written language is problematic when it comes to describing a visual or three-dimensional image. To all who use the information contained between these covers, please enjoy.

Good luck and happy scrambling.

Introduction

From mountain wisdom: Scrambling is what old climbers do, what young hikers do, and what anyone will do to have fun and visit the most beautiful places while keeping both feet on the ground.

WHAT IS SCRAMBLING?

Alpine scrambling is the use of skills for off-trail travel, often over snow and rock, with a summit as the destination. Glacier travel and the need for technical gear such as a rope, protection, or a belay over steep rock or ice are not part of the sport of scrambling. However, many backcountry skills are necessary for safe and efficient travel off the beaten track. Cross-country navigation skills are particularly important. Even those routes that follow maintained trails become scrambles when snow covered. After snowmelt, such trips are considered hikes rather than scrambles. When the difficulty of the terrain reaches a level requiring sustained use of hands for balance or a rope for protection, the trip is considered an alpine climb.

Whether a trip is a scramble or not is somewhat subjective. For this book all scrambles are primarily on class 2 terrain (involving the use of hands but not of rope). Only some routes have an occasional class 3 move or a limited section of class 3 scrambling (involving moderate exposure with frequent use of hands; a rope should be available). See How to Use This Guide, Difficulty, for a discussion of scramble ratings.

SCRAMBLING IN WASHINGTON

Washington is an infinitely varied and fascinating state with magnificent expanses of wilderness in close proximity to civilization. Two national parks, North Cascades and Olympic, are destinations for scramblers from around the world. But for those who live in or near Washington, many areas of the state yield countless treasures for endless exploration.

Many areas exhibit their own microclimates and geographic peculiarities. In general, the climate is drier east of the Cascade Crest. Convergence zones, where the climates of east and west meet, mark areas of higher than expected precipitation.

The Cascade Range is steeper and wetter than most other ranges in the lower United

Scrambling to the summit (Photo by Cliff Leight)

Rock scrambling in the North Cascades
(Photo by Chris Weidner)

States. Because Cascade peaks intercept storms sweeping in from the Pacific Ocean, they receive large amounts of rain and snow and luxuriant vegetation coats the western side of the range. Swarms of glaciers and snowfields accumulate on the higher peaks. In contrast, the eastern side of the state is desert and dense forests thin out to open timber in the huge Pasayten Wilderness in the northern part of the state adjacent to Canada.

Washington is also well known for its high volcanoes in the Cascade Range—Mount Baker, Mount Rainier, Mount Saint Helens, and Mount Adams. These peaks lie on an axis that transects the state from north to south. They are so immense that they create their own weather, which can envelop even their surrounding, satellite peaks.

The Olympic Mountains to the west are separated from the mainland of the state by the seawater expanse of Puget Sound. Their isolation has created a unique biosphere with indigenous plants and wildflowers. The Olympics are a microcosm of the whole state, with a "rain shadow" protected by the high mountains to the west and south.

The wet climate west of the Cascade Crest creates frustration for many scramblers who prefer drier weather, but the marine climate contributes to the formation of the most glaciated area of peaks in the lower United States. Although some areas are accessible only by extensive bushwhacking, there are also many fine and varied regions readily available to those with the skill, training, and motivation to travel to these outstanding alpine environments.

Washington State has a unique heritage in its local history and traditions of mountaineering. Many of the mountains were almost totally unexplored a century ago. The "mountain men" who prospected and settled the region roamed the ranges partly to hunt and fish, but partly because they loved the high country in the same sense as a modern climber or scrambler.

The Mountaineers, founded in 1906, is a non-profit outdoor activity and conservation club based in Seattle, Washington. The Mountaineers and other local organizations represent the strong community culture that greatly helps to sustain the environment and infrastructure that is required for alpine activities. These activities form a backbone for recreation in Washington State. The recreational culture of Washington supports strenuous activities for all age groups in a mountain outdoor arena.

The mountaineering tradition has also led to a strong system of roads and trails which provide easy access to almost every region within the state. The mountains are so close to the populated cities that in a single day a person can leave home, drive to a mountainous region, scramble to the top of an alpine peak in a wilderness setting, and return home in time to go to the opera. This variety of experience is possible in very few parts of the United States.

WHO SHOULD SCRAMBLE?

Although scrambling is inherently dangerous because of its location in the mountains, it is an activity available to almost anyone with the desire and the capability to use sound judgment and to learn the necessary skills. If you are just starting out it is best to join a program that sponsors scrambles that are directed by experienced leaders. But do not expect the leader to be your guide; you must be an active participant to learn the skills to become independent and safe on your own. An alternative is to find a mentor who will agree to train you in the skills you need. Don't be in a hurry. Each person has his or her own body type and personality type when it comes to risk aversion and desire to reach a summit. Find companions who are compatible and your trips will be physically and socially rewarding. It should be an aspiration for all scramblers to develop and hone their mountain skills continually. As those skills improve, your level of confidence will rise.

Enjoyment of the natural, alpine environment is part of the fabric of activities for people of all ages. Scrambling can be started at any time and continued to any age. Some families carry toddlers in backpacks on easy trips. Families, particularly those with teenagers, find scrambling a wholesome activity to enjoy together. Octogenarians are regularly seen on scrambles keeping up with the rest of the party, or even out in front, particularly if they have experienced decades of aerobic conditioning due to their scrambling habit. As people age, joints tend to ache, muscles lose their tone, and flexibility declines. Yet modern exercise physiology teaches us that much of the aging

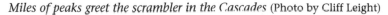

Miles of peaks greet the scrambler in the Cascades (Photo by Cliff Leight)

Scramblers enjoying Hibox summit (Photo by Mike Torok)

process is due to inactivity, and that a conditioned athlete can maintain nearly the capacity of a younger one with enough training and consistent effort. "Use it or lose it" is the rule. Scrambling is one of the most beneficial ways to maintain a youthful body and mind. The exercise is intensely aerobic, low impact, and both psychologically and spiritually rewarding.

Gender-related differences are even less of an issue in scrambling. The scrambling world is today a male-oriented domain, but this is partly due to the historic lack of female role models. Women and particularly younger women are no longer afraid to take on the challenge and can bear to get sweaty and dirty. Women in general can make a special gender-specific contribution to the party as the more conversational, conciliatory, and less macho members of the group.

Overall, scrambling is a great conditioner, burns excessive calories, provides for great camaraderie, and gives a sense of adventure and accomplishment for all who choose to try it.

SCRAMBLING FUNDAMENTALS

Many considerations and fundamental activities are important to the scrambler from conditioning to recommended scrambling skills, trip planning, navigation, and routefinding skills. The following are suggested tips and tools to use in starting, executing, and completing a scramble safely and successfully.

Conditioning

Alpine scrambles are strenuous aerobic activities, usually lasting from 6 to 12 hours. You will be carrying about 20 pounds on your back, moving at least several miles over uneven terrain, and gaining several thousand feet of elevation to reach the summit. You must be in reasonably good aerobic condition, know how to pace yourself, and have endurance for extended hours of exercise. Wide variations in aerobic power depend on the body's ability to use oxygen depending on age, gender, and training. You need to be in good physical condition so that you don't push yourself to the point of exhaustion.

Scrambling requires strength, endurance, coordination, balance, and psychological fortitude. Overall strength, with special attention to the upper body, is a prerequisite for many scrambles. Improving your functional strength and balance can help decrease injuries and enhance your enjoyment.

Aerobic power can be gained by strenuous physical activities such as jogging, swimming, bicycling, and climbing stairs or hiking. The activity should be prolonged enough to produce a sweat for at least 30 minutes, four times a week. Heart rate is a guiding factor for the intensity level of aerobic training.

However, the best exercise for scrambling is scrambling. The muscles used are fairly specific to elevation over uneven terrain, and therefore the best training is "just do it." A common measure for success on a scramble is to be able to hike up to the top of Mount Si, a local peak, hiking about 3800 feet in less than 2.5 hours. An evaluation by a physician before beginning strenuous activity may be advisable for people who fall into a high risk category for coronary artery disease or other diseases due to age, cigarette smoking, or family history.

Some people get into trouble by burning themselves out too soon. Remember that scrambles are all-day activities. The aerobic demands on your body for a 6- to 12-hour-long scramble are much different than with a short sprint. You need to learn to travel at about 60 percent of your maximum pace and replace food and water during the day to maintain a high level of energy. The better condition you are in, the more you will enjoy your journey and destination.

Scrambling Skills and Tips
Navigation skills are a prerequisite for off-trail travel. You must understand concepts of map reading, compass use, and cross-country navigation. Many

Spring snow travel on Mount Pilchuck (Photo by Chris Weidner)

Snow travel on Lost Peak (Photo by Mike Torok)

scrambles require travel on snow, even late in the summer. The snow can often be steep and icy. You must learn to kick steps, use your ice ax, plunge step, self-arrest, glissade, climb in balance, and self-belay. Some rock travel is required on most scrambles. You must master foot placement, handholds, balance, and route selection. You must learn to handle exposure. Above all, you must learn to climb safely and avoid rock fall.

Beginners often make one of two mistakes: they either walk too fast or they walk too slow. If you cannot sustain a steady pace hour after hour, you are going too fast. A very important way of controlling your pace is to use the "rest step" whenever legs or lungs need a little time to recuperate when traveling steep slopes. The rest step involves straightening your advancing leg to lock the uphill knee while swinging your back leg forward into the next step. This enables your bones to briefly hold your weight, thereby giving your muscles a rest. Remember that even the strongest and most experienced scramblers need occasional full rests.

Walking downhill is less tiring than walking uphill, but presents a mixed blessing. Tighten your bootlaces to reduce foot movement inside the boot. Maintain a measured pace that is slower than the one urged by gravity. Bend your knees to cushion the shock with each step, and place your feet lightly.

Avoid following too close. Instead of shadowing your companion, give the person ahead of you some space by staying at least a few paces back. Also, avoid following too far back so that you don't lose contact with the other members of the group or make them continually wait for you.

Rock scrambling in Mount Rainier National Park (Photo by Susan Alford)

Trip Planning

Planning a scramble can be a complicated process, but clearly the more experience you have the easier it gets. Before heading out the door, you need to go through a series of steps so that your journey will be safe and enjoyable. First, you need to pick a destination. This choice is based on talking to other people and accessing various sources such as lists circulated in the scrambling community. The choice should depend on the time of the year, the weather, the condition of the snowfall, and the abilities of the members of the party.

Gathering information is next. Talking to other scramblers who have done the trip is an excellent source of information. Look at a variety of hiking and guidebooks. Get the appropriate maps. Sketch out the route on the map and in your mind. In selecting the route, consider that the most straightforward return route is often the same as the route going in. If you plan to come back a different way, that route also needs careful advance preparation.

Anticipate any special needs, such as stream-crossing gear, or crampons, or even a hand line if the terrain looks very steep. You need to not only know the name of your wilderness destination, but also have a plan to get there. The system of Park and Ride lots in the western suburban and urban centers are a good place to leave a car to carpool for day trips with others in your party.

Backcountry Regulations and Permits. Don't let outdated information ruin your trip. Check beforehand with the appropriate agencies about roads and trails, especially closures, and about regulations, permits, and camping requirements.

In Mount Rainier, the North Cascades, and Olympic National Parks, motorized and mountain bike travel on trails is forbidden and horse travel closely regulated. Hunting is banned, but not all fishing. Pets are not allowed. Backcountry permits are required for all overnight camping in national parks and may be obtained at ranger stations on the park entry roads.

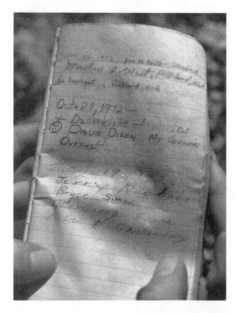

Many of the scrambles in this book are in wilderness areas within the U.S. Forest Service system of public lands, and their use is regulated to protect wilderness. Wilderness status precludes the building of roads and dams or other structures. Motorized and mechanized travel is forbidden absolutely in all designated wilderness areas, and horse travel is beginning to be regulated and in some places eliminated. Foot travel and camping are less restricted,

Summit register showing a record of previous scramblers
(Photo by Chris Weidner)

Colchuck Peak in the Alpine Lakes Wilderness (Photo by Chris Weidner)

although increasing controls may be necessary to protect fragile ecosystems.

Permits and fees are required for a scramble of Mount Adams or Mount Saint Helens. Permits are also required in the Alpine Lakes Wilderness, for day use as well as overnight camping. The Enchantments are so popular that a lottery system has been initiated and you must apply for overnight permits several months in advance. Otherwise, you take your chances with the daily permit lottery. Contact the Leavenworth Ranger Station of the Wenatchee National Forest for details and current information.

The Forest Service now requires a Northwest Forest Pass permit to park at the trailheads of most of the scrambles in this book. The permits can be purchased at U.S. Forest Service ranger stations and local outdoor equipment stores.

Neither maps nor guidebooks can keep up with changes in permits and fees. When current information about a trip is needed, visit or telephone the appropriate Forest Service or Park Service ranger station. The Washington Trails Association (WTA) publishes a handy guide called "Whom to Ask?" that is a directory of state and federal agencies providing current information on trail and road conditions, campsites, and hiking and recreation opportunities. Contact information for the WTA and state and federal agencies is listed in Appendix D. Useful websites are also listed there.

Navigation

Navigation is the science of using map, compass, and altimeter to determine the location of the objective and to keep moving in the right direction toward it. In the past, most travelers ascertained their location by sight. Navigation was achieved by detailed observation of the land and the stars and from detailed knowledge of the terrain. Today, more sophisticated technology is available to show the way. Knowing how to interpret the contour lines on a topographic map and match that information with the real terrain around you is the cornerstone to navigation. The more skilled you are at using the immense information available in a topographic map, the more effective you will be at reaching your destination.

Your brain is your most valuable navigational tool. As the party heads upward, keep asking yourself questions. How will I recognize this important spot on my return? Will I be able to find my way out in a whiteout or if snow covers our tracks? Ask the questions as you go and act on the answers. Avoid surprises and confusion by glancing back over your shoulder from time to time on the way in to see what the route should look like on the return. Fix in your mind this over-the-shoulder appearance of the route. If you can't keep track of it all, jot down times of day, elevations, landmarks, and so on, in a notebook.

Part of navigation is also having a sense of your speed. When travelling cross-country on gentle terrain with a day pack, expect to gain 1000 feet of elevation per hour.

Maps. Because scrambling is primarily the exercise of navigating off the trail, the ability to read and follow a map is essential. Maps convey a phenomenal amount of information in a convenient, easy-to-understand format and lightweight, easy-to-carry form. They are not always completely accurate, and roads, trails, and other features can change after a map is published. Still, maps are invaluable tools to the scrambler.

A number of different types of maps are available. Usually the U.S. Geological Survey maps contain the most detailed information. However, the Green Trails maps, and the Custom Correct maps for the Olympic Peninsula, are extremely useful. Other maps are also quite useful, such as U.S. Forest Service road maps, atlases, and land management and recreational maps of a region. These usually show only the horizontal relationship of natural features, without the contour lines that indicate the shape of the land. In our computer age, there are also a number of valuable programs that allow the computer literate scrambler to search for a location and to individualize a map to bring along.

Straightforward navigation on Sawtooth Ridge
(Photo by Mike Torok)

This is particularly useful when the trip covers an area at the corner of a group of maps.

Do not attempt to do any of these scrambles without an adequate map of the area. A verbal description is not enough. You must learn to match the description to the map and to use the map to enhance the description. Maps in this book are designed to help you find the trailhead and follow the general route of the scramble.

Compass and Altimeter. The compass is a very simple device that can reveal at any time the exact direction in which you are heading. An altimeter, like a compass, provides one simple piece of information that forms the basis for a tremendous amount of vital detail. The compass merely points the direction to magnetic north. The altimeter merely gives the elevation. But by monitoring the elevation and checking it against direction on the topographic map, scramblers can keep track of their progress, pinpoint their location, and find the way to critical junctions in the route. Every scrambling party should have a compass and an altimeter.

Global Positioning System. Fog and lack of visibility are often the greatest challenge to navigation that depends on a compass to take bearings and triangulate a location. The Global Positioning System (GPS) uses satellites orbiting the earth to pinpoint positions on the ground, calculating a three-dimensional position in latitude and longitude and altitude. Today GPS receivers are light enough (weighing only several ounces) that they can easily be tucked in a day pack. They are also inexpensive enough that they are available to almost anyone who scrambles.

The GPS receiver will never completely supplant the use of the compass. The compass requires no batteries and can give a reading even when the satellite transmissions are too weak to pick up. Neither will GPS ever supplant common sense, which is the ability to put all the pieces of information together to form a logical analysis of where you are and where you are going. But GPS can be critical in some situations such as during a whiteout or in heavy fog when compass readings are not feasible.

For GPS to be helpful in navigation, you must be able to match the GPS reading of your location to its location on the map. To do this you will need a map with UTM grid lines that allow you to calculate distances to correspond with your reading. You will also need a ruler and a mechanical pencil (which does not smear when wet) to be more accurate in plotting your location. Map stores stock special plastic UTM Grid Readers that are invaluable in coordinating your GPS measurements in the field with the topographic maps. Alternatively, many of the features of modern GPS receivers will allow you to go from one location to the next. The more familiar you are with the capabilities of this technology, and the more skilled you are in using it, the more confidence you will have that you will never be lost. A full description of GPS is beyond this introduction, but there are many textbooks and articles to help you learn to use this tool.

This book includes a GPS waypoint route for each scramble, with readings for landmarks along the route.

Routefinding

In contrast to navigation—the use of multiple sources of information to determine location and direction—routefinding is the art of working out an efficient route that is within the abilities of the scrambling party. Navigation points the way from where you are to where you want to be, but it takes skill in routefinding to surmount the hazards and hurdles between here and there. Keep an eye on the mountain during the approach hike, studying it for scrambling routes. The distant view reveals different information than the near perspective.

Sometimes a trail on the map may be lost in vegetation or snow, or a known boot tread is hidden from view. As a trail seeker, you become a detec-

Routefinding from Buck Creek Trail: getting the big picture (Photo by Mike Torok)

tive who combines the clues (a bit of beaten path here, a tree blaze there) with the use of map, compass, and altimeter, and with tips from guidebooks and other scramblers.

Topographic maps are seldom revised and information on forests and on roads and other manufactured features can be out of date. A forest may have been logged or a road extended or closed since the last update. Look at the map to see the easiest contours for travel; match those contours with a visual impression of your surroundings. Look for paths that match the abilities and desires of the party. Some people find it less confusing and exhausting to drop into a basin to cross over to the other side, rather than take the risk of a high, rocky traverse. Others welcome the challenge of the rock and prefer the shorter distance. Any scramble presents a range of choices of where to head next to achieve the objective. Use your common sense to define which path is the best for your trip.

When a skirmish with brush is inevitable, there are ways to minimize the hassle. Choose the shortest route across the brushy area. Use fallen trees with long straight trunks as elevated walkways. Push and pull the bushes apart— sometimes by stepping on lower limbs and lifting higher ones to make a passageway. On steep terrain, use hardy shrubs as handholds. Aim for the heaviest timber because brush is often thinnest under big trees. Use a stream channel with less brush for a passageway; dry streambeds are sometimes ideal. If water is present, consider hiking in the stream if it is shallow enough. In deep canyons, however, streams are often choked with fallen trees or interrupted by waterfalls. Look for game trails. Animals generally follow paths of least resistance.

Since people receive information and analyze situations differently, not all techniques will be practical for a single person. But the more experienced and skilled you are, the more techniques and aids you will have in your repertoire to be able to scramble effectively and safely.

WHAT TO BRING
Clothing
Clothing is an important part of your equipment. With the frequent changes in Northwest weather, including occasional snowstorms any time of the year, there is always a risk of hypothermia. Cotton does not maintain body warmth when wet and is not suitable for the mountains, therefore, wool or synthetic equivalents must always be carried. In the wet Washington climate, an outer waterproof, but breathable, layer is essential to protect you from the rain and wind.

Lightweight clothing is generally more expensive, but may be worth the savings in weight. Look for versatile equipment that can be used for several purposes. Plan to dress in layers, which are more effective at controlling your temperature.

There is a fine line between carrying too many clothes and carrying too few. Knowing the difference comes with experience. After each trip, determine what was used, what was not used, and what was really needed for a margin of safety.

Boots are perhaps the most essential item of clothing. The scrambling boot should be stiff enough for kicking steps in hard snow or making a strong platform for your foot on steep vegetated slopes; durable enough to withstand the scraping of rocks while plunge-stepping down a scree field; but comfortable enough for the approach hike. In a single day of scrambling, your boots may be exposed to streams, mud, logs, brush, scree, hard snow, and steep rock. The classic scrambling boot is made of tough leather, has high ankle support, and has a Vibram-type sole for traction. Nothing is worse than a puny boot on challenging terrain.

Equipment

With the diversity of equipment for sale, it is possible to make some expensive mistakes. You can research equipment by reviewing books and catalogs, by talking with experienced people, and by trying out gear for yourself. Do not accept any advice as final; investigate it yourself as each person has different needs and preferences, and it is solely your comfort and safety at stake. Use an equipment checklist such as the one listed in Appendix B to check before your trip that you are prepared. Nothing is worse than to reach the trailhead only to discover that some vital piece of equipment has been left behind.

The Ten Essentials are a selection of critical items that you must always take along. Some of these items may remain unused in your pack, while others will be indispensable on every trip. How much you carry to survive in an emergency is an ongoing debate. Some minimalists argue that weighing down your pack with more items causes you to climb slower, making it more likely that you will get caught by a storm or nightfall and be forced to bivouac. But most prudent scramblers (particularly those who have had to bivouac before) carry enough to survive with some degree of minimal comfort if caught out overnight. Years of experience in the mountains by thousands of people have distilled this list to the minimal amount that you need to carry to be self-reliant and safe should an emergency or accident occur.

The Ten Essentials

1. Map
2. Compass
3. Headlamp, with spare bulbs and batteries
4. Extra food
5. Extra clothing
6. Sunglasses
7. First-aid supplies
8. Pocket knife
9. Matches in waterproof container or a lighter
10. Fire starter

Additional items that most scramblers agree are essential include:

- Water and water bottles with a system for purification if additional water is required
- Altimeter
- Watch
- Emergency shelter
- Plastic sealable bags to carry out used toilet paper and garbage

An ice ax is the next most important piece of equipment that you will carry. It is useful on snow, which can sometimes surprise a scrambler even late in the summer season. An ice ax is also useful to steady your balance on talus and on steep heather or when used to keep pressure off the knees during steep descents. Carrying an ice ax without the skill to use it, however, provides a false sense of security. All too often a scrambler slips on hard snow and does not know enough about self-arrest to stop the fall. This indispensable skill comes from practicing on slopes with safe run-outs.

Crampons are warranted on higher-elevation routes where snow can be icy early in the day. Carry a helmet for steeper routes, particularly when the party is large or rock fall may be a problem. Ski poles are helpful to some on scree slopes or on a steep trail, but even when collapsible, poles can easily get caught on dense vegetation when you are bushwhacking. Of course, your pack is important; it should be nearly waterproof and give enough support but be lightweight. Additional items are necessary for overnight travel. See Appendix B for a scrambling equipment list.

For specific trips with more technical demands (see How to Use This Guide, Difficulty), it is a good idea to carry a 100-foot length of rope to serve as a hand line for steep spots, stream crossings, or other situations where a little extra security would be comforting. Perlon is an inexpensive hand line material. Seven millimeter perlon is very light, exceptionally strong, and doesn't stretch—a bad characteristic for a climbing rope but an asset for a hand line. Because it is impossible to completely anticipate the terrain in any trip, some scramblers keep the hand line coiled in their pack and bring it on every trip.

Ice axes are useful pieces of equipment for scrambling. (Photo by Jason Griffith)

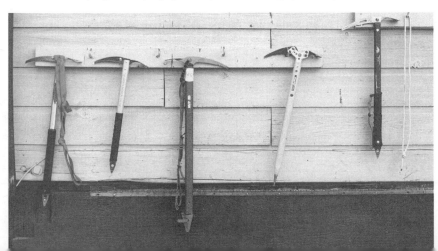

Fluid and Nutrition

If you do not replace fluid losses while exercising, you can become dehydrated and lightheaded, have poor exercise performance and stamina, and risk more serious problems such as very low blood pressure or heat-related illnesses. You can lose 32 to 64 ounces of fluid per hour of exercise. Have your water or sports drink handy and take in some fluid at least every hour so that you feel well and have relatively clear urine. Carry at least two 32-ounce containers with you and purify any water you gather along the way (see Environmental Hazards, Water).

When vigorously exercising, it is difficult to find an appetizing food that is nutritious and produces sufficient energy. The range of what scramblers bring on a trip is infinite, so follow your own judgment. Vegetables such as carrots or celery are refreshing, but are bulky, get warm quickly, and take up a lot of room for their caloric value. On a day trip this is not so critical, but on a multiday journey, the calorie-to-weight ratio will become important. Putting a sport drink or some form of electrolyte replacement in your water provides an energy-enhancing drink. Replenishing sugar as well as electrolytes while you replace fluids is usually a good way to gain more energy. Besides, on a fast-paced trip it will also save time.

SAFETY AND EMERGENCY

Hikers and backpackers may find scrambling ascents a logical and more challenging step beyond day hikes and backcountry camping. However, undertaking any trip mentioned in this guide is a potentially hazardous activity and should be treated with respect. Particular phrases in the route descriptions could be misconstrued to suggest a lack of danger and difficulty. This is not true. The mountains are dangerous and unyielding to the unprepared traveler. A beautiful day can deteriorate rapidly into hypothermic conditions. Although scrambling is considered safer than technical climbing, fatalities occur. Serious accidents can be caused by hazards in the environment, poor weather, or just poor judgment. It is your responsibility to take care of yourself and to minimize risks. Persons following any advice or suggestions contained in this guide do so entirely at their own risk. Only with attention to detail is your travel likely to be pleasurable and fun.

Scramblers face hazards of two sorts: the objective dangers of the alpine environment and the subjective factors of human aspects. The objective, physical hazards are the natural processes that exist in the environment; they are (usually) easy to recognize, are always present, and change without notice. Far harder to evaluate are the subjective factors involving the scrambler's knowledge, skill, and judgment. We cannot necessarily control these acknowledged factors, but we can act to minimize their dangerous implications. To reduce risk, you need to recognize objective hazards and learn how to avoid them. The subjective elements that must be taken into account to anticipate a problem include routefinding, skill of the scrambler, equipment quality, physical conditioning, leadership, technique, and judgment.

The best anticipation of a problem is to be prepared physically, mentally, and logistically. Before you leave, let a responsible person know the destination, trailhead, and estimated time of return. Then if for any reason you are late beyond a reasonable period, the appropriate search and rescue mechanism can be called into action. Carry the Ten Essentials to keep your safety margin bolstered. You cannot eliminate risk, but with knowledge and preparation you can reduce risk to an acceptable level.

Turnaround Time

A common form of poor judgment is underestimating the speed or skill needed to reach an objective. It is also poor judgment to let desire for the objective over-

Ice ax arrest (Photo by Chris Weidner)

whelm an accurate assessment of the risk. Desire is useful in scrambling: it calls forth your best efforts. But if it is not appropriate, it can end in a long night in the dark. Good judgment also means acknowledging when you or the members of your group are having a bad day. Scale back your plans accordingly. It's a good idea to set a time for turning back even if the summit hasn't been reached. The turnaround time will help prevent the party from pushing onward after it is too late to reach the summit so that they can get back to camp or the trailhead before nightfall.

Bivouacs

A bivouac, also called a bivy, is an unplanned stay overnight using only the equipment in your backpack. Many also use the term bivy for a planned backcountry overnight stop with minimal gear. An unplanned bivouac comes as an unpleasant surprise and often results from injury, bad weather, poor planning, or getting lost. Scrambling in the dark with a headlamp is possible, but usually only on modest terrain or on a trail. Sometimes if a party is lost or has not planned properly, nightfall and fatigue may dictate that the safest plan is to bivy until daylight.

In the mountains of Washington, the nights are chilly to downright cold at almost any elevation. It is imperative that each person brings the amount of clothing and equipment needed to be safe and survive an unplanned bivouac. Always pack raingear, even when the weather is not threatening. Raingear not only protects against rain showers, it also provides a wind barrier to protect against the loss of body heat.

When bivying, put on extra clothing and sit on your pack for insulation from the cold ground. Remove wet clothing and keep snow off your clothes. Sometimes a fire can be started to provide warmth and cheer; but it must be started only where allowed and watched by someone during the hours of the bivy. The party should be kept together, and the group should accommodate any member who lacks equipment. Sometimes huddling together will decrease heat loss. Eating and drinking is important for morale, as well as to prevent hypothermia and generate more energy for the hike out the next day.

When an Accident Happens

An injury on a scrambling trip can range from a minor sprained ankle, to a life-threatening head injury from a fall or avalanche. Each problem requires a different level of response appropriate to the situation. In dealing with an emergency, quick action may be less effective than correct action. Leadership and discipline are key to success in dealing with a crisis.

Go quickly to the aid of the injured person, but move carefully to avoid any further accidents. On difficult terrain, keep to one side to avoid the danger of knocking rocks onto the injured party. In the snow, beware of setting off an avalanche.

Begin the process of administering immediate first aid, but then sit down, pause, and take a few deep breaths. Establish a leader and ask the rest of the party to sit down to plan. Everything must be thought through to the very end, including what each person is to do under all circumstances. Every aspect of the situation needs cool analysis, including the seriousness of the injuries, the necessary measures needed for first aid, the type of terrain, the strengths and resources of the party, and the objective hazards involved in the situation. Only after careful analysis of these and other factors should your party select an appropriate course of action.

Mountain-Oriented First Aid

After administering treatment for life-threatening problems, the next step in mountain-oriented first aid is to determine whether the victim can be moved, or whether the injured party will be able to walk out. If the person is too severely hurt to walk, or if time is required before walking out, observe a few simple rules. Keep the victim warm by layering clothing, covering the head, and avoiding wind chill. Insulate the person from the ground using a pad, clothing, or a pack.

If the decision is made to go for help, appoint someone to stay with the injured person, if possible, and send at least two people for aid when they are no longer needed at the accident site. In many areas, help by helicopter is usually no more than 3 hours away once word gets to the proper authorities, although this will depend on weather, terrain, and local politics. Ground rescues often take much longer. Make sure the people going for help have a clear understanding of the party's situation and requirements so that they will know exactly what to ask for. They should take with them a list of the names and telephone numbers of everyone in the party, a report of the accident, and a map that pinpoints the accident site.

The messengers have several vital responsibilities. They need to contact the appropriate local authorities, usually the county sheriff or, if the accident occurs in the national park, the park personnel. They must ask for a rescue or relay the need for help to the local mountain rescue organization. The messenger will most likely be detained at the ranger station for the duration of the rescue, in case the need for a further interview arises concerning the location or the circumstances of the event.

Mountain-oriented first aid places much more emphasis on the "mountain," meaning how to get out of the terrain. "First aid" focuses on what it takes to stabilize an injured person so that evacuation can take place.

If You Are Lost

There are many reasons people get lost. Some people travel without a map because the route seems obvious. Others, because they are in a hurry, do not take the time to think about where they are going. Some people trust their own instincts over the compass. Others do not use the map successfully to create a good mental picture of the area. Some do not pay enough attention to the route on the way in to be able to find it on the way out. Some mistakenly rely solely on the skill of their scrambling partner.

A basic rule applies to wilderness settings: when you are lost, stop first. If you are separated from your group, use a whistle (best since the sound carries farther) or shout to attract their attention. Since panic is your greatest enemy, remain calm and conserve your energy. Have confidence that your pack contains enough to survive until you can find your way or until you are found. Carefully review the situation and the last familiar location so that you can formulate a plan to solve the problem. After mentally retracing your recent movements, mark your present location and try to backtrack to the point where the route is again familiar.

If this fails, use navigation aids to get oriented. Look at the local features of the terrain and try to match them with the map. Sometimes matching the slope of the area to the contour lines on the map will lend a clue to your specific location. Try to climb to a higher location if trees obstruct your view in identifying higher landmarks. If poor visibility is the problem, consider stopping or planning a bivouac until the situation improves.

If you need to set up a camp, choose a spot with wood and water and as much shelter as possible. It should be along the edge of open country where the smudge of a green bough fire will be visible and where searching aircraft can be signaled. Make the camp at least two hours before sunset and gather plenty of firewood for the night. Inventory your equipment, food, and other resources. Conserve your strength. If no rescuers show up after two days, consider walking out, leaving a note behind at your bivy site to indicate your direction of travel.

Consider packing a GPS unit with a gridded map that can help you out of a tough situation when you are really lost.

ENVIRONMENTAL HAZARDS
Weather Concerns

At higher elevations, weather patterns can shift with alarming speed. Temperature can vary as much as 70 degrees in a 24-hour period in the high reaches in the center of mountain ranges. It is not uncommon to experience clear skies and debilitating heat followed by fog, rain, and driving sleet in the course of a single summer afternoon. The main dangers due to weather are hypothermia and heat exhaustion.

Hypothermia. Humans maintain body comfort by creating a microenvironment of warm air next to the skin. Cold temperature, rain, and wind remove this layer of insulation, creating conditions in which hypothermia can develop. When severe, hypothermia leads to uncontrolled shivering, loss of judgment, and eventually death. The best protection is clothing that protects from the wind and that keeps you warm even when wet. A breathable waterproof material is best in the Pacific Northwest, to minimize chill from perspiration as well as to protect from rain.

Heat exhaustion. Conversely, when conditions are too hot the body suffers as well. Overexertion or excessive temperature with inappropriate clothing can result in heat exhaustion—a condition that can be just as deadly as hypothermia. The best protection is to be in good physical condition, dress appropriately, stay well hydrated, cool down when over-

Changes in weather can lead to hypothermia.
(Photo by Jason Griffith)

exertion is extreme, and avoid travelling in the intense heat of the day.

Lightning. Although not one of the principal perils of scrambling, lightning has caused a number of serious and mostly avoidable accidents. The most frequent targets for lightning are also the places the scrambler most frequently seeks—high peaks and ridges. Scramblers should avoid travelling during thunderstorms and leave high spots when the warning signs occur, such as the buzzing of metal or feel of static electricity in the air. If you are caught in the midst of a storm, sit on an insulated pack, put all metal objects far away, and make yourself as small as possible.

Rock Fall

Why are people so afraid of rock fall? Besides the awful sound, rock fall portends extreme danger. First, there is the immediate danger of a head injury. With the right trajectory and speed, the impact of even a rather puny-sized chunk of talus can be fatal. Next, there

Storm approaching on Big Craggy Peak
(Photo by John Roper)

is the danger of bodily damage: broken bones, cuts, and bruises. The hands are particularly at risk when a handhold fails and rock from above pins the hand beneath the rockslide below it.

The Cascades are notorious for their friable rock and disintegrating scree and debris in many gullies and on upper high slopes. Rocks frozen together in winter can plummet when melting releases them. Gullies often act as chutes for debris from above. Massive scree and talus slopes provide simple routes to the top of many peaks, but footholds can fail and handholds can unexpectedly pull out in your hand. A sharp thump to the rock with the palm of the hand will usually indicate whether or not a hold is solid.

However, the most likely source of rock fall may be from the party itself. Since it may be next to impossible to avoid dislodging rocks while moving over the terrain, it is imperative that people avoid scrambling immediately above or below others. When going down a slope, travel side by side so as to minimize the danger of being hit. The smaller the party, the less chance that a rock will be loosed.

The best way to be safe from rock fall, of course, is to wear a helmet when scrambling. You should always climb with a helmet when the danger is extreme, although helmets are not usually needed on easier routes.

Avalanches

The public generally associates avalanche accidents with skiers. This is far from true: travelers in the backcountry figure high in avalanche accident statistics even in seasons other than winter, particularly in the spring thaw cycle. Avalanches catch and very often kill the unwary who literally trigger their own destiny when they venture onto unsafe snow. It is important that you learn avalanche awareness and safety.

Nevertheless, the chance of being caught by a naturally triggered slide is remote unless you are travelling during or immediately after a heavy snowfall or when the temperature suddenly rises and a major thaw results. A large percentage of accidents have occurred when avalanche hazards were known to be high. Avoid avalanche hazard by using good routefinding skills, by recognizing and avoiding hazardous slopes, and by staying out of avalanche terrain during high hazard periods. In particular, avoid steep or open slopes or gullies when the snow pack is unstable. If you are unsure, contact a local avalanche center to determine whether your risk traveling in the area is worth it.

Stream Crossings

On selected scrambles, there is a possibility that you will have to ford a stream or river. The water obstacles range from a small, ankle-deep brook to a tumultuous snow-fed stream. Avoid the largest and most dangerous rivers by back-

tracking to higher ground and crossing at a less dangerous point. However, if you must get by the obstacle, first check the water temperature. The cold water could temporarily paralyze you. In this case, try to make an improvised bridge by pushing logs or branches over the waterway.

If you are attempting to ford, move to high ground and examine the stream for level stretches where it breaks into a number of channels. Pick a spot on the opposite bank where travel will be easy and safe. Avoid a ledge or rocks that indicate the presence of rapids. Timber growths show where the channel is deepest.

When you select your fording site, choose a course leading across the current at about a forty-five-degree angle downstream. Never try to ford a stream directly above or close to a deep or rapid waterfall or an abrupt channel. Instead, always ford where you would be car-

Avoiding the open slope on Baring Mountain
(Photo by Chris Weidner)

Suspended bridge in Mount Rainier National Park (Photo by Susan Alford)

ried to a shallow bank or sandbar should you lose your footing. Remember that, except in still water, the shallowest part is generally where the current is widest. A stout pole is useful during the actual wading for balance and as a support against the tugging current. Sometimes it is best to take off your socks and put your boots back on for the crossing to avoid injuries to your feet. Wipe out your boots when you are safely on the other side, and they will be only briefly uncomfortable when you put back on your dry socks.

Wildlife
Apart from rattlesnakes found during summer days in eastern Washington, few animals except bears represent a threat to the scrambler. When camping, hang anything that smells even remotely edible about 15 feet up a tree and 10 feet out from the tree trunk or between two trees well away from camp. Keep your camp clean. Avoid a bear if you should see one. Bears are particularly prevalent in the Olympic Mountains and in the North Cascades National Park.

Mountain goats present another nuisance in many regions. They will follow you to lick up patches of urine (for the salt) that are left on the ground. They will also gnaw on sweaty clothing or pack straps. Keep such materials out of reach, and do not be surprised if a muscular white goat follows you when you separate from the group.

Insects
Mosquitoes are annoying and swarm with a vengeance throughout most of Washington's mountains from late June to early September. Even more troublesome are black flies and horse flies that do not seem to be repelled by ordinary insecticides and can inflict horribly painful bites. The best way to avoid biting insects is to keep to higher elevations, wear lightweight, protective clothing, and carry a kerchief for swatting.

Bees and hornets are another matter. Usually they are not plentiful. The first person in line is sometimes the one who stirs up the nest, but is not the one who gets stung. Take an epinephrine kit along to prevent a severe allergic reaction if anyone in your group has a venom allergy. Antihistamine tablets will also help in this situation.

Ticks are another arthropod of particular disdain. Active in the spring and summer, ticks can be repelled with chemicals, particularly those with DEET. But if they land and set their proboscis, they can transmit infections. After travelling in a tick-infested area, you should examine your hair, body, and clothing to make sure that a wayward tick is not still attached.

Avoid the painful bite of black flies.
(Photo by Chris Weidner)

Water

High peaks are often parched or frozen, so you usually need to carry enough water to prevent dehydration. Usually two quarts of fluid per day for the hiker are sufficient, but many scramblers especially in warmer weather need as much as two to three times that amount.

You will need to treat all water, including snow, from natural sources in the backcountry. Far gone are the days when you could drink heartily from a clear running stream. Today *Giardia lamblia,* a waterborne protozoan, has tainted nearly all the water sources in Washington, and it takes only one swallow of contaminated water to get sick.

Iodine tablets or crystals are one method of water treatment, but the water then tastes quite chemical and unappealing. Vitamin C, citric acid tablets, or even lemonade can be carried as an antidote. But the difficulty with iodine is that it takes at least an hour at ordinary temperatures for a tablet to purify one quart of water and *Giardia* cysts can prove highly resistant to iodine. Many parties now carry a water filtration device in the form of a pump. Filters treat water by physically removing contaminants. If you choose this method, be sure that the filter removes *Giardia*.

Boiling water is still the only 100 percent certain water purification method, although unless the water is boiled for at least 20 minutes, viruses may not be killed. Boiling drinking water can also be cumbersome unless you are on an overnight scramble.

WILDERNESS ETHICS
Responsibilities of the Scrambler

Everywhere in the United States user impact is spreading faster than land managers can control it. Recreational use of America's wildlands has exploded in the past forty years. People visit the backcountry because they value and enjoy it, but in the words of one observer, "We are loving our wilderness to death." As the number of backcountry visitors grows, the responsibility to the land changes. We need to be concerned about damage to the integrity of the land and conserving the wilderness experience for future generations.

Restrictions enforced by land management agencies are unavoidable. Many of us seek the solitude and freedom of wildlands as temporary relief from a restrictive society. An underlying premise of a new way of thinking is that most damage to wilderness is the result of lack of education, not malice. Minimum-impact backcountry use is a practical approach to caring about land while also caring about people. This ethic depends more on awareness than on rules and regulations. We have a responsibility to change our techniques and attitudes about what is appropriate behavior in the outdoors. When you travel off trail in remote backcountry, you must accept a special responsibility for your impact. Off-trail areas are special because they have seldom been visited. These areas require a commitment of extra care.

Wilderness solitude in Mount Rainier National Park (Photo by Mike Torok)

Human Waste Disposal

The most responsible, though perhaps not the most practical, way to deal with solid human waste is to pack it out. For the backcountry traveler, the three objectives are to minimize the chance of water pollution, minimize the chance of anything or anyone finding the waste, and maximize the rate of decomposition. There is no single solution for every situation. Use toilets or latrines where they have been provided. In an area where the use is extremely low and soils are absent, there is little chance that someone will contact your feces before it has decomposed. Choose a site that is not likely to be visited by others and is more than two hundred feet from water with a dry open exposure. Scatter or smear the feces with a rock or stick to maximize exposure to the sun and the air. In more popular places that are regularly visited by people, bury waste in cat holes. Even though decomposition is slower than at the surface, it is important to bury it to decrease the likelihood of contact with others. Those traveling in a group should disperse their waste sites and not concentrate them.

Camping without Trampling

Where routes are on bare rock or snow, the effects of trampling are negligible. But in sparsely vegetated, boulder-covered areas, campers often move rocks to create more comfortable tent sites. Unfortunately, once the rocks are moved, the vegetation dies and a permanent scar is created. You should camp at well-worn sites and not cause further impact.

Camping on a more heavily vegetated or pristine site demands much

more care. Choose a resistant surface with no evidence of previous use. Concentrate most camp activities and place your tent on a hard surface—snow, rock, and mineral soil are best. Dry grass and sedge meadows are moderately resistant, whereas areas of low shrubs or succulent plants are fragile. Never pitch your tent on fragile, herbaceous plants. Disperse your traffic widely, trying not to step on the same places. Don't use the area more than one night, and don't congregate with others in your party in one location unless it is on a hard surface. Everything you do on a pristine site should minimize the

Camping on snow
(Photo by Jason Griffith)

Spread out to avoid creating a worn path. (Photo by Mike Torok)

number of times the area is trampled. Carry a stove and never start a fire unless there is a significant need while on an unplanned bivouac.

Leave No Trace

The Leave No Trace program expresses the basic principles of minimum-impact camping, stressing the need to camp in durable areas, to leave what you find, to remove what you pack in, and to properly dispose of what you cannot pack out. Visitors must consider the specifics of each decision concerning the soil, vegetation, wildlife, moisture, amount and type of use the area receives, and overall effect of their own use, and then use judgment to determine which practices to apply.

In general when traveling cross-country, do not mark the route with cairns or leave messages for members of your group in the dirt. Select a route that best avoids the most fragile vegetation. Spend as much time as possible on durable surfaces such as bare rock, gravel, snow, or the deep duff of the forest floor. Watch where you put your feet and try to step on as few plants as possible. Step on rocks when you can. When hiking with others spread out rather than follow the same route. However, where places are so fragile that even the passage of a single person leaves a trail, it is better to walk single file so that only one lane is created. Follow all restrictions, rules, and permit requirements.

Be a role model to other visitors to the backcountry, and politely point out areas of improvement when others violate these principles. Become a teacher to the youngsters you know to give them the ethic of Leave No Trace travel.

Conservation

It is no delusion that larger numbers of visitors to the backcountry increase the impact on wildness. However, we have also learned that threatened areas can only be saved if they are widely known and treasured, otherwise they will disappear forever to another interest group. Washington State is well known for its grassroots organizations who in 1976 helped pass the act that created the Alpine Lakes Wilderness. In 1984 that same alliance won passage of the Washington Wilderness Act, encompassing more than one million acres. This legislation established these new wilderness areas: Clearwater, Norse Peak, William O. Douglas, Glacier View, Tatoosh, Indian Heaven, Trapper Creek, Wonder Mountain, Mount Skokomish, The Brothers, Buckhorn, and Colonel Bob, plus additions to Goat Rocks and Mount Adams.

Nevertheless, the job is not done. It is our obligation to be stewards of the land and to work toward a wilderness vision. As the human population burgeons and the demands on the land increase, it is even more important to preserve the diminishing portion of the state that is still truly wild. The paradox is that to save the wilderness, it must be used. Treat the land responsibly, speak of its beauty and spirit to others, and do everything that you can to preserve it forever so that you, your children, and others can always experience it.

How to Use This Guide

The scrambles in this book are grouped into twelve geographical regions around the mountainous areas of the state. Note that a particular scramble in this book might be considered to be in any of several different scrambling areas. This is particularly true for peaks or destinations that have multiple, common approaches. Therefore, use the scrambling areas in this book to give a rough estimate of the time it takes to arrive at the trailhead, the common geographic and climatic conditions that are involved, and the typical weather to expect at a particular time of year.

Each scramble begins with the following summary information:

Elevation gives the height in feet and meters for each of the peaks; heights for multiple peaks follow the same listing order as that in the scramble title.

Difficulty provides a two-part rating with which to evaluate the trip. Although subjective, it is meant to convey practical information so that the trip chosen most closely matches the experience, skills, and desires of the members of the party.

Mountain travel is traditionally divided into classes. Class 1 is a hike on a rocky gradient where hands are not needed. Class 2 involves the use of hands but not the use of a rope. Class 3 involves moderate exposure with frequent use of hands, and a rope should be available. Class 4 terrain has significant exposure, and most climbers want a rope because an unprotected fall could be serious or fatal. Class 5 describes technical rock climbing, where rope, climbing aids, and helmet are required. Scrambles in this book are primarily class 2, with only several that have an occasional class 3 move or a limited section of class 3 scrambling.

In this guide, the two-part difficulty rating listed provides more detail. The first measure is labeled "S" for strenuousness and is followed by a number from

1 to 5. The higher the number, the more strenuous the trip. Strenuousness measures the amount of exertion that the scramble requires and is based on a composite impression of the total distance, the portion of trip that is off trail, the ruggedness of the terrain, and the elevation gained. A trip that is rated S3 might be a stretch for someone who scrambles only infrequently; the same trip might be effortless for someone who scrambles every weekend. The scale is relative, but will give a rough idea of the physical effort needed to complete the trip in comparison to others.

The second measure is labeled "T" for technique and is also followed by a number from 1 to 5, with 5 requiring the most skill. This measure rates the more technical aspects of the scramble, and factors in the degree of exposure on a route, the type of terrain (the amount of loose rock, for example), the degree of caution needed, and the need for use of hands for balance or vertical movement. This number is generally related to the degree of composure and skill that is needed to complete the trip. As this scale goes up, the scrambling more closely approaches true climbing. For example, a T5 trip might have some class 3 moves (moderate exposure, requiring use of hands) and some party members might appreciate a hand line for safety. This measure of technique required is included because many people differ with regard to their tolerance of exposure and risk of falling. Beginning scramblers might be alarmed by the vertical nature of the terrain, whereas other more experienced scramblers would be minimally concerned.

The combined rating is meant to give a general impression of the trip as a whole. To illustrate, a trip that is rated S5/T2 might be very long and require many hours of constant movement, but be free of any anxiety. In contrast, a trip that is rated S2/T5 might involve less overall exertion, but require movement over nearly vertical terrain.

Distance is the total round trip mileage of the trip, unless otherwise noted.

Elevation gain is total feet gained over the course of the entire trip including ups after partial descents.

Trip time is round trip time given in hours for 1-day trips and given in days for multiple-day scrambles. Trip time is based on an average group with a modest 10-minute break per hour, and about half an hour on the summit. The average speed is approximated at 1000 feet of vertical gain per hour without heavy snow, which would delay progress.

Time to summit measures the one-way time it takes to achieve the summit. Unless stated otherwise, time to the summit is calculated from the trailhead.

Best time of year describes the optimal months for making the trip. Because of seasonal variation year to year, these recommended times are rough guides. The time of November to April (winter season) was specifically left out, since scrambles during these months are primarily snowshoe trips that require a different set of skills. Although some of the trips listed in this book can be done in winter, most of the peaks are at an elevation high enough that a winter scramble could present significant avalanche danger or be inaccessible due to snow on the access road. See Appendix A for a list of scrambles by season.

Alpine scrambling in Washington (Photo by Chris Weidner)

Maps are listed for the general area by type and title. They are generally U.S. Geological Survey (USGS), Green Trails, or Custom Correct maps. Contour maps are also included for each scramble to give an overview of the described route. Use these maps to orient you to the trip as a whole; always carry a more detailed topographic map to use for accurate navigation.

Contact lists the governing agency of the scramble area. Contact information for each agency is listed in Appendix D.

Special considerations lists important features, objective difficulties, or recommended special gear to safely complete the scramble. Please read the route descriptions carefully for more detailed considerations.

Following the summary information, you will find an overview of each scramble and **trailhead directions** for driving directions to the start of the scramble. The miles and hours listed at the end of trailhead directions refer to the one-way distance and driving time from Seattle.

Each scramble chapter then has a description of the **standard route** to the summit, followed by **alternate routes** where applicable. These descriptions are often more detailed than those in a standard hiking guide, which describe routes on established trails. A good portion of each of these scrambles is off trail or on a snow-covered trail in early season.

Written descriptions are only rough guides. Words can be misleading and the appearance of the terrain changes over time and with season. A tarn may be completely covered with snow and invisible in spring. A ridge trivial to scramble in July might be covered in ice and exceedingly dangerous to scramble in June. There are typically many routes that lead to a summit. Your choice depends on the condition of the terrain at the time of travel and how well the route fits the abilities and desires of the party.

Each scramble description also contains a **GPS waypoint route** approximating the standard route. GPS waypoints were obtained from a computer-generated topographic program whose settings were adjusted to use the NAD 27 map datums, and if you use the waypoint routes you will need to adjust the settings of your GPS receiver to this datums preference.

GPS waypoints should be used only as a rough guide and may not correspond exactly to what you feel is the best trajectory for your route. To use the waypoint routes in this book, enter the waypoint you want to reach. Your GPS receiver will calculate your position and a bearing which you can follow on your compass, or you can use the pointer on the display to indicate when you are on course. GPS is particularly useful when determining which peak of several is the one to head for or when visibility is too poor to get an accurate compass reading.

Note that elevations in the GPS waypoint route are rounded to the nearest 100 feet for trailheads and passes, and to the nearest 20 feet for other readings. Summit elevations and other features noted on the USGS map are given as an exact number. The distances are cumulative and are calculated visually from the map.

As a final note, the photographs in this book augment the text descriptions and maps to give an overview of the summit routes described. However, not all photographs are taken from the route itself. They are meant to convey a peak in the context of its total environment. For example, a photograph might be taken from the top of a nearby peak to show what to expect at the summit. Also, since each season is vastly different than the next, do not expect all the pictures to match the scenes you might witness.

A NOTE ABOUT SAFETY

Safety is an important concern in all outdoor activities. No guidebook can alert you to every hazard or anticipate the limitations of every reader. Therefore, the descriptions of roads, trails, routes, and natural features in this book are not representations that a particular place or excursion will be safe for your party. When you follow any of the routes described in this book, you assume responsibility for your own safety. Under normal conditions, such excursions require the usual attention to traffic, road and trail conditions, weather, terrain, the capabilities of your party, and other factors. Because many of the lands in this book are subject to development and/or change of ownership, conditions may have changed since this book was written that make your use of some of these routes unwise. Always check for current conditions, obey posted private property signs, and avoid confrontations with property owners or managers. Keeping informed on current conditions and exercising common sense are the keys to a safe, enjoyable outing.

The Mountaineers Books

1 CHURCH MOUNTAIN

Elevation: 6315 ft (1925 m)

Difficulty: S3/T5

Distance: 9.2 miles

Elevation gain: 4100 ft

Trip time: 9 hours

Time to summit: 6 hours

Best time of year: August to September

Maps: USGS Bearpaw Mountain, Glacier; Green Trails Mount Baker 13

Contact: Mount Baker–Snoqualmie National Forest, Mount Baker Ranger Station

Special considerations: Beware of loose rock in gullies and moderate exposure on summit approach.

GPS WAYPOINT ROUTE
1. Church Mountain trailhead: 2300 ft (10U 583794mE 5418120mN)
2. Deerhorn Creek: 3.8 miles, 4940 ft (10U 583317mE 5419724mN)
3. Trail end lookout: 4.2 miles, 5920 ft (10U 582456mE 5419700mN)
4. Church summit: 4.6 miles, 6315 ft (10U 581927mE 5419883mN)

Church Mountain benchmark (Photo by John Roper)

Positioned between Canyon Creek to the north and North Fork Nooksack River to the south, Church Mountain rises from an elevation of 1200 feet at the river to its highest point in less than 2 miles. The abandoned lookout near the top is a popular trail trip, but the summit farther on is an even lovelier viewpoint that encompasses the meandering Fraser River valley and the dazzling glaciers of Mount Baker.

Early settlers named the mountain for its spire appearance. Primarily a trail trip, the final scramble to the summit is moderate when the proper course is unveiled, but dicey and forbidding if the party wanders off the route. Hikers who are not familiar with off-trail travel can stop at the lookout site to soak in the views, while the scramblers forge on to the summit and back.

Trailhead Directions: Drive I-5 north to the Mount Baker Highway (SR 542). Head east for 34 miles to the Glacier Ranger Station and 5 miles farther to FS Road 3040. This unimproved road starts at 1200 feet and continues to Church Mountain Trail 671. (130 miles, 3 hours from Seattle)

Standard Route: From the Church Mountain trailhead at 2300 feet, ascend many switchbacks to about 4600 feet where the trail flattens and traverses

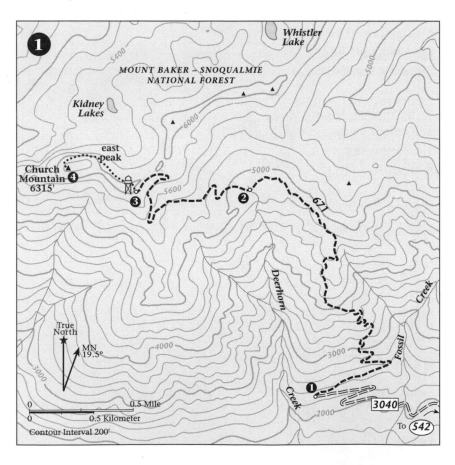

west around the basin of Deerhorn Creek. At about 4800 feet the trail crosses the creek and continues to the west above tree line. Continue up longer switchbacks to the end of the trail and the remnants of an old lookout, just east of the true summit.

From the lookout, head north on a beaten path and drop 125 feet into the basin. Trend northwest on a rising traverse past the last gendarme heading up to a notch in the ridge. Cross the ridge to the south and traverse 80 feet to a gully that is difficult to go across (class 3). On the other side of the gully, continue at the same elevation about 300 feet to a flat area (you might find a cairn here). Scramble up 40 feet and then trend rightward up the vegetated slope to the ridge crest. Cross the ridge to the north and follow a level beaten path almost to the summit. Expect some exposed sections where you must be careful. The final push to the top is easier (class 2).

There is a way through the summit region that is a scramble, but getting off the route will lead to difficult climbing. The basin of Kidney Lakes is to the north of the small rock-and-heather summit.

2 YELLOW ASTER BUTTE

Elevation: 6241 ft (1903 m)	
Difficulty: S1/T1	
Distance: 8 miles	
Elevation gain: 2800 ft	
Trip time: 7 hours	
Time to summit: 4 hours	
Best time of year: July to October	
Maps: USGS Mount Larrabee; Green Trails Mount Shuksan 14	
Contact: Mount Baker–Snoqualmie National Forest, Mount Baker Ranger Station	
Special considerations: Occasional fog makes routefinding difficult.	

GPS WAYPOINT ROUTE
1. Tomyhoi Lake–Yellow Aster Butte trailhead: 3600 ft (10U 598045mE 5421821mN)
2. Yellow Aster Butte Trail: 1.5 miles, 5200 ft (10U 597780mE 5422825mN)
3. Spur trail: 3.4 miles, 5800 ft (10U 596221mE 5422477mN)
4. Yellow Aster summit: 4 miles, 6241 ft (10U 596594mE 5423026mN)
5. Tarns: 4.3 miles, 5540 ft (10U 595906mE 5422788mN)

Yellow Aster Butte is a favorite late season scramble when the hills are luminous with the brazen hues of autumn. If the time is right, a party can heartily graze on ripe huckleberries. The trip to Yellow Aster Butte is delightful and easy, with beautiful small tarns and lakelets dotting the countryside. Tomyhoi

Peak, American Border Peak, and Mount Larrabee stand nearby, while the jagged peaks of Canada and formidable Baker and Shuksan tower farther on. In late season a trail is present nearly to the summit. Yellow Aster Butte therefore makes a gentle trip when time is short or the party is less experienced.

The old Keep Kool Trail once led to the butte, but was subject to severe erosion. Now a newer trailhead leaves from the same starting point as the Tomyhoi Lake Trail farther down the spur road.

Trailhead Directions: Drive I-5 north to Bellingham. Take the Mount Baker Highway (SR 542) east for 34 miles to the Glacier Ranger Station. Continue for 13 miles and turn north on the Twin Lakes Road (FS Road 3065) marked by a forest service sign. At 2.3 miles is the old Keep Kool Trail 699 (3000 feet). Continue about 2 miles to the Tomyhoi Lake-Yellow Aster Butte Trail No. 686 trailhead (3600 feet). (140 miles, 3.5 hours from Seattle)

Standard Route: Start on the Tomyhoi Lake Trail No. 686. At 1.5 miles (5200 feet), just shy of Gold Run Pass, go left on the new Yellow Aster Butte Trail No. 686.1 that contours south around Yellow Aster Butte. At 5800 feet, just before dropping down to the middle of a group of small ponds, turn right up a spur trail. Ascend northeast along the butte, where a climber's trail leads to the summit at the ridge end. The true summit is west of the named summit on the map. On the descent, if visibility permits, leave the ridge just below the summit slabs and descend westerly on talus and scree to the tarns. Go southeast to connect with the Yellow Aster Butte Trail for the return.

Yellow Aster Butte in winter (Photo by John Roper)

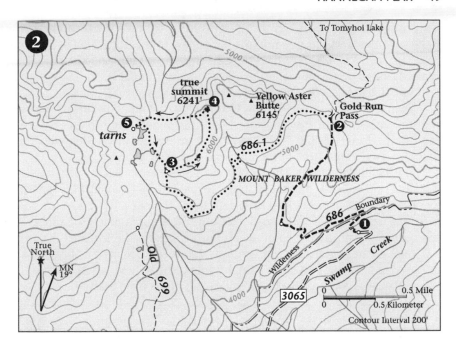

ろ HANNEGAN PEAK

Elevation: 6187 ft (1886 m)

Difficulty: S2/T1

Distance: 10 miles

Elevation gain: 3100 ft

Trip time: 8 hours

Time to summit: 4.5 hours

Best time of year: late June to August

Maps: USGS Mount Sefrit; Green Trails Mount Shuksan 14

Contact: Mount Baker–Snoqualmie National Forest, Mount Baker Ranger Station

Special considerations: This is a scramble only in early season as a trail leads to the top after the snow melts in late July or August.

GPS WAYPOINT ROUTE

1. Hannegan Campground: 3100 ft (10U 603360mE 5418253mN)
2. End of traversing trail: 3.3 miles, 4660 ft (10U 607158mE 5415124mN)
3. Hannegan Pass: 4 miles, 5080 ft (10U 607558mE 5415280mN)
4. Hannegan summit: 5 miles, 6187 ft (10U 607538mE 5416301mN)

Hannegan Pass is the prime entry into the Chilliwack and Picket section of the North Cascades National Park. The trail along Ruth Creek traverses above a striking valley dominated by the glittering ice-clad Ruth Mountain. Hannegan Pass and Hannegan Peak offer a view of the north wall of Mount Shuksan, the Pickets, and a chain of peaks floating off into the horizon. The exalted landscape encompasses the kingly domains of Baker, Shuksan, Ruth, Triumph, Challenger, Redoubt, and Slesse.

This trip is best done with snow to make it a true scramble; in late season the trail to Hannegan Pass and on to the ridge makes the trip an easy one even for beginners. Still it is well worth the minimal effort to link with the marvelous wilderness that lies just beyond this tame gateway.

Trailhead Directions: Drive north on I-5 to Mount Baker Highway (SR 542) and continue east past the Glacier Ranger Station. At about 13 miles and just before the highway crosses the North Fork Nooksack River, turn left and continue traveling east on FS Road 32. Continue approximately 1.5 miles; at the next fork stay left and continue on Ruth Creek Road (FS Road 32) about 4.5 miles to the Hannegan Campground. Hannegan Pass Trail 674 begins at the parking lot at the end of the road, leading ultimately to Whatcom Pass in North Cascades National Park. (150 miles, 3.8 hours from Seattle)

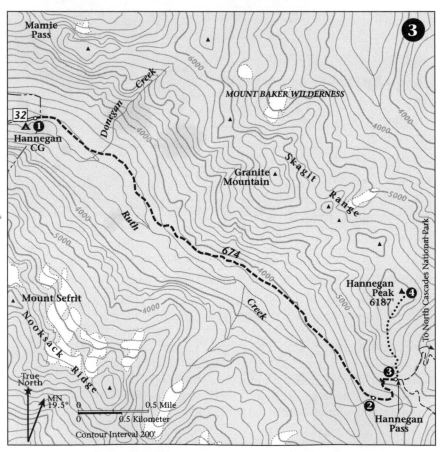

View from Hannegan Peak (Photo by Mike Torok)

Standard Route: Begin at Hannegan Campground, 3100 feet, and ascend gently through trees and avalanche paths along Ruth Creek. Mount Sefrit is clearly visible to the south along the cliffs and waterfalls. Mount Ruth is visible at about 1 mile. Continue traversing along the creek for about 3 miles until the trail swings back into the forest and starts to climb.

The final 0.5 mile of the trail advances in the forest to just before Hannegan Pass at 5080 feet. After the snow is gone, a trail leads from Hannegan Pass to the ridge. In summer a meadow of heather and flowers comes into view, vividly coating the summit plateau of Hannegan Peak (6187 feet). A car camp is suggested at the trailhead.

HADLEY PEAK

Elevation: 7515 ft (2291 m)	
Difficulty: S5/T4	
Distance: 14 miles	
Elevation gain: 4700 ft	
Trip time: 11 hours	
Time to summit: 7 hours	
Best time of year: August to early October	
Maps: USGS Mount Baker, Groat Mountain; Green Trails Mount Baker 13	
Contact: Mount Baker–Snoqualmie National Forest, Mount Baker Ranger Station	
Special considerations: Expect loose rock on some ridge traverses.	

GPS WAYPOINT ROUTE
1. Skyline Divide trailhead: 4400 ft (10U 583320mE 5415568mN)
2. Saddle: 4.5 miles, 6300 ft (10U 584088mE 5410491mN)
3. Chowder Ridge: 5 miles, 6340 ft (10U 584447mE 5408827mN)
4. Hadley summit: 7 miles, 7515 ft (10U 586562mE 5407232mN)

Located where Dobbs Cleaver joins the northern slope of Mount Baker, Hadley Peak is the high point of Chowder Ridge. The approach is over the Skyline Divide Trail, a superb stroll through emerald meadows. The convoluted glaciers of the north wall of Mount Baker accentuate the southern vista. The Border Peaks and the Cheam Range present rugged spires to the north. The openness and grandeur of the scene is exhilarating, as the scramble rolls up and down the ridge, approaching the summit. Indeed, Hadley Peak and the whole of Chowder Ridge provide high alpine scrambling at its best. But this is an area of sensitive and unique flora: Be careful to tread lightly and respect the fragile vegetation.

Trailhead Directions: Drive I-5 north to the Mount Baker Highway (SR 542). Continue east past the Glacier Ranger Station until you reach the first

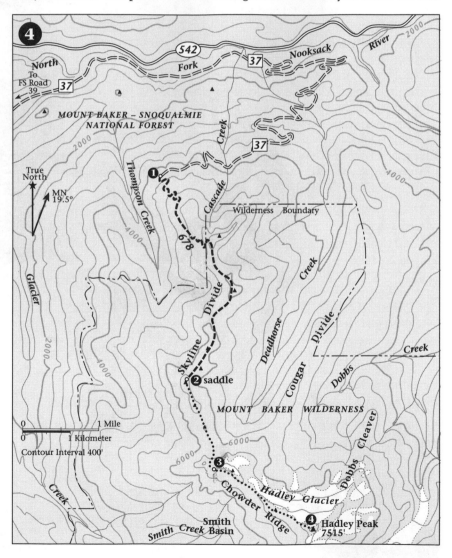

The summit of Hadley Peak (Photo by Mike Torok)

large road to the south, FS Road 39. Almost immediately turn left onto FS Road 37, and drive along the North Fork Nooksack River for about 4 miles. The road climbs and crosses Cascade Creek and then Deadhorse Creek. At the end of the road find Skyline Divide Trail 678. (140 miles, 3.5 hours from Seattle)

Standard Route: From the Skyline Divide trailhead at 4400 feet, ascend a moderately steep trail 2 miles to a huge ridge-top meadow. At the 5900-foot saddle the trail splits; take the right fork that continues along the tundra crest 2 miles to a higher 6300-foot saddle.

In late season, at the start of the upward leg to Chowder Ridge, water is available at a lake set at the foot of the Hadley Glacier. Follow the contours of Chowder Ridge, keeping to the south of the crest. A rocky gendarme can be bypassed by dropping 100 feet in elevation and traversing below to the south. At the end of the ridge reach Hadley Peak, a praiseworthy spot for admiring the colossal cone of Mount Baker.

5 RUBY MOUNTAIN

Elevation: 7408 ft (2258 m)

Difficulty: S5/T2

Distance: 7 miles

Elevation gain: 5600 ft

Trip time: 10 hours

Time to summit: 6 hours

Best time of year: June to November

Maps: USGS Ross Dam; Green Trails Diablo Dam 48

Contact: North Cascades National Park, Ross Lake National Recreation Area

Special considerations: Difficult routefinding

GPS WAYPOINT ROUTE
1. Boulder field at road: 2100 ft (10U 642563mE 5398749mN)
2. Ruby ridge: 2.5 miles, 5680 ft (10U 643665mE 5396331mN)
3. Ruby summit: 3.5 miles, 7408 ft (10U 644121mE 5395116mN)

Ruby Mountain is a bulky mass that is smack in the middle of the North Cascades. The mountain rises steadily 6200 feet above Thunder Arm in just over two miles. As such Ruby renders a queenly stance toward the Pasayten Wilderness, Ross Lake, and the Picket Range. The true summit on the western end connects to the lower eastern peak with a curving ridge. Despite its hulking appearance, Ruby is quite reasonable on the northwest side where scramblers can readily access a towering perch at this outpost of the resplendent sea of peaks of the North Cascades.

As one emerges high on Ruby's open alpine slopes, the scene is impressive in all directions and just keeps getting better. Either with or without snow, Ruby is a true gem of a scramble. But beware: Ruby can be treacherous,

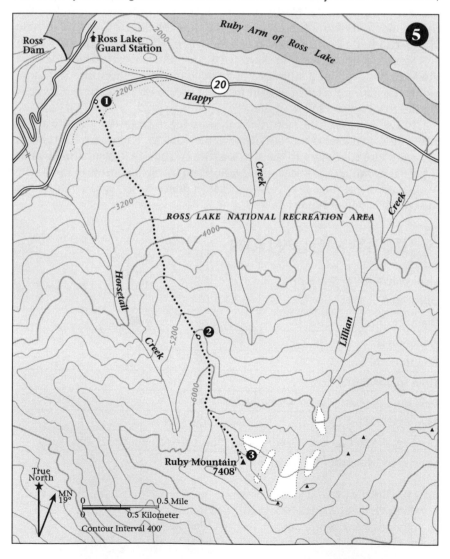

for it is a long, physical trip that requires routefinding skills to avoid steep belts and cliff bands.

Trailhead Directions: Drive I-5 north, then take the North Cascades Highway (SR 20) east to Colonial Creek Campground. Drive past the campground for 2.8 miles and park opposite a boulder field coming off Ruby Mountain. (120 miles, 2.5 hours from Seattle)

Standard Route: From the road at 2100 feet, ascend sharply to the left of the boulder field at the base of Ruby Mountain for about 500 feet. Continue up and slightly left to gain the ridge, climbing through timber, then onto open slopes. Follow the ridge up to the summit block. The last 300 feet is a rock scramble; bear left near the top.

Alternate Route: Hike the Thunder Creek Trail from Colonial Creek Campground for 2.1 miles. Turn left (east) on the Panther Creek Trail and hike upward 2.5 miles, gaining 2000 feet to Fourth of July Camp. A free backcountry permit from the North Cascades National Park office in Marblemount is required to camp here. Continue 0.7 mile to Fourth of July Pass.

Leave the trail, or try to find a very old way trail, and ascend to the north, gradually gaining the long and broad south ridge. Continue working up to the north. The summit is at the western end of the curved summit ridge. The way trail is helpful and fast at times, but is easily lost.

This route adds 10 miles and 600 feet for a total of 17 miles and 6200 feet elevation gain, and usually takes 2 days to complete.

On Ruby Mountain (Photo by Jason Griffith)

6 NORTH GARDNER MOUNTAIN AND GARDNER MOUNTAIN

Elevations: 8956 ft (2730 m); 8898 ft (2712 m)

Difficulty: S5/T4

Distance: 27 miles

Elevation gain: 8100 ft

Trip time: 3 days

Time to summit: 5 hours from meadow camp to North Gardner; 2.5 hours from North Gardner to Gardner

Best time of year: May to October

Maps: USGS Midnight Mountain, Mazama, Silver Star Mountain; Green Trails Buttermilk Butte 83, Stehekin 82, Washington Pass 50, Mazama 51

Contact: Okanogan National Forest, Methow Valley Ranger District

Special considerations: After the snow has melted, extensive loose scree; some class 3 moves

GPS WAYPOINT ROUTE
1. Wolf Creek trailhead: 2900 ft (10U 701745mE 5400000mN)
2. Gardner Meadows: 10.5 miles, 5700 ft (10U 685684mE 5373425mN)
3. Basin: 11.5 miles, 6880 ft (10U 684882mE 5374654mN)
4. South ridge: 12 miles, 8400 ft (10U 684407mE 5375825mN)
5. North Gardner summit: 12.5 miles, 8956 ft (10U 684604mE 5376379mN)
6. Gardner summit: 15 miles, 8898 ft (10U 685620mE 5375496mN)

Gardner and North Gardner Mountains form the highest point in the Methow Mountains. The slightly higher of the two peaks, North Gardner, is wide when seen from the northwest or southeast, but from other directions it emerges as a narrow triangle. Although it has a rough profile, the softer rock of North Gardner creates a less conspicuous appearance than that of adjacent Kangaroo Ridge and Silver Star Mountain. In contrast to its pointed brother, Gardner is sprawling and broad. It is well above the timber zone on all sides with a precipitous northeast face. Composed of sedimentary and volcanic rocks, Gardner is more desolate than most of the surrounding peaks. Of its two summits, the northern point is the highest.

Both peaks have high elevation scree basins, some of which hold firm snow late into summer. But because of their eastern location and relatively benign approach, this prominent duo can also be explored early in the season when kicking steps is easier than struggling on scree. The combined trip of North Gardner and Gardner can be best accomplished in 3 days, combining the scramble ascents of both peaks on the second day. The logical time for the scramble is late spring or early summer; a Memorial Day weekend

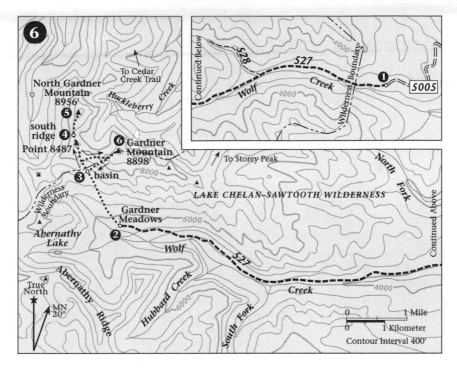

often provides a multiday high snow outing with a laudable aerial outlook.

Trailhead Directions: Drive I-5 to the North Cascades Highway (SR 20) and continue east to Winthrop. After driving through town cross over the Methow River and immediately turn right on Twin Lakes Road (County Road 9120). In about 1.5 miles turn right on Wolf Creek Road (County Road 1131) and after 3 miles turn left on road signed "L. Fork Wolf Creek Road." Shortly thereafter turn right on a dirt road signed "Wolf Creek Trail," FS Road 5005. At 3.5 miles, stay left at a fork in the road and descend for 0.5 mile until reaching the Wolf Creek Trail 527 trailhead. (205 miles, 4.5 hours from Seattle)

Standard Route:

Day 1: From the Wolf Creek trailhead at 2900 feet, hike 10.5 miles on good trail to campsites in Gardner Meadows at 5700 feet (7 hours).

Day 2: For North Gardner, ascend north up the broad open slopes of Gardner Mountain from Gardner Meadows. Do an ascending traverse northwest into the mouth of the small basin at 6880 feet. Reach the saddle between Point 8487 and North Gardner by dropping down to scree or snow on either side of the ridge. The eastern side is probably better with snow, whereas the western side is probably better without snow. From the saddle ascend the obliging crest on the south ridge to the summit of North Gardner (5 hours from camp). To reach Gardner from North Gardner, return to the same basin but higher, at about 7200 feet, traversing open slopes at this elevation southeast onto the broad open slopes of the south side of Gardner. Ascend directly up easy rock and talus slopes to the summit. Total scrambling time on day 2 adds up to about 9 hours.

On the ridge to North Gardner Mountain (Photo by Mike Torok)

After the snow has melted, extensive loose scree impedes quick progress, especially on Gardner Mountain. If a western approach is used, the ascent from the central saddle at 8160 adjacent to North Gardner offers no technical problem if the path is kept south of the crest. Between Point 8487 and its saddle with North Gardner, part of the ridge is class 4. This portion is by-passed by dropping down to the talus and scree slopes on either the western or the eastern side of the ridge.

Day 3: Hike from campsite back to Wolf Creek trailhead (6 hours).

Alternate Route: North Gardner can be approached from the Cedar Creek Trail, crossing the creek at about 3950 feet. Go up the north ridge to 5300 feet. Continue on a rising traverse (water here) to a steep gully (6000 feet). Ascend to 7200 feet. This portion of north ridge involves more difficult climbing and cannot be bypassed on its eastern side; scramblers bypass it to the west. Regain the crest of the north ridge at 7800 feet and continue south to the summit (class 2).

7 HOCK MOUNTAIN

Elevation: 7750 ft (2362 m)

Difficulty: S5/T4

Distance: 18 miles

Elevation gain: 4500 ft

Trip time: 12 hours; 1-2 days

Time to summit: 6 hours

Best time of year: July to September

Maps: USGS McAlester Mountain; Green Trails Washington Pass 50, Stehekin 82

Contact: North Cascades National Park

Special considerations: Long and arduous day trip

GPS WAYPOINT ROUTE
1. Rainy Pass: 4800 ft (10U 667350mE 5376159mN)
2. Stiletto Spur Trail: 3 miles, 4240 ft (10U 669611mE 5373564mN)

3. McAlester Trail: 5 miles, 3900 ft (10U 669096mE 5370560mN)
4. Leave McAlester Trail: 7 miles, 4440 ft (10U 670756mE 5368605mN)
5. Summit ridge: 8.2 miles, 7200 ft (10U 672349mE 5368589mN)
6. Hock summit: 9 miles, 7750 ft (10U 672605mE 5368907mN)

Positioned on the Chelan crest less than 2 miles southwest of Twisp Pass, Hock Mountain lies at the head of the South Fork Twisp River. The north face of Hock is steep granite rock, but the western slope is wooded and moderate. Nearby Twisp Mountain, Lincoln Butte, and Stiletto Peak form a series of high points that surround Twisp Pass. The pass itself is noted for its gardens, glacier-smoothed boulders, dramatic rock peaks, and views down into Bridge Creek and across to Mounts Goode and Logan. This area is dotted with

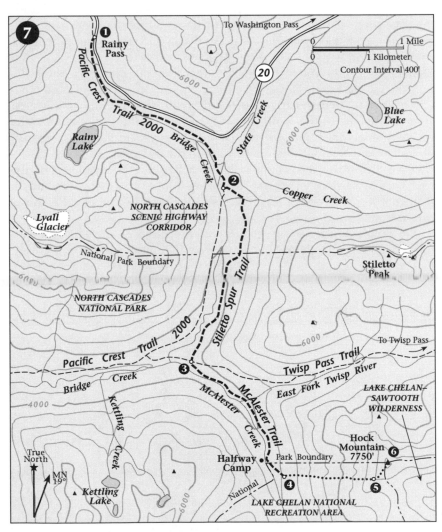

larch trees and there are also old lookout sites steeped in history.

Hock is on the southern and western boundary of the Twisp Pass region, yet just southeast of SR 20, the North Cascades Scenic Highway. Thus Hock suffers some of the convergence zone weather features of so-called "Rainy Pass," but the aspect to the east gives way to the dry and boundless Chelan territory.

Trailhead Directions: Drive I-5 north to the North Cascades Highway (SR 20). Drive 38 miles past Newhalem to Rainy Pass. To cut about 1.5 miles from the trip, drive east of Rainy Pass and park near milepost 159 just east of Bridge Creek. Follow the connector trail downslope to the Pacific Crest Trail. Otherwise, begin at the Pacific Crest Trail 2000 trailhead at Rainy Pass. (150 miles, 3 hours from Seattle)

Standard Route: From Rainy Pass at 4800 feet, follow the Pacific Crest Trail heading south. Continue until a junction with the Stiletto Spur Trail after crossing State Creek. Go south on the Stiletto Spur Trail past Copper Creek until reaching the junction with the Twisp Pass Trail. Just west of this junction is an intersection with the McAlester Trail at 3900 feet. Continue south on McAlester Trail until you pass Halfway Camp, a suitable camp on a 2-day trip.

Any ascent eastward toward the Hock summit ridge is feasible, but probably the best travel path starts about 0.3 mile past Halfway Camp in the forest after crossing two nearly confluent large streams. Continue ascending to the east to intersect the summit ridge at about 7200 feet. From here it is an easy scramble along the south spur northward to the summit.

Note that if this trip is done from Rainy Pass, the extended hike on the trail leads to a seriously long day. If starting from east of Rainy Pass and directly north of the Pacific Crest Trail, locating the trail south of the highway can be troublesome.

Alternate Route: Instead of starting from Rainy Pass, drive on SR 20 until encountering a southward bulge at the southernmost part of the highway. Park the car and go cross-country directly south until intersecting the Pacific Crest Trail at about 4400 feet. This saves 2 miles of trail hiking each way.

Hock Mountain (Photo by John Roper)

𝟪 SNOWKING MOUNTAIN

Elevation: 7433 ft (2266 m)

Difficulty: S5/T4

Distance: 11 miles

Elevation gain: 6500 ft

Trip time: 1-2 days

Time to summit: 11 hours from trailhead; 5 hours from camp at Cyclone Lake

Best time of year: June to September

Maps: USGS Snowking Mountain, Sonny Boy Lakes; Green Trails Cascade Pass 80, Snowking Mountain 79

Contact: Mount Baker–Snoqualmie National Forest, Mount Baker Ranger Station

Special considerations: Avalanche danger in early season

GPS WAYPOINT ROUTE
1. Climber's trailhead: 2400 ft (10U 630996mE 5368692mN)
2. Point 5116: 2 miles, 5116 ft (10U 630239mE 5366706mN)
3. Cyclone Lake: 4 miles, 5350 ft (10U 629191mE 5364031mN)
4. Summit ridge: 5 miles, 6800 ft (10U 627627mE 5362733mN)
5. Snowking summit: 5.5 miles, 7433 ft (10U 627520mE 5362923mN)

Tucked into the interior of the North Cascades, Snowking Mountain forms an altitudinous crown between the Cascade and Suiattle Rivers. Snowking presents a gentle facade that culminates in four small summits, the highest of which is the eastern peak. Despite its wilderness quality, Snowking is visible from the North Cascades Scenic Highway. Due to its western location in the range, snowfall is heavy on Snowking creating an uncommon amount of glacier ice for a peak its size. In this respect the mountain is akin to Mount Buckindy, Mount Daniel, and Bacon Peak.

The Snowking Glacier covers the northern slopes over a mile from east to west, and most times of the year the broad summit shimmers with snow. The top of Snowking provides a premium vantage of the North Cascades from Kangaroo Ridge, Mount Goode, the Picket Range, and beyond to Mounts Shuksan and Baker. Even Olympus, Rainier, Chimney Rock, and Fernow give the impression of being next door. The route up the glacier is a climb requiring crevasse-rescue skills, yet a scramble route can be forged from near Cyclone Lake to the summit.

Trailhead Directions: Drive I-5 north to the North Cascades Highway (SR 20). Drive to the town of Marblemount and cross the bridge onto the Cascade River Road. Drive 14.5 miles to FS Road 1570. Cross the river and drive as far as possible; a 4WD may be needed to get to the end of road. The last 2 miles are rough and may need to be walked to where a climber's trail begins. (100 miles, 3 hours from Seattle)

Standard Route:

Day 1: From the end of the road find a well-defined climber's trail at 2400 feet. Take it up to the ridge crest and the saddle south of Point 5116. From the north, the climber's trail skirts the eastern side of Point 5116 to the saddle on the south. Continue on the path to the saddle and ascend the next high point of the ridge. Follow the crest south to the area near Cyclone Lake, or use the wide section of the ridge just above the two small lakes to the north for a better camp. (5 hours)

Day 2: Follow the granite ridge east of Cyclone Lake southwest toward

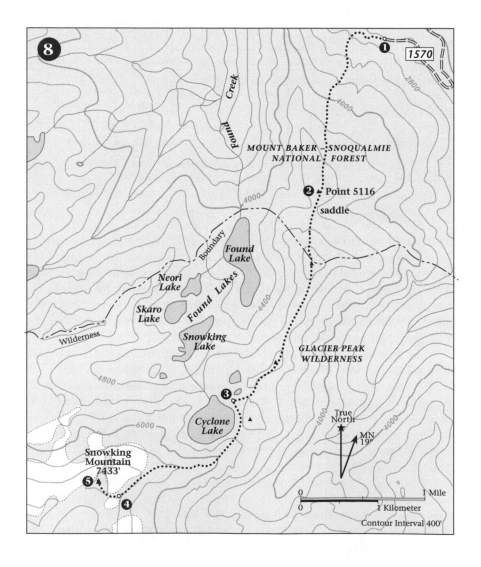

Snowking Mountain (Photo by John Roper)

Snowking's east peak. Hike over comfortable slabs and some heather sections. Avoid the glacier, which is on your right to the northeast, by scrambling upward on steep snow or rocks, keeping to the left side of the summit area where the glacier trends toward the summit. Thereafter scramble up the southeast rock slope to the summit. (4 hours from camp to summit)

Due to complex navigation on the approach to Cyclone Lake, Snowking is best done after mid-July when the snow is patchy or gone. Some loose snow can be encountered near the summit; in early season beware of avalanches.

Alternate Route: Snowking can be done in 1 day from the road end, taking 10 to 12 hours for a small party of people in good physical condition. From Cyclone Lake, cross the stream at the outlet and attain the ridge west of the lake. Connect with the standard route to avoid the glacier. This way is shorter than the standard route and makes a commendable round trip.

OSCEOLA PEAK, MOUNT LAGO, AND MOUNT CARRU

Elevations: 8587 ft (2617 m), 8745 ft (2666 m), 8595 ft (2620 m)

Difficulty: S5/T4

Distance: 40 miles

Total gain: 11,500 ft (8300 ft in plus 3200 ft out)

Trip time: 4 days

Times to summit: 2 hours from Lake Doris to Osceola; 3 hours from camp to Lago; 2 hours from Lago to Carru

Best time of year: July to October

Maps: USGS Mount Lago, Pasayten Peak; Green Trails Washington Pass 50, Pasayten Peak 18

Contact: Okanogan National Forest, Methow Valley Ranger District

Special considerations: Beware of loose scree and talus and slippery lichen-covered rocks.

GPS WAYPOINT ROUTE
1. Slate Pass: 6900 ft (10U 671613mE 5400182mN)
2. Lake Doris: 11.8 miles, 6975 ft (10U 676961mE 5410265mN)
3. Osceola summit: 13 miles, 8587 ft (10U 677942mE 5411280mN)
4. Camp west of Shellrock Pass: 17 miles, 6340 ft (10U 680519mE 5409869mN)
5. Lago summit: 18.5 miles, 8745 ft (10U 680830mE 5411186mN)
6. Lago-Carru saddle meadow: 19 miles, 7100 ft (10U 680084mE 5410830mN)
7. Carru summit: 19.5 miles, 8595 ft (10U 679579mE 5411447mN)

The Pasayten Wilderness has the reputation of being the "Sunny Pasayten" because it lies east of the Cascade Crest. The region is attractive to scramblers particularly during unsettled weather when the west side of the mountains is wrapped in thick fog or steady rain. Yet the Pasayten is not immune to showers, and can sometimes fall prey to an extended deluge. Do not despair; usually the weather will clear enough to enjoy an athletic scramble to rugged peaks surrounded by stunning views of craggy and frozen spires from Canada to the heart of the North Cascades.

Osceola Peak and Mounts Carru and Lago constitute a triple crown of jewels in the Pasayten Wilderness. On Osceola, the dry and gradual, northwest-facing scree slopes contrast with the shaded and precipitous, recently glaciated slopes of its northeast ridge. Located between Osceola and Lago, Carru features cirques and ice remnants and is one of the most significant formations on the Lease-Eureka Creek divide. Lago has the distinction of having the easternmost glacier in the Cascade Range. Osceola is an agreeable, straightforward scramble from Lake Doris with a royal perspective from the top. The route on Carru is varied and engaging with sections of delightful scrambling on decent rock. Nearby Lago is an added bounty.

Certainly for the avid peakbagger a sensible trip is to combine the triplets

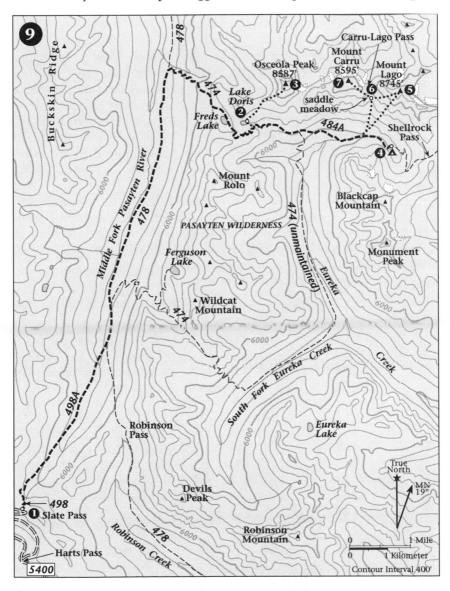

for a multiday outing. Many possibilities exist depending on the available time and energy of the party. Scrambling Carru and Lago together rather than separately makes an excellent day trip from the trail. Assuredly the combined scramble of these three Pasayten giants is a regal trip for those seeking an extended outing of wilderness travel.

Trailhead Directions: Drive I-5 north to the North Cascades Highway (SR 20), and drive it east to 1.5 miles past Early Winters Campground. Turn left and drive 0.4 mile to Mazama. Turn left on Harts Pass Road (County Road 9140) and drive, continuing on FS Road 5400, about 20 miles to Harts Pass. Turn right and drive 2 miles to Slate Pass and the Buckskin Ridge Trail 498 trailhead. (205 miles, 5 hours from Seattle)

Standard Route:

Day 1: From Slate Pass at 6900 feet, hike north on Buckskin Ridge Trail 498 for 0.6 mile. Turn right on Middle Fork Pasayten Trail 498A (also Trail 575) and descend 3.1 miles until it joins with Robinson Pass Trail 478 at 5200 feet, just after crossing the middle fork of the Pasayten River. Hike north down the river valley continuing on Trail 478 for 5.1 miles, and turn right at a junction with the north end of Ferguson Lake Trail 474. Hike 3 miles east up Trail 474 past Freds Lake and on to Lake Doris. Lake Doris is slightly north of the trail at 6975 feet. Camp at cozy Lake Doris and savor the high vista of the peaks ahead. (7 hours from trailhead)

Day 2: From Lake Doris, begin the scramble of Osceola. Travel cross-country northeast easily for about 0.6 mile through scattered forest, ascending gradually. Gain 1400 feet on a generally settled talus and boulder field, although there are loose sections. More troublesome are the black lichen-covered rocks

On the summit of Osceola Peak (Photo by Mike Torok)

which are extraordinarily slippery when wet. Pick either the southwest ridge or the south face and ascend broken rock and talus fields to the summit of Osceola. The southwest ridge has sections of decent boot track. Return to Lake Doris in ample time to disassemble camp and move to a more suitable site to access Lago and Carru. Travel east 4 miles toward Shellrock Pass on nearly level terrain, staying left on Trail 484A after Trail 474 (unmaintained) heads south down Eureka Creek. Find a suitable camp in the meadow at 6340 feet just west and below Shellrock Pass. If the party has time and energy, hike up a well-traveled pack trail 1100 feet on switchbacks to the pass panorama and watch as the setting sun projects a fiery glow. (8 hours camp to camp)

Day 3: A scramble of Lago begins a combined summit day of Mounts Lago and Carru. From the meadow camp, hike west 0.5 mile back down Trail 484A along Eureka Creek. Note the pass between Lago and Carru at 7600 feet. Just east of the pass is a rock buttress and then to the right, a major gully of reddish talus. Directly opposite this gully, leave the trail going north at the creek crossing and ascend the lower gully, a broad avalanche track, about 400 vertical feet. Before the gully narrows into a bowling alley-sized slot, traverse west below the rock buttress and above most of the trees. Rising slightly, easily traverse the buttress to the southwest face directly above a small meadow in the Lago-Carru saddle. Ascend directly up scree, talus, and broken rock to the west ridge. Traverse up and east, on the south side of the west ridge, to the Lago summit. The scramble route is neither troublesome nor exposed but the way is impeded by abundant talus.

To obtain the summit of Carru, descend the scrambling route of Lago to the ascent meadow at the 7100 feet level of the saddle. Traverse west onto Carru through broken forest and around the first rock buttress. Note the upper section of a large western summit gully, and travel an ascending traverse northwest directly to it. The party can experiment with many variations of enjoyable rock scrambling. A high gully tops out with a 2-foot-wide saddle about 400 feet below the summit and just east of the summit gully. From this saddle traverse into the summit gully, to follow it, scrambling to the summit ridge. The true summit of Carru is a small, sharp pinnacle 200 feet east along the ridge crest. Descend the scrambling route back to the saddle meadow; the recommended path traverses to the lower ascent gully on Lago to descend to the trail. A direct descent to the trail from the saddle is possible, but the creek bed narrows, the sides get steeper, and the forest thickens as one descends. (8 hours round trip)

Day 4: From the camp below Shellrock Pass, the party can return on the trail 17 miles to Slate Pass (10 hours). Alternatively, the trip can continue eastward over Shellrock Pass to access other glorious scrambles in the Pasayten region.

Alternate Routes: The northwest ridge to Osceola is long and inconvenient but a feasible scramble. Because of loose scree sections and pinnacles to be bypassed, this route is less pleasant than the standard southern route.

On the south flank of Lago, there are three moderately broad scree gullies which can be scrambled. On Carru, the western spur facing Osceola is composed of scree and appears the easiest route from that direction.

10 PTARMIGAN PEAK

Elevation: 8614 ft (2626 m)

Difficulty: S4/T1

Distance: 38 miles

Elevation gain: 7200 ft

Trip time: 3 days

Time to summit: 3 hours from camp at Tatoosh Buttes meadow

Best time of year: June to October

Maps: USGS Mount Lago, Tatoosh Buttes; Green Trails Washington Pass 50, Pasayten Peak 18

Contact: Okanogan National Forest, Methow Valley Ranger District

GPS WAYPOINT ROUTE
1. Slate Pass: 6900 ft (10U 671613mE 5400182mN)
2. Tamarack Ridge: 17 miles, 7120 ft (10U 680195mE 5419072mN)
3. Ptarmigan summit: 19 miles, 8614 ft (10U 681066mE 5415305mN)

Just a stone's throw to Canada, Ptarmigan Peak is one of the highest summits of the northern Pasayten Wilderness. Ptarmigan is flagrantly lopsided with gradual southwest slopes encircling a sheer and cavernous northeast cirque. In contrast to the gentle crest, the precipice to the east is dizzying. To the northeast of the summit, Ptarmigan Lake nestles at the base of rippling grooves speckled with occasional ice patches.

The scramble of Ptarmigan Peak is primarily an extended backpacking trip with a simple walk-up to the summit added on. Yet the approach over Tatoosh Buttes and Tamarack Ridge reveals vast unenclosed alpine meadows where the sky is as big as creation. It is difficult to find such a great hulk of a mountain that is so lenient. Moreover, it is a shame to hike all the way in to high meadows and not spend enough time to relish in and explore the area. Added gifts are the striking views of the rutted north faces of Osceola, Lago, and Carru right next door.

Trailhead Directions: Drive I-5 north to the North Cascades Highway (SR 20) and head east to 1.5 miles past Early Winters Campground. Turn left and go 0.4 mile to Mazama. Turn left on Harts Pass Road (County Road 9140), which becomes FS Road 5400, and drive about 20 miles to Harts Pass. Continue 2 more miles to Slate Pass and the Buckskin Ridge Trail 498 trailhead. (205 miles, 5 hours from Seattle)

Standard Route:

Day 1: Take Buckskin Ridge Trail 498 north from Slate Pass at 6900 feet. After 0.6 mile, take the right spur, Trail 498A (also Trail 575), down to the crossing of the Middle Fork Pasayten River (5200 feet). Intersect Robinson

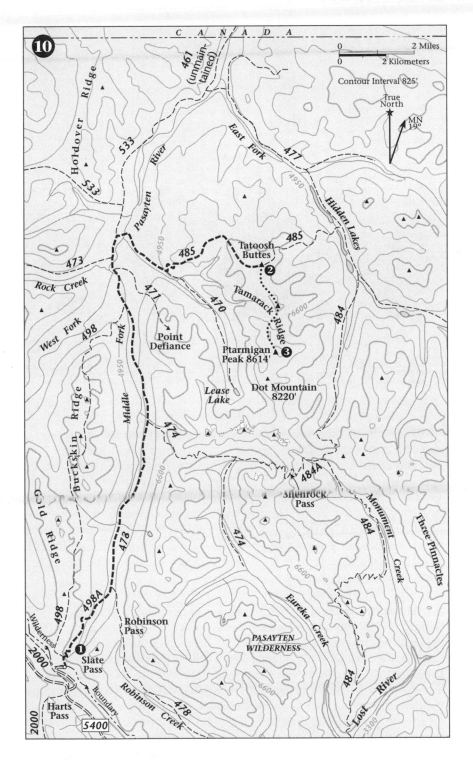

CANADA

10

2 Miles
0
0
2 Kilometers

Contour Interval 825'

True
North

MN
19°

Holdover Ridge
461
(unmaintained)
533
Pasayten River
East Fork
471
4950
Hidden Lakes
533
473
Rock Creek
485
Tatoosh Buttes
485
471
470
Tamarack Ridge
6600
484
West Fork
498
Middle Fork
Point Defiance
Ptarmigan Peak 8614'
Lease Lake
Dot Mountain 8220'
4950
Buckskin Ridge
474
484A
6600
Sherrock Pass
Monument Creek
484
Three Pinnacles
Gold Ridge
478
474
6600
498A
Robinson Pass
Eureka Creek
PASAYTEN WILDERNESS
484
Lost River
Wilderness
2000
498
Slate Pass
1
Harts Pass
2000
Boundary
Robinson Creek
478
5400
6600
3300

2

3

Ptarmigin Peak (Photo by John Roper)

Pass Trail 478 and continue north. At 9.3 miles, pass Point Defiance Trail 471 and continue 0.2 mile. Take a right at the junction and hike east on Tatoosh Buttes Trail 485 for 1.4 miles. Go left, north, and up for about 4 miles to the open meadows below Tatoosh Buttes where camping is available.

Day 2: The next day, hike cross-country southward along open and easy Tamarack Ridge for about 1.5 miles, then scramble up onto rocks and talus slopes for a mile-long traverse on the eastern side of the ridge top to the Ptarmigan summit. If desired, one can continue scrambling another mile south to Dot Mountain (8220 feet). On the second day camp may be moved to a lower location to shorten the hike out on the third day.

Day 3: Return to Slate Pass.

Alternate Route: A shorter approach can be made from Canada, but as there is no customs at the border, officials frown upon this route, and little information is therefore available. For the approach from Canada, hike south on unmaintained Trail 461, which begins near the border, go east on Hidden Lakes Trail 477, then south and west up Tatoosh Buttes Trail 485 to the Tatoosh Buttes. This approach is somewhat less hiking, but a lot more driving, and the trailhead in Canada is unmarked and not well maintained. Prior arrangements with both Canadian and U.S. customs must be made in advance for the border crossing.

11 REMMEL MOUNTAIN

Elevation: 8685 ft (2647 m)

Difficulty: S4/T1

Distance: 32 miles

Elevation gain: 5400 ft

Trip time: 2-3 days

Time to summit: 10 hours; 2 hours from Four Point Creek camp

Best time of year: June to October

Maps: USGS Coleman Peak, Bauerman Ridge, Remmel Mountain; Green Trails Coleman Peak 20

Contact: Okanogan National Forest, Methow Valley Ranger District

Special considerations: Tricky ford when Chewuch River is running high

GPS WAYPOINT ROUTE
1. Chewuch trailhead: 3600 ft (10U 718917mE 5412436mN)
2. Chewuch River ford: 5.2 miles, 4400 ft (10U 716208mE 5419300mN)
3. Four Point Creek camp: 15.5 miles, 7120 ft (10U 706467mE 5423270mN)
4. Remmel summit: 16 miles, 8685 ft (10U 705430mE 5422522mN)

High in the Pasayten Wilderness just south of the Canadian boundary, Remmel Mountain is nearly in the middle of the rugged land where neither roads nor even motor powered saws to clear the trails are permitted. Remmel is one of the most colossal and exceptional mountains in the Okanogan Range. The immense hulk displays multiple cirques to the east with scenic alpine lakes.

Nevertheless, Remmel is basically a trail trip, as a rudimentary path leads almost all the way to the summit, thus requiring minimal cross-country rambling in high, open country. But the area is so lovely, the views so outstanding, and the feeling of solitude and remoteness so great, that a visit to Remmel is gratifying. The best time to scale the peak is at sunset, when the trudge up the talus slope leads to a serene respite at the very tiptop.

Trailhead Directions: Drive I-5 north past Mount Vernon. Take the North Cascades Highway (SR 20) east to Winthrop. From Winthrop drive 30 miles on the West Chewach River Road (FS Road 51) north to its end as FS Road 5160 at Thirtymile Campground and the start of Chewach River Trail 510. (240 miles, 5.5 hours from Seattle)

Standard Route:

Day 1: From the Chewuch trailhead at 3400 feet, hike along the Chewuch River north for 5.2 miles to Fire Creek Trail 561. At 4400 feet ford the Chewuch River. This is no easy feat in early summer; consider bringing aqua-socks or wading shoes for comfort, safety, and to preserve dry boots. Regain the Fire Creek Trail, and follow it with some difficulty at times for 5.6 miles to the junction with Coleman Ridge Trail 505. Continue west, then north for 5 miles along open and scenic Coleman Ridge. Good camping is available in several places on Coleman Ridge, at Four Point Lake, and along the Chewuch River. The most favorable camp is found at the headwaters of Four Point Creek.

Day 2: The next day climb west into a small basin. Go up the old way trail, on the north side of the basin, all the way to the summit.

Day 3: Return to the trailhead. Remmel can be done in a fast-paced 2 days but allowing for 3 days will grant time to savor the high country along Coleman Ridge.

Alternate Routes: For a pleasing loop trip and a shorter return time as it is entirely on trail, hike down to Four Point Lake. Pick up Coleman Ridge

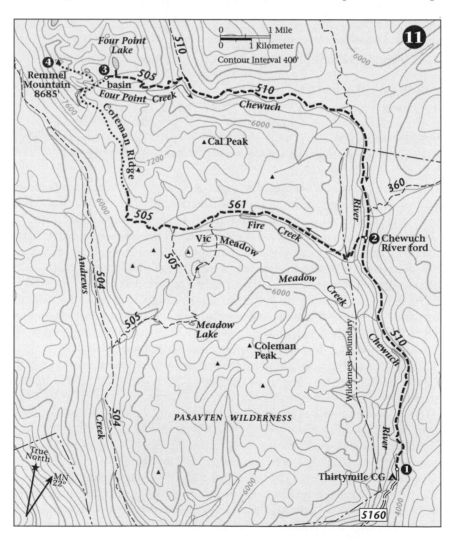

Remmel Mountain (Photo by John Roper)

Trail 505 and descend 2.4 miles east to the Chewuch River Trail where there is a bridge across the river. Hike east and south 12 miles back to the trailhead.

In early season Remmel is best done in reverse, by following Trail 510 first and forgoing Coleman Ridge and the ford of the Chewuch River. Instead use the bridge over the Chewuch River at Fire Creek. Camping is easily established at Four Point Lake, and a side trip to explore Coleman Ridge is still available to those with the energy and desire. Without Coleman Ridge, the round trip is 30 miles.

12 BIG CRAGGY PEAK AND WEST CRAGGY PEAK

Elevations: 8470 ft (2582 m), 8366 ft (2550 m)

Difficulty: S4/T4

Distance: 9 miles

Elevation gain: 3600 ft

Trip time: 1-2 days

Time to summit: 9 hours to Big Craggy, 5 hours from Copper Glance camp; 2 hours from Big Craggy to West Craggy

Best time of year: July to October

Maps: USGS Billy Goat Mountain, Sweetgrass Butte; Green Trails Mazama 51, Billy Goat Mountain 19

Contact: Okanogan National Forest, Methow Valley Ranger Station

Special considerations: Dangerous rock fall in places, helmets recommended

GPS WAYPOINT ROUTE
1. Copper Glance Creek trailhead: 3800 ft (10U 699159mE 5402022mN)
2. Leave trail to head up southeast ridge: 2 miles, 5900 feet (10U 697432mE 5403001mN)

3. Big Craggy summit: 3 miles, 8470 ft (10U 696445mE 5404345mN)
4. Saddle: 3.5 miles, 7600 ft (10U 695851mE 5404159mN)
5. West Craggy ridge: 4 miles, 7660 ft (10U 695410mE 5403852mN)
6. West Craggy summit: 4.5 miles, 8366 ft (10U 695112mE 5404273mN)

The Craggys are a lofty and jagged twosome standing as watchdogs at the southern border of the Pasayten Wilderness. The higher of the two, Big Craggy, sports a heterogeneous northern face mixed with steep rock gullies and cliffs. In contrast, its south side manifests a middle-of-the-road, mellow scree slope. Equally as rough, West Craggy emanates an elevated ridge that extends north to Eightmile Peak.

The Craggys represent the quintessential Pasayten trip with far-reaching vast spaces expanding to rocky panoramas under gleaming skies. The terrain is honest, straightforward, and guileless. Roam free and unrestricted in this welcoming land to view miles of broad valleys and open ridges. Carry plenty of water and start early before the sun gets hot. This is big-scale country at its best.

Big Craggy and West Craggy are best accomplished in 1 lengthy day, with a car camp the night before. But the trip described here is for parties who wish to extend the wilderness delight to enjoy good camping at Copper Glance Lake, beneath the cliffs of Isabella Ridge and 8204-foot Sherman Peak. A patch of water that by itself might scarcely be considered worth the walk, Copper Glance Lake is the portal to spectacular scenery and expansive meadows that reward the sweat of the steep approach.

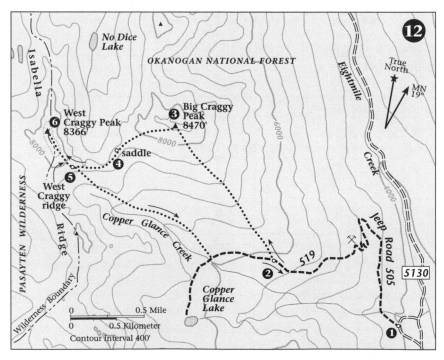

On the summit of Big Craggy Peak (Photo by Mike Torok)

Trailhead Directions: Drive I-5 and take the North Cascades Highway (SR 20) east to Winthrop. Continue north on the West Chewuch River Road (FS Road 51) for 9.7 miles and turn left on Eightmile Creek Road (FS Road 5130). Drive 12.3 miles to Copper Glance Creek Trail 519, which begins at Jeep Road 505. (220 miles, 4 hours from Seattle)

Standard Route: From the Copper Glance Creek trailhead at 3800 feet begin hiking up a precipitous mining road. At 1.5 miles and 5200 feet find a mineshaft and the end of the mining road. At about 2 miles journey through a lush meadow dotted in season with wildflowers. The way returns to the woods, at 2.6 miles passing a small pond. Begin a steep ascent of a rockslide to top out at 6400 feet. For a suitable camp go down 300 feet to the shore of Copper Glance Lake (6100 feet).

To summit Big Craggy, hike the Copper Glance Trail to a point just before the trees in the large meadow. After the crossing of Copper Glance Creek and at about 5900 feet leave the trail and head up the southeast ridge. At 7800 feet the route is abrupt and the scree is troublesome, but persevere to gain the summit. Watch for dangerous rock fall in the dirty gully above the southeast scree slope on the last 500 feet of Big Craggy.

For West Craggy, traverse past the saddle between Big Craggy and West Craggy at 7600 feet. Continue southwest just west of the gendarme on the eastern ridge of West Craggy at about 7660 feet. Contour to a gully that appears to proceed almost to the high point on the ridge and continue up the gully. At the apex, follow a scree slope to the top: almost any route is reasonable from the basin southeast of the summit. Although some routes have more loose scree than other routes to impede forward progress, those same scree slopes provide an excellent down-route where "scree skiing" accelerates the descent.

Alternate Route: For a single day trip, hike the Copper Glance Creek Trail to about 6100 feet. Before the crossing of Copper Glance Creek, leave the trail and head up the valley on the right side in the lightly brushy terrain. At 6550 feet, head north to the saddle at 7600 feet, then follow the west ridge to the summit of Big Craggy, navigating goat trails along the way. Beware: The black lichen on the west ridge is treacherous when wet.

13 PASS BUTTE AND LOST PEAK

Elevations: 8140 ft (2481 m), 8464 ft (2580 m)

Difficulty: S5/T2

Distance: 42 miles one way

Elevation gain: 14,200 ft

Trip time: 3 days

Time to summit: 3 hours from base camp to Pass Butte; 2 hours from Pass Butte to Lost Peak

Best time of year: June to October

Maps: USGS Lost Peak, Mount Lago; Green Trails Washington Pass 50, Mazama 51, Billy Goat Mountain 19, Pasayten Peak 18

Contact: Okanogan National Forest, Methow Valley Ranger District

Special considerations: Slippery boulders on parts of the scramble; intensely strenuous

GPS WAYPOINT ROUTE
1. Monument Creek trailhead: 2400 ft (10U 683419mE 5392020mN)
2. Pistol Pass: 10.4 miles, 7200 ft (10U 683862mE 5403826mN)
3. Camp east of Shellrock Pass: 16.8 miles, 6840 ft (10U 682282mE 5409906mN)
4. Butte Pass: 17.9 miles, 6900 ft (10U 682903mE 5410423mN)
5. Pass Butte summit: 19.4miles, 8140 ft (10U 685073mE 5410210mN)
6. Lost Peak summit: 20.9 miles, 8464 ft (10U 686701mE 5409560mN)
7. Camp west of Shellrock Pass: 26 miles, 6340 ft (10U 680519mE 5409869mE)
8. Slate Pass: 41.8 miles, 6900 ft (10U 671613mE 5400182mN)

Deep in the core of the Pasayten Wilderness are situated Pass Butte and Lost Peak, the gentle giants. This vicinity of the Pasayten Wilderness provides delightful wandering, because the terrain is open and unfettered by the dense brush that causes scramblers to curse the notorious bushwhacks of the wetter, western regions.

Pass Butte is a moderate hump connected by a ridge to a more striking yet smaller and unnamed 8211-foot summit to the northwest. Up close, Lost Peak is tall and rounded, mostly covered with scree and small blocky rock sections on its southern slopes. But despite this modest demeanor, the northern side is ominously steep with a small ice gully and ice remnant.

The combination of Pass Butte and Lost Peak makes a first-rate day trip from a campsite from either direction. Because the duo is a long way from the closest trailheads, a loop trip is recommended for its variety and aesthetics. Most of the travel is along trails paralleling long riverbeds and thus provides a logical introduction for the backpacker transitioning into a scrambler. Delight in your progress from hiking on the trail to superb strolling along enormous hillsides where the views explode.

Trailhead Directions: Drive I-5 north and then drive east on the North Cascades Highway (SR 20) to 1.5 miles east of Early Winters Campground. Turn left and drive 0.4 mile to Mazama. Turn left on Harts Pass Road (County Road 9140), which becomes FS Road 5400. This trip requires a car shuttle. To reach the start of the trip at the Monument Creek trailhead, drive Harts Pass Road about 7 miles from Mazama. After crossing the Lost River, turn right and go 0.3 mile to a parking lot. Leave the other car 2 miles beyond Harts Pass at Slate Pass and the trailhead for Buckskin Ridge Trail 498. (205 miles, 5 hours from Seattle)

Standard Route:

Day 1: Begin on Monument Creek Trail 484 at 2400 feet, which travels along Lost River. Camp at the trailhead the night before and start early in the morning as the day will be ambitious and long. The tread is in forest for 2 miles to the high point of 2700 feet. At 4 miles, after entering the Pasayten Wilderness,

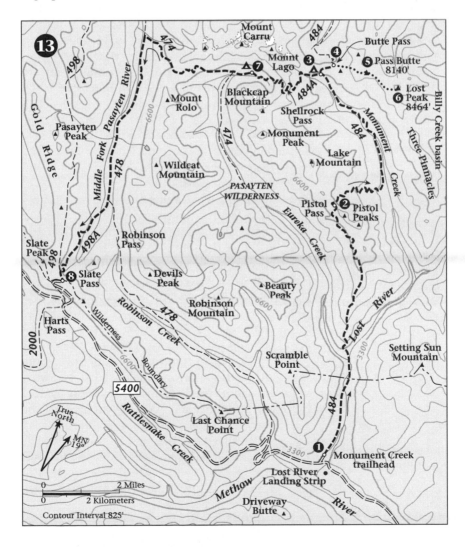

discover the dramatic confluence of two gorges, Eureka Creek from the west and Lost River from the east. Peer into the black hole of the mouth of the legendary and wild Lost River Gorge, a dividend on the way to more aerial sights.

Cross over Eureka Creek on the bridge, and travel on a rough trail across many blowdowns for another 4 miles. Then ascend 4600 feet up the hogback between two canyons to 7200-foot Pistol Pass. This open, south-facing slope is blazing hot and bone dry in the summer sun. Beware, as parties can suffer from heat exhaustion carrying heavy packs if the bearers are not well hydrated. The path then drops 2800 feet to Monument Creek, a tributary of the Lost River. Trudge onward toward Shellrock Pass, heading due west past the continuation of Trail 484 to Butte Pass. But stop short at a meadow with a small lake and creek at 6800 feet, 0.5 mile east of Shellrock Pass. Put up the tents and relax. Congratulations are in order for accomplishing a lengthy but rewarding hike to base camp. (Monument Creek trailhead to camp: 17 miles, 6800 feet, 12 hours)

Day 2: Summit day provides a kind-hearted scramble in a loop from east camp across Pass Butte, to Lost Peak, and then back. From your camp east of Shellrock Pass, hike Trail 484 east to a junction. Trail 484 continues north to Butte Pass and Ptarmigan Creek. Cruise this trail north to Butte Pass (6900 feet). Stroll cross-country eastward through open forest, going over Point 7275, or traversing its north side, to gain the west ridge of Pass Butte. Follow the ridge top southeast to the summit of Pass Butte (the eastern of the two bumps) at 8140 feet. An easy 1.5-mile, 1.5-hour traverse can be made to Lost Peak along

the eastern ridge of Pass Butte and the northwest ridge of Lost.

Point 8107 along the way is easily bypassed with a traverse on its south slope. On Lost Peak, much of the northwest ridge, especially on the south side, consists of boulders covered with black lichen that is severely slippery when wet. But long sections of clean solid rock are attained on the ridge crest by edging onto the steep north side of the ridge. After enjoying the summit, return to your camp east of Shellrock Pass. (7 hours round trip)

Day 3: To complete the trip, break camp and continue beyond Shellrock Pass to a western camp at 6340 feet just west of the pass (or add 1.5 hours and 1000 feet each way if the party is energetic enough to attain this camp on the first day). Hike west on Trail 484A to its junction with Ferguson Lake Trail 474. Travel west, following Trail 474 to the junction of Trail 478 at the Middle Fork Pasayten River.

Lost Peak (Photo by Mike Torok)

Continue south to Trail 498A (also Trail 575) and return to the cars at Slate Pass on Trail 498. (Camp to Slate Pass: 16 miles, 4400 feet, 11 hours)

Alternate Route: The west slope and the southwest flank of Lost Peak are gentle and can be scrambled. Also, the basin of Billy Creek presents a straight-forward scramble with a long cross-country descent from the summit of Lost Peak at 8464 feet to Lost River at 3760 feet via the Billy Creek basin.

14 MONUMENT PEAK AND LAKE MOUNTAIN

Elevations: 8592 ft (2619 m), 8371 ft (2552 m)

Difficulty: S5/T4

Distance: 33 miles

Elevation gain: 10,400 ft

Trip time: 3 days

Time to summit: 4 hours from camp to Monument; 4 hours from Monument to Lake

Best time of year: June to October

Maps: USGS Mount Lago, Lost Peak; Green Trails Washington Pass 50, Mazama 51, Billy Goat Mountain 19, Pasayten Peak 18

Contact: Okanogan National Forest, Methow Valley Ranger Distict

Special considerations: Much of the route is dry and waterless.

GPS WAYPOINT ROUTE
1. Monument Creek trailhead: 2400 ft (10U 683419mE 5392020mN)
2. Pistol Pass: 12 miles, 7200 ft (10U 683862mE 5403826mN)
3. Lake of the Woods camp: 13 miles, 6620 ft (10U 683856mE 5404896mN)
4. Basin: 15 miles, 6400 ft (10U 681794mE 5405804mN)
5. Monument summit: 16.3 miles, 8592 ft (10U 680609mE 5407285mN)
6. Lake summit: 18.3 miles, 8371 ft (10U 682889mE 5405981mN)

Monument Peak and Lake Mountain are situated in the rugged and wild heart of the Pasayten Wilderness. To the north tower the lined faces of the Mount Osceola-Lago-Carru group. Ranged by Pistol Pass and the Lost River, certainly the names of these surrounding features suggest something more ominous than the feasible scrambling that provides access to such remote giants. Monument has a long southern ridge that protects a steep north face laced with cliffs. Less than 2 miles away, the north face of Lake is nearly as abrupt. An open, glacier-scooped basin nestles in the arm between the two.

This rocky scramble is very strenuous and athletic. The high, alpine landscape is wild, alien, and lonely. Few people visit the area because it is so much work to get there, and parts of the trail have not been well maintained in recent years. The trail up to Pistol Pass gains about 4800 feet elevation on a south-facing slope with little shade, and therefore can be hot and parching. Plan accordingly: travel early, carry enough water, and stop when heat exhaustion threatens.

Trailhead Directions: Drive I-5 north past Mount Vernon and take the North Cascades Highway (SR 20) east. One and a half miles east of Early Winters Campground, turn left, cross the Methow River, and go 0.4 mile to Mazama. Turn left on Harts Pass Road (County Road 9140). Cross the Lost River and at about 7 miles from Mazama, turn right, and go 0.3 mile to a parking lot at Monument Creek Trail 484. (190 miles, 4.5 hours from Seattle)

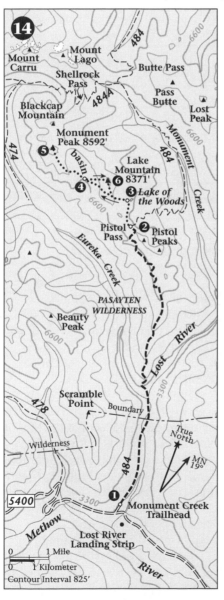

Standard Route:

Day 1: From the trailhead at 2400 feet, hike Monument Creek Trail 484 north for 3.6 miles to the bridge across Eureka Creek and the last dependable water. For the next 7 miles the trail goes sharply up the ridge southwest of Pistol Peaks and then traverses northwest to Pistol Pass. Drop 600 feet and hike 0.7 mile north through open woods to a good camp at Lake of the Woods (6620 feet). (7 hours from trailhead)

Day 2: To attain Monument Peak, scramble up to the low point at about 7400 feet on the long south ridge of Lake Mountain. Traverse northwest across numerous rock fields and gullies then descend sharply into the south end of the basin between Monument and Lake. Cross the basin at roughly 6400 feet and scramble directly up onto the southeast ridge of Monument. Hike and scramble northwest up the ridge top for about 1.3 miles. A final short, steep rock scramble gains the summit. For Lake, return to the basin. Approach Lake from the west or from its northwest ridge. The slope is moderately steep but straightforward. From the summit scramble down the eastern ridge and hike back to camp. (9 hours round trip)

Day 3: Return to the trailhead.

Monument Peak first ascent (Photo by John Roper)

15 ROBINSON MOUNTAIN

Elevation: 8726 ft (2660 m)

Difficulty: S5/T5

Distance: 14 miles

Elevation gain: 6500 ft

Trip time: 12 hours; 1-2 days

Time to summit: 7 hours from trailhead; 3 hours from base camp

Best time of year: June to October

Maps: USGS Robinson Mountain; Green Trails Washington Pass 50

Contact: Okanogan National Forest, Methow Valley Ranger District

GPS WAYPOINT ROUTE
1. Robinson Pass trailhead: 2600 ft (10U 681094mE 5392911mN)
2. Beauty Creek: 2.3 miles, 3580 ft (10U 679991mE 5396018mN)
3. Meadow creek outlet: 3.8 miles, 5200 ft (10U 680881mE 5397865mN)
4. Camp: 5 miles, 6700 ft (10U 679739mE 5398333mN)
5. Robinson summit: 7 miles, 8726 ft (10U 678436mE 5399704mN)

Located at the confluence of the Pasayten Wilderness and the North Cascades, Robinson is the mammoth peak that is visible from many distant viewpoints. Awesome swaths from avalanches sweep down from the crest over 4000 feet to Robinson Creek that surges below. The northwest face is precipitous and cliffy. In contrast, the southwest slopes support extended snow gullies that reach to the summit. Yet in later summer these same regions expose lengthy, dry expanses of talus and scree. The geography here is not one of big-glacier, monster crags. Yet this country is spectacular, showing imposing stony ridges coupled with enormous U-shaped glacial-trough valleys.

Robinson Mountain (Photo by John Roper)

A favorite with horse people especially in the fall hunting season, Robinson Creek is a main thoroughfare into the Pasayten Wilderness. Yet the summer is lonesome, and the high country above timberline is empty even when the hunters are stalking below. Robinson is a peak that can be scrambled early in the season on snow, or in October when the countryside is luminous with golden, fuzzy larches. The summit ridge is blocky and exposed; therefore it is best attempted when dry. But the airy roaming is splendid with the extra recompense of a charming camp at a high alpine tarn, if an overnight trip is preferred over a strenuous 1-day excursion.

Trailhead Directions: Drive I-5 north to the North Cascades Highway (SR 20) and head east to 1.5 miles beyond Early Winters Campground. Turn left and go 0.4 mile to Mazama. Turn left on Harts Pass Road (County Road 9140) and drive 8.1 miles to Robinson Creek Campground and Robinson Pass Trail 478. (190 miles, 4.5 hours from Seattle)

Standard Route:

Day 1: Begin at the Robinson Pass trailhead (2600 feet) and travel about 2.3 miles to the second major bridge at the crossing of Beauty Creek. About 50 feet after the crossing, find the Beauty Creek path, which is fairly well defined, but not maintained and not on the map. Follow the tread about 1.5 miles to where it crosses a creek at 5200 feet. Cross the creek and head northwest up the open meadow. Ramble up the slope through the forest about 1 mile to a tarn at 6700 feet. A suitable campsite is found here when snow-melt provides water. Otherwise camp lower at 6300 feet in the less rocky forest.

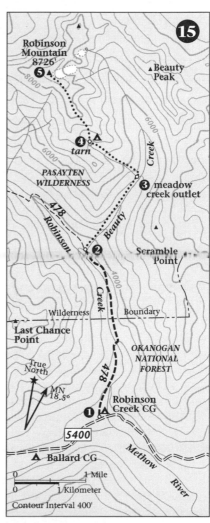

Day 2: From the alpine tarn, attain the southeast ridge either on snow or scree, and follow the ridge northwest to Robinson's summit. The ridge is deceptive with several false summits. The last false summit requires scrambling up a dirty gully (class 2) and followed by an airy 60-foot section of absorbing knife-edge rock that could be troublesomely slick in rain or snow. From here it is an easy rock scramble to the summit.

16 GILBERT MOUNTAIN

Elevation: 8023 ft (2445 m)

Difficulty: S4/T4

Distance: 14 miles

Elevation gain: 4600 ft

Trip time: 13 hours; 2 days

Time to summit: 8 hours from trailhead; 3 hours from North Lake camp

Best time of year: July to October

Maps: USGS Gilbert; Green Trails Stehekin 82

Contact: Okanogan National Forest, Methow Valley Ranger District

Special considerations: Rotten rock in gullies

GPS WAYPOINT ROUTE
1. North Creek trailhead: 3700 ft (10U 680024mE 5370193mN)
2. Trail fork to North Lake: 4 miles, 5740 ft (10U 678240mE 5373617mN)
3. Ridge: 6 miles, 7260 ft (10U 677555mE 5371934mN)
4. Gilbert summit: 7 miles, 8023 ft (10U 678831mE 5372373mN)

Gilbert Mountain resides at the end of the Twisp River Road in a sector that was well explored during the heyday of the Gilbert and North Lake mining boom. A prospector-built trail once reached claims high on the south and west flanks. The uppermost ridge on Gilbert forms a stony cirque around the head of North Creek, making a connection with the south end of Kangaroo Ridge. Of Gilbert's two high points, the south peak is the true summit. This apex can be fairly easily approached from any direction, but the most straightforward route is the ascent via North Lake.

The zone near the summit embraces some of the most exalted wandering in all the North Cascades. Draw near this region through picturesque pines and larches. For even larger views ascend on granite knobs, comely ledges, slabs, and buttresses. The open forests are aromatic, but scrambling on the steep heather meadows and rockslides that lead to Kangaroo Ridge is intoxicating. At the very top of Gilbert, revel in the spectacle east to Abernathy

Peak, south to the Chelan Crest and pyramid-shaped Reynolds Peak, and north to Silver Star Mountain. Look closer and see if you can distinguish Big Snagtooth, Willow Tooth, Cedar Tooth, Dog Tooth, and of course, the debris on Decayed Tooth, which together comprise the crumbling smile of Snagtooth Ridge.

Trailhead Directions: Drive I-5 to Exit 208 at Arlington and continue past Darrington to the North Cascades Highway (SR 20). Continue over Washington Pass through the town of Winthrop to Twisp. Turn west onto the Twisp River Road (County Road 9114). At Mystery Campground the way becomes FS Road 4440. At 21.6 miles (3180 feet) find the Scatter Creek Trail 427 trailhead, but continue 3.8 miles past the South Creek Campground. There is an old trailhead here, near a cabin at the intersection of North Creek and the

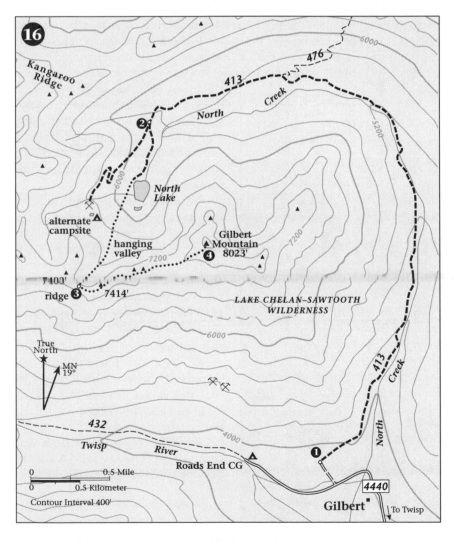

Twisp River Road. Do not be deceived, however—the newer trailhead is about 0.5 mile farther. A short spur road extends from FS Road 4440 north to the newer North Creek Trail 413 trailhead. (240 miles, 5.75 hours from Seattle)

Standard Route:

Day 1: From the new trailhead at 3700 feet, travel along the deep forests of North Creek, crossing the creek at about 5080 feet. At 3 miles continue past a junction with Trail 476 (5430 feet) and stay on Trail 413 for another mile to a second fork. Pleasant camps are found at North Lake at 4.7 miles. Alternatively, take the right fork to explore relic mines on a stream at 5.6 miles (6500 feet). Continue to a decrepit miner cabin at 5.7 miles (6600 feet). An option is to camp here where plentiful water is available at a small larch-bound lake.

Day 2: From North Lake camp in the morning, traverse slightly southeast to a hanging valley where snow collects in early season. Once in the hanging valley, proceed slightly southwest at about 6 miles to gain the west ridge of Gilbert between Points 7483 and 7414. Rock scrambling is necessary to gain the ridge, particularly for the last 100 feet (class 3). The remaining 1-mile push to the summit passes over numerous, airy small gaps. At 7800 feet the true summit lies to the northeast. At or near this point, leave the ridge crest and scramble just to the right and below the true summit. The final approach above 7900 feet is a classic rock scramble before gaining the summit.

Alternate Route: Any flank of Gilbert provides a route. From Twisp Pass Trail 432, which begins at the campground at the end of FS Road 4440, an abandoned mine trail begins after 0.5 mile. Ascend this mine trail to about 5900 feet, and then climb a gully or a rock slope to the ridge just west of the summit. From here follow the same path as for the standard route. The alternative course is through dense forest until nearly to the top, but expansive views from the ridge and summit reward the persistent scrambler.

For an enjoyable weekend trip, climb Gilbert one day and Abernathy Peak (Scramble 17) the next.

Kangaroo Ridge from Gilbert Mountain
(Photo by Mike Torok)

17 ABERNATHY PEAK

Elevation: 8321 ft (2536 m)

Difficulty: S5/T4

Distance: 10 miles

Elevation gain: 5200 ft

Trip time: 11 hours

Time to summit: 7 hours

Best time of year: July to October

Maps: USGS Gilbert; Green Trails Stehekin 82

Contact: Okanogan National Forest, Methow Valley Ranger District

GPS WAYPOINT ROUTE

1. Scatter Creek trailhead: 3100 ft (10U 683541mE 5367491mN)
2. Drainage creek: 3.4 miles, 6040 ft (10U 684543mE 5370508mE)
3. Scatter Lake: 4.2 miles, 7047 ft (10U 683696mE 5371282mN)
4. Abernathy summit: 5 miles, 8321 ft (10U 683035mE 5372152mN)

Abernathy Peak is situated just east of the North Cascades Scenic Highway at the head of the Twisp River. Although it borders the often soggy and rain scoured North Cascades National Park, the peak has more in common with the landscape to the east. Situated beyond the major North Cascades crest, an arid climate with its correlating vegetation gives the feeling of a distant world. Abernathy's flanks tend to be rocky, with extensive scree slopes above timberline. There is a mine near the north ridge at about 7400 feet and a cabin was once located at the 7680-foot saddle. The Scatter Lake area on the southeastern flank is a gorgeous spot in early October when the landscape shimmers with a golden coat of larch.

The route is steep above timberline after Scatter Lake, but is easily visualized. The strenuous ascent culminates in a zenith of views. To the

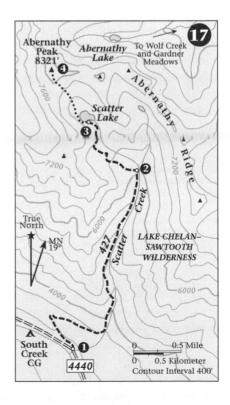

southwest, the deep valley of the Twisp River underscores Gilbert Mountain, while to the northeast are poised the craggy summits of Gardner and North Gardner Mountains. Note that car camping the night before at South Creek Campground off FS Road 4440 makes this scramble a feasible 1-day trip.

Trailhead Directions: Drive east on I-90 and then north on US 97 over Blewett Pass and through Wenatchee to Pateros. Continue north on SR 153 to Twisp and the North Cascades Highway (SR 20). Alternatively, drive I-5 north to the North Cascades Highway and continue east over Washington Pass through the town of Winthrop to Twisp.

From Twisp, turn west onto the Twisp River Road (County Road 9114). At Mystery Campground the way becomes FS Road 4440. At 21.6 miles, park at the Scatter Creek Trail 427 trailhead. (215 miles, 5.5 hours from Seattle)

Standard Route: Begin at the Scatter Creek trailhead at 3100 feet and gently ascend along the pack trail after a long traversing switchback at 3400 feet. At 6040 feet approach the drainage creek from Scatter Lake. Make a direct turn northwest and continue upslope, out of sight from the creek, until the trail ends at Scatter Lake at 4.2 miles (7047 feet).

Continue around either side of the lake and ascend the rock ridge directly toward Abernathy Peak, or scramble the scree slope just to the right of the summit. The scree slope does not pose any rock fall danger, but makes any fast forward progress an arduous undertaking. Do not try to scramble up the eastern ridge from Point 8360 because the ridge is not a scramble. The scree slope is the preferred way to descend back to Scatter Lake.

Alternate Route: Although the approach to Abernathy Peak is much more direct from Scatter Creek, an alternate route can be accomplished from Gardner Meadows. Drive I-5 to the North Cascades Highway (SR 20) and continue east to Winthrop. Drive through town, cross a bridge over the Methow River, and immediately turn right on Twin Lakes Road 9120. In about 1.5 miles turn right on Wolf Creek Road 1131 and shortly thereafter turn right on a dirt road signed "Wolf Creek Trail." At 3.5 miles, remain left at a fork in the road and descend for 0.5 mile until reaching the Wolf Creek Trail 527 trailhead (2900 feet).

Hike the trail 10.5 miles to Gardner Meadows where there is level ground and good camping (5700 feet). Cross the creek and follow a sketchy old trail

Abernathy Peak (Photo by John Roper)

to Abernathy Lake. Continue past the mines to the ridge, and then follow the north ridge to the summit. Because the round trip is 26 miles with 5800 feet gain, an overnight camp at Gardner Meadows is necessary.

18 HOODOO PEAK

Elevation: 8464 ft (2580 m)

Difficulty: S3/T3

Distance: 11 miles

Elevation gain: 4500 ft

Trip time: 9 hours; 1-2 days

Time to summit: 6 hours

Best time of year: June to October

Maps: USGS Hoodoo Peak, Martin Peak; Green Trails Buttermilk Butte 83, Prince Creek 115

Contact: Okanogan National Forest, Methow Valley Ranger District

GPS WAYPOINT ROUTE
1. Libby Creek trailhead: 4400 ft (10U 701142mE 5350345mN)
2. Libby Lake: 6 miles, 7618 ft (10U 697734mE 5346391mN)
3. South saddle: 5.6 miles, 8080 ft (10U 697064mE 5346742mN)
4. Hoodoo summit: 6 miles, 8464 ft (10U 697351mE 5347508mN)

Hoodoo Peak provides a princely portal to the tiara of the Sawtooth Ridge, which stretches north to Purple Pass high above Lake Chelan, and south to the end of the divide at the Navarre Peaks. Located at the head of East Fork Buttermilk Creek, Hoodoo is a great blocky mound with an extended northwest slope. Raven Ridge, a spur just southeast of Hoodoo, surpasses it in height. Nonetheless, at 8464 feet Hoodoo is one of the major summits in the region.

The straightforward and quick approach makes a scramble of Hoodoo an amiable day trip to a major peak in the Lake Chelan–Sawtooth Wilderness. But for the scrambler who seeks a longer span of solitude, Libby Lake affords a dramatic overnight camp. Because the trail is so steep in places as to be a notorious horse-killer, Libby Lake is not plagued with the residue of horse packers as are other nearby lakes in the district. Nestled beneath the cliffs of the confluence of the spurs of Raven Ridge and Hoodoo Peak, the tarn displays massive rockslides on three sides and giant larch trees on the fourth.

Hoodoo makes a striking trip in early October when the larch needles flicker with shades of yellow and gold. But the flowers of early July are brilliant as well, for those who crave a variety of color.

Trailhead Directions: Drive east on I-90 to Blewett Pass Exit 85. Then drive north on US 97 to US 2. Go east to Wenatchee, and then north on US 97 to Pateros. Turn left on SR 153 and continue 20.5 miles to Blackpine Road

(County Road 1049). Follow it for 2.5 miles to FS Road 43 where the pavement ends. Continue left at a fork and go 4.9 miles to FS Road 4340. Continue 1.2 miles on FS Road 4340 to FS Road 700, turn right, and go 1.5 miles to FS Road 750. Turn left and proceed 0.9 mile to the end of the road and Libby Creek Trail 415. (220 miles, 5 hours from Seattle)

Standard Route: From the Libby Creek trailhead at 4400 feet, hike Trail 415 for 4.3 miles to 7100 feet, leaving the trail at the first large boulder field below Hoodoo Peak. Head up the valley to around 7400 feet, then ascend the southeast slope to the summit. Alternatively, from the southeast slope continue west to the south saddle at 8080 feet and then follow the ridge to the summit. A loop can incorporate both sections. Either way is a sporting rock scramble on large blocks, with a few steep sections. Note that the east slope of Hoodoo Peak is not a scramble.

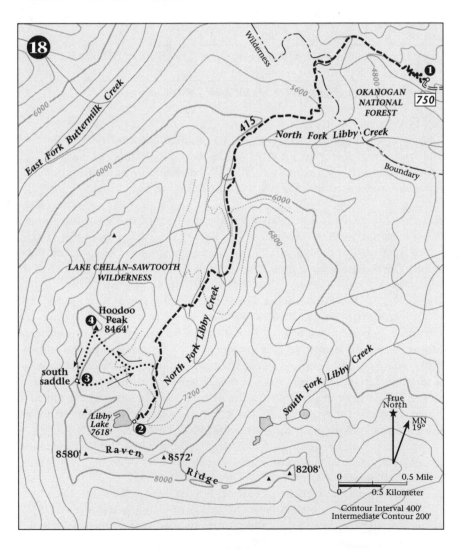

Hoodoo Peak from Raven Ridge (Photo by John Roper)

19 SAWTOOTH RIDGE

Courtney Peak, Buttermilk Ridge, Oval Peak, Star Peak, Cheops, Martin Peak, Cooney, Mount Bigelow

Elevations: 8392 ft (2558 m), 8267 ft (2520 m), 8795 ft (2681 m), 8690 ft (2649 m), 8270 ft (2521 m), 8375 ft (2553 m), 8321 ft (2536 m), 8444 ft (2574 m)

Difficulty: S5/T3

Distance: 41 miles one way

Trip time: 5 days

Elevation gain: 17,800 ft

Best time of year: June to September

Maps: USGS Oval Peak, Prince Creek, Martin Peak, Crater Creek; Green Trails Buttermilk Butte 83, Prince Creek 115

Contact: Okanogan National Forest, Methow Valley Ranger District

Special considerations: Steep snow slopes early in the season, potential for avalanches

GPS WAYPOINT ROUTE
1. Courtney summit: 9.7 miles, 8392 ft (10U 689830mE 5348229mN)
2. Buttermilk Ridge summit: 10.5 miles, 8267 ft (10U 690412mE 5348888mN)
3. Oval summit: 12.7 miles, 8795 ft (10U 691104mE 5351214mN)
4. Star summit: 17.1 miles, 8690 ft (10U 690999mE 5347148mN)
5. Cheops summit: 26.7 miles, 8270 ft (10U 697086mE 5341357mN)
6. Martin summit: 27.7 miles, 8375 ft (10U 696963mE 5340454mN)
7. Cooney summit: 28.7 miles, 8321 ft (10U 696492mE 5338987mN)
8. Bigelow summit: 33.7 miles, 8444 ft (10U 696641mE 5343746mN)

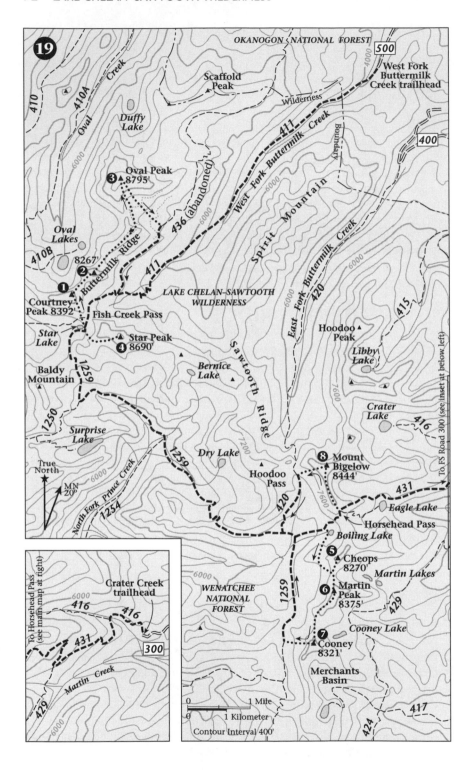

The Sawtooth Ridge is a palisade of peaks along the Chelan Crest that include the major summits in the region. Oval's rounded profile forms the apex. Gentle saddles separate the ridges of other peaks, whereas Cheops, Martin, and Cooney almost blend together. The entire locality takes on a stony, desolate tone by midsummer covered by the dry coniferous forest characteristic of eastern Cascade slopes. The windswept, often-treeless ridges support extensive alpine vegetation with many rare species.

The scrambles of the Sawtooth Ridge parallel and lie east of the Chelan Summit Trail. The trail itself offers miles and days of easy-to-roam ridges with spectacular views westward to the main Cascades range over the deep trench of mostly hidden Lake Chelan. Sawtooth Ridge can be easily traversed from end to end, with many variations of entry and exit on trails that strand outward to the east. Innumerable fine outings of multiple days can be devised with high roaming, peak bagging, and excellent camping interspersed.

Because this grouping of scrambles includes relatively easy yet significant peaks, it provides a superb introduction to a multiday trip for the beginning scrambler. To maximize the variety and uniqueness of the journey, create a loop trip. Two cars are required to connect the ends of the loop, or a family member can be recruited for drop-off duty. Each section of the Sawtooth Ridge can be accomplished in a shorter time if needed, but this country is so distinguished by the proximity of numerous high scrambles, that the serious peakbagger can accomplish much in a condensed outing.

Much of this region has great potential for early season scrambling. Most travel is on decent talus, which is not excessively loose. Minimal routefinding skills are required. But if the snow is deep, the scrambler must be acutely aware of the potential for avalanches. Traveling on ridges and in trees is generally safer than traveling on open slopes; but remember that small bands of forest often give only a false sense of security. Generally the best time to scramble in this spectacular province is late spring, when avalanche activity is most predictable. June is the finest time of year here, graced by gigantic green meadows, plenty of water, snowfields for ascending and descending, no dust, no heat, no people—just immense expansive wildlands stretching to infinity.

Trailhead Directions: This trip is described from north to south, although clearly a reversed direction is feasible. A car must be left at each trailhead to make this a one-way trip. From Seattle, drive west on US 2 over Stevens Pass to Wenatchee. Drive north on US 97 to Pateros. Go northwest on SR 153 to Twisp. Alternatively, from Seattle, drive north on I-5 then east on the North Cascades Highway (SR 20) to Twisp.

Turn west on Twisp River Road (County Road 9114) and then left on Buttermilk Creek Road (FS Road 43) toward Black Pine Lake Campground. At 3.5 miles from the Twisp River crossing and before the campground, turn right on FS Road 500 and drive to the end of the road at West Fork Buttermilk Creek Trail 411.

Leave a car at the end of FS Road 300 at Crater Creek Trail 416 for the return. You can access FS Road 300 by continuing south from Black Pine Lake on FS Road 43 to FS Road 4340, and then west on FS Road 300 to Crater Creek trailhead. (235 miles, 5 hours from Seattle)

Standard Route:

Day 1: From the West Fork Buttermilk Creek Trail 411 trailhead at 4000 feet, hike 8.7 miles to Fish Creek Pass. Continue over the pass and camp at Star Lake at 7173 feet. (8.7 miles, 3480 feet, 6 hours)

Day 2: Pack for the summit day push of Courtney, Buttermilk Ridge, and Oval. From Fish Creek Pass, ascend directly up the southeast ridge of Courtney Peak, following an easy gradient, mostly on a way trail, with a short rock scramble at the summit. From the 7680-foot saddle between Courtney Peak and Buttermilk Ridge, scramble directly up the southwest ridge on large, solid blocks to Buttermilk Ridge summit. In contrast to Courtney Peak, this rock scramble is steeper and rock moves are necessary. From Buttermilk Ridge, continue along the ridge tops to the summit of Oval Peak. The only questionable spot is the northwest ridge of Point 7978, which can be bypassed by descending the eastern ridge of Point 7978 and traversing across its northern slope in an open basin. The south ridge of Oval is not very steep, but the continuous rock field of large, solid blocks provides a good rock-scrambling workout. Return to Star Lake camp by descending to a pleasant tarn in the basin southeast of Oval at 7000 feet. From there follow an abandoned but usable old tread (Trail 436) south to Fish Creek Pass and back to camp. (6 miles, 6461 feet, 9 hours from Star Lake)

Day 3: To reach the summit of Star Peak from Star Lake, ascend steeply south for 600 feet to the obvious saddle on the western side of Point 7912. Go over or around Point 7912 and traverse onto the main southwest spur of Star Peak, traveling mostly on scree or snow in early season. Ridge crests to the summit have solid rock for ascending. Faces and open slopes have pleasant dirt and scree for descending. From the summit, return to Star Lake camp and pack for the next leg of the trip.

Go to Summit Trail 1259 and hike southeast 7.2 miles to a junction where the Summit Trail makes a 90-degree turn south. Instead, go east, slowly ascending Eagle Lake Trail 431 for 1 mile to Boiling Lake, where picnic tables create an excellent spot to relax. (10.8 miles, 3220 feet, 6 hours from Star Lake)

Day 4: A combined scramble of Cheops (Point 8270), Martin Peak, and Cooney (Point 8321) makes for an excellent day of scrambling. From Boiling Lake camp, ascend south for 0.5 mile to the saddle (7440 feet) on the west ridge of Cheops. Because the north side of the west ridge is steep and exposed, it does not provide an easy scramble route. Drop 100 feet from the saddle, and traverse southeast into the upper meadow. Then ascend directly up to the saddle between Martin Peak and Cheops. Scramble north up the south ridge toward the Cheops summit. The rock on the west side of the ridge is generally solid, but has some slippery lichen. The east side is cleaner but loose.

From the summit of Cheops, drop again to the saddle between Cheops and Martin Peak. Perform an ascending traverse south on the west side of Martin's north ridge. About 200 to 300 feet directly below the summit of

Sawtooth Ridge (Photo by Mike Torok)

Martin, scramble satisfactory solid rock diagonally up and left onto the north ridge. Scramble the ridge to Martin's summit.

Alternatively, when directly below the summit on Martin's west slope, continue an ascending traverse south on loose scree, to a small pass on Martin's south ridge. Scramble up the ridge or go through a pass to the east side of the ridge for an easier scramble up to Martin.

To attain Cooney from Martin Peak, hike easily south on broad uplands to the saddle with Cooney at 7840 feet. Scramble south, directly up the ridge on pleasant rock. Return to Boiling Lake camp by descending south to the Summit Trail 1259. (6 miles, 3230 feet, 7 hours)

Day 5: From Boiling Lake, ascend Eagle Lake Trail 431 to Horsehead Pass (7560 feet). From the pass, ascend north on a way trail directly up the ridge about 400 vertical feet. Traverse left, onto the west slope of the ridge. Scramble north on solid boulder fields and talus, traversing 1 mile below the top of the ridge to the summit of Bigelow. One can descend the west face of Bigelow directly to the meadow below returning to Boiling Lake using in part the East Fork Buttermilk Creek Trail 420.

Break camp at Boiling Lake, and continue east back over Horsehead Pass via Eagle Lake Trail 431 for 4.9 miles to Crater Creek Trail 416. Head east 0.7 mile to reach the car left at the trailhead at FS Road 300. (8.2 miles, 1440 feet, 6 hours)

Alternate Routes: If the peaks are done individually, the following routes are feasible.

Courtney southeast ridge: Hike West Fork Buttermilk Creek Trail 411 for 8.7 miles to Fish Creek Pass (7480 feet). From the pass, ascend directly up the southeast ridge. The path has an easy gradient, with a short rock scramble at the summit. *Courtney northeast ridge:* In the meadow north of Fish Creek Pass, leave Trail 411. Go northwest 0.5 mile to the saddle at the bottom of the northeast ridge. Scramble talus and rock fields up the eastern side of the ridge to the summit. (Round trip: 19 miles, 4400 feet)

Buttermilk Ridge southwest ridge: Hike Trail 411 for about 8 miles to meadows just north of and below Fish Creek Pass. Leave the trail and hike northwest for 0.5 mile to the saddle between Courtney Peak and Buttermilk Ridge at 7680 feet. From this saddle, scramble directly up the southwest ridge on large, solid blocks. (Round trip: 18 miles, 4300 feet)

Star southwest spur: Hike Trail 411 for 8.7 miles to Fish Creek Pass (7480 feet). Descend 0.6 mile past Star Lake (good camping) to Summit Trail 1259. Turn left and hike 0.5 mile up to a pass at 7400 feet southwest of Star Peak and northeast of Baldy Mountain. From this pass, ascend a secondary southwest spur ridge of Star Peak. Traverse east around a second minor ridge, then north onto the main southwest spur. Scramble broken rock and talus up to the summit ridge and then east up the summit pyramid. (Round trip: 22 miles, 5200 feet)

Oval south ridge: Hike Trail 411 for 7.7 miles to about 7000 feet in forest north of Fish Creek Pass. Turn right on an abandoned trail (Trail 436). Look carefully for the turn-off; a partially cut log blocks the path about 15 feet off the main trail. Hike this decent old trail (reasonably easy to follow) about 2 miles to a lake (good camping) in a basin at 6900 feet just southeast of the summit. From the lake, ascend to the saddle on the south ridge. Scramble the solid rock field on the ridge top to the summit. It might be possible to follow abandoned Trail 436 from its northern trailhead at 4800 feet, at the end of a logging road that branches north from FS Road 500, saving mileage and elevation gain. (Round trip: 24 miles, 4800 feet)

Bigelow west ridge: Hike 6 miles south on East Fork Buttermilk Creek Trail 420 from its trailhead at the end of FS Road 400 to Hoodoo Pass. From the pass, or just south of the pass, ascend the west ridge of Bigelow to reach the south slope and an easy ascent of scree, heather, and talus to the summit. (Round trip: 14 miles, 3700 feet)

Cheops south ridge: Hike 6.8 miles from the Crater Creek trailhead first on Trail 416 and then on Trail 431 near the end of FS Road 300 to Horsehead Pass (7600 feet). Hike down the trail 1 mile to a good camp at Boiling Lake (6960 feet). From camp, ascend south for 0.5 mile to an obvious saddle (7440 feet) in the west ridge of Cheops. Drop 100 feet and traverse southeast in the upper meadow, then ascend directly up to the saddle between Martin Peak and Cheops. Travel north up the south ridge. The rock on the western side of the ridge is more solid than the eastern side, which is cleaner of lichen, but loose. (Round trip: 18 miles, 4200 feet)

Martin west slope: Follow directions above for Cheops south ridge to the saddle between Martin Peak and Cheops. Then do an ascending traverse south on the western side of Martin's north ridge. About 200 to 300 feet directly below the summit, scramble good, solid rock diagonally up and left onto the north ridge. Scramble the solid ridge to the summit. A variation exists: when directly below the summit on the west slope, continue an ascending traverse south on loose scree to a small pass on Martin's south ridge. Scramble up the ridge or go through the pass to the eastern side of the ridge for an easier scramble up. (Round trip: 19 miles, 4300 feet)

Cooney south slope: Hike Foggy Dew Trail 417 for 7.2 miles to the southeast shoulder of Cooney at about 8000 feet. Scramble up the shoulder to the summit. (Round trip: 15 miles, 4700 feet)

GLACIER PEAK WILDERNESS

20 FORTRESS MOUNTAIN AND BUCK MOUNTAIN

Elevations: 8674 ft (2644 m), 8573 ft (2613 m)

Difficulty: S5/T5

Distance: 40 miles

Elevation gain: 10,900 ft

Trip time: 4 days

Time to summit: 3 hours from Buck Creek Pass to Fortress; 5 hours from High Pass to Buck

Best time of year: July to September

Maps: USGS Trinity, Suiattle Pass, Clark Mountain; Green Trails Holden 113

Contact: Wenatchee National Forest, Lake Wenatchee Ranger District

Special considerations: Complex routefinding

GPS WAYPOINT ROUTE
1. Buck Creek trailhead: 2800 ft (10U 660005mE 5326758mN)
2. Chiwawa River Trail 1550: 1.5 miles, 3200 ft (10U 658845mE 5328616mN)
3. Buck Creek Pass: 9.6 miles, 5800 ft (10U 651629mE 5334096mN)
4. Pass No Pass: 11 miles, 6400 ft (10U 652517mE 5335217mN)
5. Fortress summit: 12.5 miles, 8674 ft (10U 653776mE 5335892mN)
6. High Pass: 20 miles, 7000 ft (10U 652490mE 5330431mN)
7. Mount Berge: 21 miles, 7953 ft (10U 653258mE 5329782mN)
8. Pass between Buck and Berge: 22 miles, 6640 ft (10U 654031mE 5328849mN)
9. Buck summit: 23 miles, 8573 ft (10U 655554mE 5328615mN)

Fortress and Buck Mountains are the highest and second highest summits of the Chiwawa Mountains. Fortress has a steep northeast face adorned by the Fortress Glacier and a terminal lake. Notwithstanding, Fortress is reasonably gentle when approached from the southeast. Buck dominates the divide between the upper Napeequa and Chiwawa Rivers. There are three distinct summits; the middle point above King Lake is the highest. Like Fortress, the northern facade of Buck is formidable and dangerous whereas the upper south slope is largely filled by perennial snow.

The gateway to this duo is through legendary Buck Creek Pass. This spot is famed for the close, intimate appearance of Glacier Peak; it's as if you can reach out and touch its hanging glaciers. The trail farther along the divide above Buck Creek to High Pass is even more airy and splendid. High Pass has a wild, glacial appearance, with moraines and snow cover late into fall.

Many parties follow the trail to High Pass, but scrambling Fortress and Buck present a better opportunity to experience dramatic high-country roaming. An energetic party can scramble the subsidiary summits of Helmet Butte, Flower Dome, and Liberty Cap as easy side excursions. These grassy knolls magnify the splendor of the perspective of icy peaks, which give contrast to the fragile beauty of surrounding meadows.

Herders once heavily used Buck Creek Pass on an old trail crossing from the Chiwawa to the Suiattle River. A century ago about 2500 sheep grazed the

area, resulting in harsh meadow damage before pasturing declined in the 1930s. Nowadays horse packers and hunters overcrowd the region. During September, first bear and then deer fall prey to modern weapons. Horses straddle the trail, and a constant human parade reaches to timberline. It is therefore prudent to avoid this sector during the opening of the hunt. But farther on, the highest reaches are still lonesome.

In autumn, yellow, red, magenta, and purple hues of foliage create a multi-colored cover. Particularly in September, wandering in the resplendent high country can be exceptional if you are prepared to wear bright orange, to dodge the bullets, and to steel your ears to the staccato of distant gunfire at dawn and dusk. The sensation of kaleidoscopic freedom and space justifies the distraction.

Trailhead Directions: Drive US 2 to Coles Corner at the junction with SR 207 (also called Lake Wenatchee Road). Drive SR 207 for 3.8 miles to a major fork. Take the Chiwawa Loop Road along the south shore of Fish Lake east to Chiwawa River Road (FS Road 62). Take a left going north; FS Road 62 becomes FS Road 6200 and extends 23.5 miles to Trinity. The final leg of the road goes around Trinity to the west on public property to Buck Creek Trail 1513. (135 miles, 3 hours from Seattle)

Standard Route:

Day 1: Begin at the Buck Creek trailhead at 2800 feet and follow the trail around the private property of Trinity. Continue past the junction with Chiwawa River Trail 1550 at 1.5 miles. Good campsites are found along Buck Creek and on the east side of Buck Creek Pass at 9.6 miles. Because of heavy use at Buck Creek Pass, overnight campers may choose to camp below the pass on the east slope below Liberty Cap in the large meadow at 5800 feet. For an evening stroll, Flower Dome (6300 feet) can be readily reached, also from the trail northwest of Buck Creek Pass; hike west along a trail spur to the rounded summit. Return to the pass to savor the spectacle of the glittering diamond of Glacier Peak in the sunset. (9.6 miles, 3040 feet, 5 hours)

Day 2: To gain Fortress, the apex of Helmet Butte can be crossed on the way to Pass No Pass, the grassy saddle between Helmet Butte and Fortress (6400 feet). Alternatively, from Buck Creek Pass, follow the path contouring the southeast slopes of Helmet Butte; when it bears south, leave and ascend the gentle lower southwest flank of Fortress. Ascend to a wide snow-patched basin under the rocky summit area. Take the principal snowfield to its narrowing apex, and then continue on a snow finger to the high southwest ridge. Turn left and scramble talus and ledges readily to the summit. Note that Fortress has some steep snow patches in the basin just beneath the summit that can be avoided later in the season; but the scree impedes quick progress to the gully system immediately below the summit ridge.

Return to camp and pack up for the scenic traverse to High Pass. While you continue south on Trail 1562.2 toward Liberty Cap southwest of the pass, the summit of Liberty Cap (6700 feet) can be accessed by a trail along the mountain's north ridge and west slope. Continue near the crest of the ridge,

High Pass (Photo by Mike Torok)

sometimes to the east and sometimes to the west, with spacious views in either direction. The terrain tops out above timberline, with the distinctive flavor of glacial territory, at High Pass (7000 feet). Find a suitable camp near, but not right at, High Pass. (7.2 miles, 4065 feet, 7 hours)

Day 3: To attain Buck Mountain from High Pass, first traverse at 6800 feet around the west shoulder of Mount Berge (Point 7953 on the Green Trails map and Point 7948 on the USGS Clark Mountain map). Reaching the summit of Mount Berge is more than a scramble and should be bypassed. Ascend to the ridge at 7640 feet, and then drop leftward traversing to the southeast trending ridge to a pass at 6640 feet, above Louis Creek and between Buck and Berge. The ascent is now a long, gentle hike with possible snow up the west shoulder of Buck to the summit area. The most prominent of three summits is the middle one. Approach this high point from near the right notch. Scramble loose rock leftward to the summit on or near the ridge crest (class 3).

Reverse the route to return to camp. Note that on Buck, the routefinding is complex in finding the appropriate system around Berge. When approaching the final Buck summit, remain to the center or to the right of the path to avoid fourth class climbing. (7 miles, 3788 feet, 6 hours)

Day 4: Reverse the trail route back to the cars. Dropping down with packs from High Pass is possible, but to avoid crossing Buck Creek, it is probably faster, although longer in distance, to return via Buck Creek Pass on the established trail. (12.6 miles, 4240 feet descent, 8 hours)

Alternate Routes: The most direct route down from Buck leaves from about 0.3 mile south of the summit. Descend into the basin of Alpine Creek, keeping to its left (the least brushy flank). Descend forested terrain to the Chiwawa River, about 1 mile from Trinity.

21 CHIWAWA MOUNTAIN

Elevation: 8459 ft (2578 m)

Difficulty: S5/T5

Distance: 18 miles

Elevation gain: 5700 ft

Trip time: 11 hours; 2 days

Time to summit: 5 hours from camp

Best time of year: July to September

Maps: USGS Suiattle Pass; Green Trails Holden 113

Contact: Wenatchee National Forest, Lake Wenatchee Ranger District

GPS WAYPOINT ROUTE
1. Buck Creek trailhead: 2800 ft (10U 660005mE 5326758mN)
2. Chiwawa River Trail 1550: 1.5 miles, 3200 ft (10U 658845mE 5328616mN)
3. Trail 1505B: 4.6 miles, 4900 ft (10U 656389mE 5334129mN)
4. End Trail 1505B: 5.6 miles, 4900 ft (10U 656384mE 5334133mN)
5. Chiwawa Basin: 7.4 miles, 6300 ft (10U 656734mE 5335825mN)
6. Summit basin: 8.4 miles, 7460 ft (10U 655970mE 5336186mN)
7. Southwest slope: 8.6 miles, 7000 ft (10U 655464mE 5335739mN)
8. Chiwawa summit: 9 miles, 8459 ft (10U 655661mE 5336339mN)

The approach to Chiwawa Mountain along the Chiwawa River has been touched and some would even say ravaged by the tradition of mining in the district. Early in the century, a wagon road to the head of the valley penetrated the range. Now Trinity, private property at the end of the Chiwawa River Road, is near the site of the Royal Development Mine, a previously active copper mining venture. In former days, prospectors worked high on Red Mountain and mining operations battered the fragile subalpine terrain. Not all is lost, however—the surviving meadows are partially reclaimed, and the views of the upper Chiwawa River basin are impressive.

Chiwawa's northeast face boasts a popular ice climb on the Lyman Glacier. This technical route is one way to the summit, but a scramble up the south side reaches the same spot. From the uppermost rocks, observe the cliffs and hanging glaciers on the north wall of nearby Buck Mountain. Look toward Spider Meadow, Red Mountain, Ten Peak Mountain, and Mount Rainier. Peer down to the shrinking Lyman Glacier, the upper Lyman Basin, and the lush green of the basin below. Survey the exceptional sight of the grand ice streams of Glacier Peak, seen across the broad, forested valley of the Suiattle River, and just next door, behold the dusky summit of mighty Mount Maude.

Trailhead Directions: Drive US 2 to Coles Corner at the junction with SR 207 (also called the Lake Wenatchee Road). Drive SR 207 for 3.8 miles to a

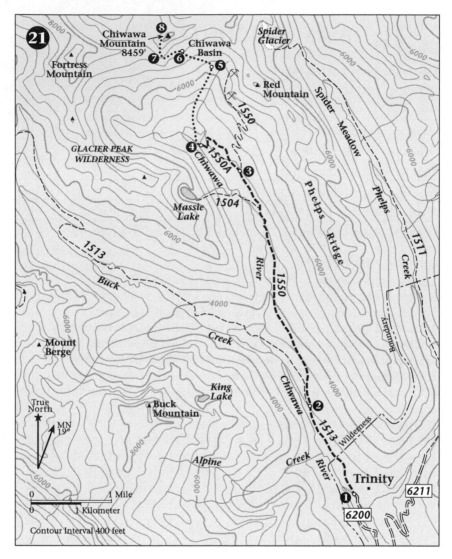

major fork, and then go on the Chiwawa Loop Road along the south shore of
Fish Lake and east to Chiwawa River Road (FS Road 62). Take a left going
north; FS Road 62 becomes FS Road 6200. The way extends 23.5 miles to
Trinity, which is private property. Take the final leg of the road past Trinity to
Buck Creek Trail 1513. (135 miles, 3 hours from Seattle)

Standard Route:

Day 1: Begin at the Buck Creek trailhead at 2800 feet and walk Buck
Creek Trail 1513, skirting around Trinity. Follow signs to the Glacier Peak
Wilderness at 0.6 mile. At 1.5 miles is a junction. Continue rightward on the
road, which becomes Chiwawa River Trail 1550. Steadily ascend the valley on
the flanks of Phelps Ridge. Pass a junction with Trail 1504, which leads leftward to Massie Lake.

At 5.6 miles (4900 feet) the route splits. The left fork is Chiwawa Basin Trail 1550A, which is filled with brush a mile farther into the basin. Camp in the meadow at the end of Trail 1550A for an early morning start for the cross-country approach to Chiwawa's summit. Note that there is a large avalanche swath about half way up the cross-country approach. The field of blown down trees makes for difficult and strenuous travel.

Alternatively, for a higher camp stay right at the fork on Chiwawa River Trail 1550 and climb onto the shoulder of Red Mountain. For the Red Mountain variation, stick with the road, climbing through avalanche brush, then timber, in a series of long switchbacks. The Red Mountain trail is no longer maintained and is fairly overgrown with alder. At the top of the last switchback is a fine campsite at the edge of a large green basin. From here look upward at the brightly colored rock slopes of Red Mountain.

Day 2: Travel to Chiwawa Basin at about 6300 feet from either camp. Traverse west at 6500 feet toward the Fortress-Chiwawa saddle. Before the saddle and on the southwest slope of Chiwawa, go northeast on snow slopes or talus to the west ridge of Chiwawa near the summit. From here, the rock and talus is loose but easy to the top (class 2).

Alternate Route: Use the approach for Fortress Mountain (Scramble 20), heading toward the Fortress-Chiwawa saddle. Just before the saddle go northeast on snow slopes that lead into the face between the west ridge of Chiwawa and a rock spur on the right. At the upper end of the snow, exit on the right and follow easy talus and brownish rock to the summit. Loose rock presents a difficulty on this approach. Using this route, Chiwawa Mountain can be attained from Buck Creek Pass in 1 day.

Summit ridge of Chiwawa Mountain (Photo by Jason Griffith)

22 MOUNT MAUDE AND SEVEN FINGERED JACK

Elevations: 9082 ft (2768 m), 9077 ft (2774 m)

Difficulty: S5/T4

Distance: 14 miles

Elevation gain: 6900 ft

Trip time: 3 days

Time to summit: 4 hours from camp to Maude; 4 hours from Maude to Seven Fingered Jack

Best time of year: July to October

Maps: USGS Trinity, Holden; Green Trails Holden 113

Contact: Wenatchee National Forest, Lake Wenatchee Ranger District

Special considerations: Moderate rock fall. Beware of snow avalanches in early season.

GPS WAYPOINT ROUTE
1. Phelps Creek trailhead: 3500 ft (10U 661369mE 5327623mN)
2. Leroy High Route Trail 1512: 2.5 miles, 4200 ft (10U 660786mE 5332452mN)
3. Leroy Basin: 4 miles, 6000 ft (10U 661776mE 5333917mN)
4. Maude south shoulder: 5.2 miles, 8000 ft (10U 663191mE 5332999mN)
5. Maude summit: 5.7 miles, 9082 ft (10U 663484mE 5333716mN)
6. Saddle: 7.7 miles, 7860 ft (10U 662655mE 5334556mN)
7. Seven Fingered Jack summit: 8.2 miles, 9077 ft (10U 662659mE 5335126mN)

For the altitude seeker, Mount Maude and Seven Fingered Jack are two of the highest scramble peaks of Washington. They loom above Leroy Basin and together comprise the western rim of the Entiat Mountains. Maude and Jack make an odd couple: Maude is the elegant queen, whereas Jack is the tattered courtier. Yet both are among the few Cascade nonvolcanic peaks above 9000 feet.

Maude is a dominating hulk, a true empress of the range. Maude's southern and western slopes are gentle, but the South Entiat Glacier on the steep north face is the most dramatic in the region. Maude is connected to Seven Fingered Jack by a ragged rib. Once called "Entiat Needles" by miners, Seven Fingered Jack is an appropriate name for its spiked formation of steep granite pinnacles. The true summit is the least rugged and most northerly of the group.

Maude and Jack provide a prime spot for scramblers of all levels. Beginners can enjoy peace on an extended walk-up of one of the tallest mountains in the state, intermediates can ascend a loose scree field to ragged spires, and experienced highlanders can create a strenuous and colossal loop with an honor roll of elevated glacial lakes.

The vantage points from the summits are unparalleled in the region. From the top spy the icy monarchs of Bonanza, Logan, Goode, plus the peaks surrounding the Inspiration Glacier to the north, and glittering Glacier Peak to the west. This is a fine larch trip that many parties explore in October.

Tucked in between the Entiat River to the east and Phelps Creek to the west, Maude can be approached from either side, but the easiest ascent of Seven Fingered Jack is from Leroy Basin on the west. The trip can be accomplished in 2 days by scrambling Maude the first day, and Seven Fingered Jack the second. But if done individually, the elevation to gain the saddle between the two is repeated, therefore a 3-day trip is common with the middle summit day providing a giant loop of extended rambling. An optional dividend is

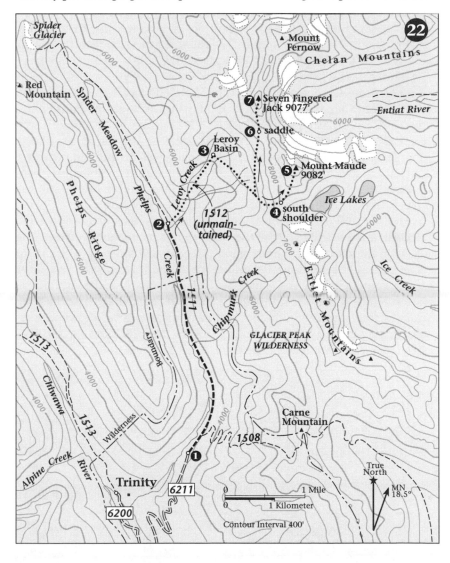

a visit to the austere gems of Ice Lakes at the southeastern foot of Maude where alpine trees stand out starkly in a barren, glaciated landscape.

This country is dry, so whenever water is available take advantage of it. Go in late season to avoid biting, carnivorous ladybugs that swarm on the summits. Also beware: particularly on Seven Fingered Jack the gullies are filled with loose rock. Wear helmets, keep the party small, and follow one another closely to avoid dangerous rock fall. Nevertheless the sumptuous spectacle of formidable peaks in all directions is well worth the risk.

Trailhead Directions: Drive US 2 to Coles Corner and the junction with SR 207 (also called Lake Wenatchee Road). Drive SR 207 3.8 miles to a major fork, and then go on the Chiwawa Loop Road along the south shore of Fish Lake and east to Chiwawa River Road (FS Road 62). Take a left going north; FS Road 62 becomes FS Road 6200. At 22 miles go right on the Phelps Creek Road (FS Road 6211) and continue 2.5 miles to a parking area for Phelps Creek Trail 1511. (135 miles, 3 hours from Seattle)

Standard Route:

Day 1: From the Phelps Creek trailhead at 3500 feet, hike Phelps Creek Trail 1511 past Carne Mountain Trail 1508, which forks to the right uphill. Leroy High Route Trail 1512 leaves Trail 1511 on the north side of Leroy Creek at 2.5 miles (4200 feet) and closely follows Leroy Creek to Leroy Basin in 1.5 miles (6000 feet). This portion of the trail is well defined but no longer maintained. Leave Trail 1511 and ascend along the stream to timberline meadows and good camping at 6000 feet in the basin. Take caution: Leroy Basin has much avalanche evidence so beware of slides in early season.

Day 2: To gain Maude from camp, traverse southeast and ascend a boulder field and west-facing gully to the south shoulder at about 8000 feet. The route from there to the summit is moderately angled scree. To continue to Seven Fingered Jack, descend the upward route, and then traverse northwest to the prominent gully at the Maude–Seven Fingered Jack saddle. At the large bench at 7800 feet, traverse north up the talus, keeping just south of the long, thin, left-slanting snow gully, heading toward the summit that is the northern-

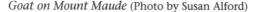

Goat on Mount Maude (Photo by Susan Alford)

most point seen from the basin. The final ascent is largely scree. (Round trip: 5.5 miles, 4360 feet, 8 hours)

As a bonus side trip on summit day, Ice Lakes can be reached via the 6800-foot level near the saddle between Leroy and Chipmunk Creeks. Cross the saddle at 7600 feet south of Maude. From here descend snow and boulders to the lakes. After enjoying the scene and gathering water, ascend easily to the shoulder of Maude on talus. There is no need to rise to the saddle west of the lake. Return to camp.

Day 3: Walk out and drive home.

23 ENTIAT CREST
Cardinal Peak, Emerald Peak, Saska Peak, Pinnacle Mountain

Elevations: 8590 ft (2618 m), 8422 ft (2567 m), 8404 ft (2562 m), 8402 ft (2561 m)

Difficulty: S5/T5

Distance: 42 miles

Elevation gain: 14,000 ft

Trip time: 5 days

Time to summit: 2 hours from camp to Cardinal; 2 hours from camp to Emerald; 3 hours from Emerald to Saska; 6 hours from camp to Pinnacle

Best time of year: June to October

Maps: USGS Pyramid Mountain, Saska Peak, Pinnacle Mountain; Green Trails Lucerne 114

Contact: Wenatchee National Forest, Entiat Ranger District

Special considerations: Severe rock fall in places, helmets recommended

GPS WAYPOINT ROUTE
1. North Fork Entiat River trailhead: 3900 ft (10U 681169mE 5320182mN)
2. Pyramid Mountain Trail 1433: 8 miles, 6600 ft (10U 676749mE 5329329mN)
3. High camp: 9.2 miles, 6900 ft (10U 676225mE 5331004mN)
4. Cardinal summit: 9.5 miles, 8590 ft (10U 677826mE 5330321mN)
5. Emerald summit: 10.2 miles, 8422 ft (10U 676559mE 5331605mN)
6. Saska summit: 11.4 miles, 8404 ft (10U 675580mE 5331248mN)
7. Saska Pass: 12.4 miles, 7440 ft (10U 675402mE 5330479mN)
8. Emerald Park Trail 1230: 13.8 miles, 5800 ft (10U 673952mE 5330918mN)
9. 45-Mile Sheep Drive Trail 1432: 14.6 miles, 6080 ft (10U 674365mE 5331613mN)
10. Borealis Pass: 15.6 miles, 7660 ft (10U 673181mE 5332383mN)
11. Pinnacle summit: 16.6 miles, 8402 ft (10U 673435mE 5333392mN)

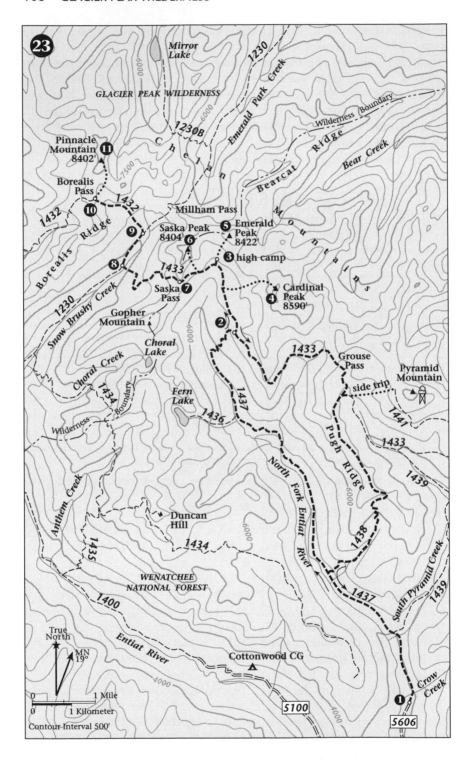

Situated in the Entiat region between Lake Chelan and the Entiat River, the peaks of Cardinal, Emerald, Saska, and Pinnacle form the crest and crown of the Chelan Mountains. This sector can be entered from the north by taking a boat ride on the famed "Lady of the Lake" up Lake Chelan to Lucerne and then to the region via Domke Lake. But if the extra logistics and travel time create a problem for a party with more activity in mind, the Entiat Crest is also accessible from the North Fork Entiat River to the south.

This country offers miles of on- and off-trail travel, dramatic sights, flower-rich meadows, and loud streams. The spectacle of the imperial lords of the Entiat Crest is a joy, and they are only part of the landscape. This region is a paradox of extremes, with barren alpine crags contrasting with lush meadows and dazzling blossoms. Diverse loop trips and various outings are possible because of the many trails that lace the vicinity from all directions. A consummate choice is to make a single camp for the entire trip high in the Emerald-Saska valley and perform day scrambles from camp. When the party is satiated with rugged and exalted scrambling, a return trail loop can be concluded to further enhance the scenery.

A side trip to Pyramid Mountain along Pugh Ridge is highly recommended for its perspective on the region. From the site of an old fire lookout, the vista extends from the mountain ranges of the Glacier Peak Wilderness to the plateaus of the Columbia River Basin. Lake Chelan sits 7000 feet below, so far away that binoculars are needed to spot the "Lady of the Lake." Pyramid Mountain is an unlikely site to choose for a fire lookout—the scenery is all rock, ice, and water. But a lightning strike fire burned in the area as recently as July of 1994. The massive blaze extended to Leavenworth and continued to smolder for months. Even into winter, red stains of fiery points were visible at night dotting the hillsides—a serious lesson about this parched land and the violent forces of nature.

Trailhead Directions: Drive to Wenatchee, and then continue 19 miles north on US 97 to the town of Entiat. Turn left on the Entiat River Road (FS Road 51). Just after Entiat Falls, and before the North Fork Campground, the North Fork Entiat Road (FS Road 5606) forks right at 32.5 miles. In about 2 miles at the end of the road find North Fork Entiat River Trail 1437. (190 miles, 4.5 hours from Seattle)

Standard Route:

Day 1: From the North Fork Entiat River trailhead at 3900 feet, the trail immediately crosses Crow Creek. After some ups and downs, boulder-hop South Pyramid Creek at 1 mile; in June the creek is difficult to cross because of melting snow. At 1.2 miles Pyramid Creek Trail 1439 forks to the right, and at 2.7 miles Pugh Ridge Trail 1438 goes right. At about 4 miles, small meadows begin to appear in the forest. At 5 miles the trail steepens until the Fern Lake Trail 1436 junction (5300 feet), and at 6 miles you come to a delightful camp by the river. The best plan, however, is to press on. After another mile upstream the path tilts steeply, gaining 1000 feet in 0.7 mile. At 8 miles the trail comes to a junction with Pyramid Mountain Trail 1433 at 6600 feet near

Cardinal Peak. Stay left several hundred yards to a pleasant camp in a meadow, on the right side of the trail, or continue up 1.2 miles to fine high camps in a large meadow in the basin between Emerald and Saska at 6900 feet. (9.2 miles, 2900 feet, 6 hours)

Day 2: To climb Cardinal, backtrack on Trail 1433 to the end steep trail at 6700 feet. Aim toward the middle summit, which is rounded, set back on the ridge, and not easily seen through the blocky crest. Ascend through open forest to the wide talus slope and continue up the gully to the ridge notch between the middle and north summits. Follow the ridge south to the middle summit. Avoid the south summit that presents difficult climbing. Later on enjoy the afternoon with an optional stroll, taking the trail west to Saska Pass, 7440 feet, with views down Snow Brushy Creek and the North Fork Entiat River valley. (Round trip from camp: 3.5 miles, 1600 feet, 5 hours)

Day 3: Emerald is located midway between Cardinal Peak and Millham Pass, with a steep, alpine north rock face laced with snow patches until late summer. Saska is less than 1 mile south of Millham Pass. It is a rugged peak that stands out southwest of the Chelan Mountains crest between the drainage of Snow Brushy Creek and the north fork of the Entiat. There is a steep cliff on the northwest flank. Both Emerald and Saska can be easily accomplished in a day from high camp. Note that on Emerald, and especially on Saska, the rock fall danger is severe. Most handholds are loose. Therefore, the party should include no more than six people. Helmets are desirable and rock fall management is imperative.

To attain Emerald, leave the trail at the basin between Emerald and Saska, at about 6900 feet. From the basin, scramble north to the upper basin just below the ridge between Emerald and Saska. Stay high enough to see the broad gully leading to the summit. There appear to be three summits. Climb to the notch between the left and middle summit. Turn right and climb a short rock step (8250 feet) to the upper talus field. Walk easily to the middle summit. Beware of the gully that is full of loose rock.

For Saska, return to the trail in the basin and follow it west 0.5 mile to 300 feet short of the first switchback to Saska Pass. Leave the trail and scramble up the hill into the basin south of Saska. A broad gully leads steeply up and left to the ridge. Climb to the notch to the right of an area of red rock. Go over the ridge and drop slightly, traversing north about 300 feet. A series of benches and a steep gully leads up to the south ridge. Beware of serious rock fall danger and loose handholds. Scramble on the south ridge on the left to the airy summit. Several gullies on the south and southeast sides are feasible. (Round trip from camp: 4 miles, 2600 feet, 6 hours)

Day 4: Pinnacle is a twisting bedrock row of granite rock summits, the highest being about 1.3 miles northwest of Millham Pass and east of the upper Entiat River. The two highest summits are at the top northwest end; the most southern of these is the true summit. From high camp, take Trail 1433 west over Saska Pass and down to Emerald Park Trail 1230 at 5800 feet. Then hike

Emerald Peak (Photo by Mike Torok)

on the trail northeast toward Millham Pass for 0.6 mile.

At a junction with 45-Mile Sheep Drive Trail 1432, the trail becomes hard to find. Angle up the western slope to a pass between two rocky buttresses and a saddle west of the 6767-foot knob. The trail reappears from time to time. After passing the knob, continue north into the meadows, beginning at about 6800 feet. At the second meadow at 7100 feet, turn west and ascend a heather and grassy slope with a short bit of talus. The trail reappears above the talus and makes an easy path to Borealis Pass at 7660 feet.

From the pass, drop north into a meadow. Follow the stream to an upper basin. Scramble 300 feet up a loose, rocky gully, then trend right 200 feet up steep, grassy slopes to the top of the headwall at 7600 feet just south of Pinnacle. The final push to the summit is on the ridge (class 2). Descend to the 7100-foot meadow east of the pass through steep, loose talus and scree. Return to camp. (Round trip from camp: 12 miles, 6800 feet, 10 hours)

Day 5: To return, first retrace tracks to the junction of Trail 1437 with Trail 1433. Head southeast on Trail 1433 and at about 5.5 miles there is a junction with Trail 1438 at 6500 feet. From here drop packs for a side excursion to Pyramid Mountain. Return to pick up the packs and continue southward to rejoin Trail 1437, 2.7 miles from the trailhead. (From camp: 13 miles, 2900 feet descent, 9 hours)

24 CARNE MOUNTAIN

Elevation: 7085 ft (2160 m)

Difficulty: S2/T1

Distance: 8 miles

Elevation gain: 3600 ft

Trip time: 7 hours

Time to summit: 5 hours

Best time of year: July to October

Maps: USGS Trinity; Green Trails Holden 113

Contact: Wenatchee National Forest, Lake Wenatchee Ranger District

GPS WAYPOINT ROUTE
1. Phelps Creek trailhead: 3500 ft (10U 661369mE 5327623mN)
2. Carne Mountain Trail 1508: 0.2 mile, 3400 ft (10U 661575mE 5327931mN)
3. Saddle: 3.6 miles, 6700 ft (10U 663863 mE 5327843mN)
4. Carne summit: 4 miles, 7085 ft (10U 663698mE 5328256mN)

A mild, wide crest in the Entiat Mountains, Carne Mountain stands high above the Chiwawa River. In times past, the summit had a lookout cabin reached from the main trail by a path from the south. The top of Carne

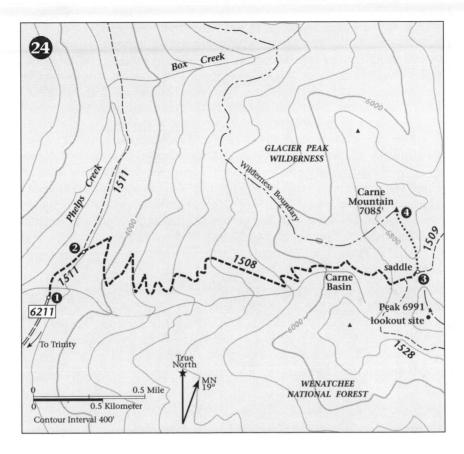

can also be approached from the Rock Creek Trail 1509 and the Estes Butte Trail 1528. Carne is an easy jaunt when the weather seems too threatening at the trailhead to make a greater commitment for a longer trip on the same drainage.

Although Carne is scarcely a scramble in summer when the snow has melted, it is still a worthy pilgrimage in autumn, when the larches are glowing and the bugs are gone. Carne is also a junket to enjoy when the party prefers to dawdle and enjoy the views rather than work up a sweat or push their pulses. Loll around an enchanting basin, enjoying the seclusion among soaring peaks. Then climb to the summit and gaze west to the towering peaks of Chiwawa Ridge, and north to the face of the empress of the Entiat, mighty Mount Maude.

Trailhead Directions: Drive US 2 to Coles Corner at the junction with SR 207 (also called the Lake Wenatchee Road). Drive SR 207 for 3.8 miles to a major fork, and then go on the Chiwawa Loop Road along the south shore of Fish Lake and east to Chiwawa River Road (FS Road 62). Take a left going north; FS Road 62 becomes FS Road 6200. Phelps Creek Road 6211 exits right at 22 miles; continue up it 2.5 miles to a parking area for Phelps Creek Trail 1511. (135 miles, 3 hours from Seattle)

Standard Route: From the Phelps Creek trailhead at 3500 feet, go 0.2 mile to Carne Mountain Trail 1508. Turn uphill, taking the rightward fork. At 3 miles enter Carne Basin (6100 feet). The basin contains one of the world's largest subalpine larches. The trail disappears in the meadow and reappears on the far side. At 3.5 miles the trail splits in two. The right fork, Estes Butte Trail 1528, climbs to a nearby saddle and then heads south past Old Gib Mountain and meets the Chiwawa River Road at Rock Creek.

Take instead the left fork, Rock Creek Trail 1509, passing a trail at the first switchback to the former site of a fire lookout on top of Peak 6991. Continue to an open saddle. Stroll north to Carne's summit for wide views of the Rock Creek valley, impressive Chiwawa Ridge, the Entiat Mountains, and queenly Mount Maude. This is a trail trip once snow is gone. It is also a long day trip because of the drive time. Consider car camping the night before and scramble another peak on the next day.

On Carne Mountain (Photo by Mike Torok)

25 MOUNT INDEX

Elevation: 5979 ft (1822 m)

Difficulty: S5/T4

Distance: 8 miles

Elevation gain: 4100 ft

Trip time: 11 hours

Time to summit: 6 hours

Best time of year: June to September

Maps: USGS Gold Bar, Index; Green Trails Index 142

Contact: Mount Baker–Snoqualmie National Forest, Skykomish Ranger Station

Special considerations: Finding the appropriate access road is difficult. Steep snow may present problems in spring.

GPS WAYPOINT ROUTE
1. Park on FS Road 6220: 2800 ft (10U 603097mE 5292814mN)
2. Index-Persis ridge: 1.5 miles, 5100 ft (10U 604505mE 5292076mN)
3. Index summit: 4 miles, 5979 ft (10U 606456mE 5291995mN)

Mount Index needs little introduction; its three peaks render a dazzling sight from the highway. The most dramatic portion of the main and highest peak is the great cliff above Lake Serene, which features the renowned Norwegian Buttresses. The only scramble is the main peak, despite its vertical and corrugated face. The Index Town Wall is a famous local climbing area known for its clean granite cracks. The nearness of the peaks to civilization has contributed to accidents due to the steep and sometimes treacherous terrain.

The scramble of Index follows a brushy ridge, but leads to a spectacular overlook of the rugged north face plunging below. Some of the greatest difficulty of this trip is identifying and gaining access to the proper starting place. The approach to the scramble route is confusing and requires travel over private roads that are gated during the week. A Weyerhauser map available at the North Bend Ranger Station is essential. But the scramble is clearly more achievable than scaling the sheer cliff to the east.

Trailhead Directions: Go east on US 2 past the town of Gold Bar and past milepost 33. Turn right (south) on Proctor Creek Road (FS Road 62). This road may be gated at US 2, but is sometimes open. Go about 3.5 miles and take the left fork at FS Road 6220. At the next junction in about 1.5 miles, a small spur leads upward to the end of the road. This is south of the usual beginning of the climber's trail to Mount Persis. (60 miles, 1.5 hours from Seattle)

Standard Route: From the start at FS Road 6220 (2800 feet), the Index-Persis ridge can be attained along the Proctor Creek drainage through brush and rock bands. In general, stay right and below the cliffs until you have reached the top of the spur ridge. At about 4400 feet at the southernmost point of the Index-Persis ridge, start traversing right up to a low point on the ridge ahead (5100 feet) from which the summit can be seen. Drop 250 feet to a saddle and then ascend the western ridge about 1200 feet to the summit. Expect class 3 scrambling and steep snow traverses.

Alternate Route: The shortest approach to Mount Index is via the southwest route from the North Fork Tolt River via the Proctor Creek Road (FS Road 62) on private land. This bypasses the start at the usual approach to Index and also shortens the trip. At 3.5 miles past the entry to FS Road 62, find a junction. The left fork leads to the traditional Index-Persis approach, but instead bear right and pass through the Proctor Creek Gate if it is open.

In general, stay on the main track despite numerous spurs. A few miles farther come to a T intersection and go left (the right is the main road that will eventually go as far as North Bend). After crossing a creek on an improved concrete culvert, arrive at a junction. The right fork passes through another gate that is usually closed. Proceed on the less traveled road to the left until arriving at another T. The route is to the left, but the road begins to deteriorate.

Mount Index (Photo by John Roper)

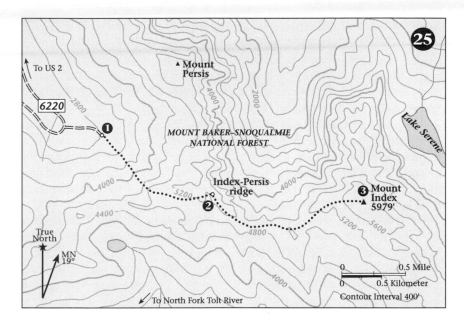

Parking is found at 2100 feet. Walk on the road until it ends at a creek (3900 feet). From here, ascend to the Index-Persis ridge, and approach Index from the southwest. Index can also be approached from the east from Lake Serene.

26 BARING MOUNTAIN

Elevation: 6125 ft (1867 m)

Difficulty: S4/T5

Distance: 9 miles

Elevation gain: 4000 ft

Trip time: 9 hours

Time to summit: 5 hours

Best time of year: June to September

Maps: USGS Baring; Green Trails Monte Cristo 143

Contact: Mount Baker–Snoqualmie National Forest, Skykomish Ranger Station

Special considerations: Hand line recommended

GPS WAYPOINT ROUTE
1. Barclay Creek trailhead: 2200 ft (10U 615522mE 5294236mN)
2. Ridge: 2 miles, 4000 ft (10U 615600mE 5293314mN)
3. Baring summit: 4.5 miles, 6125 ft (10U 617279mE 5292746mN)

Baring Mountain is best known for its striking vertical north face that appears suddenly when you are driving toward Stevens Pass. In contrast, the southern slope of Baring is a relatively benign forest with minor rocky cliffs. The higher north summit is clearly distinct from the south summit. From the west or south the scramble of Baring is mostly in the trees. But at the top above the timber, Baring offers excellent views of nearby uplands.

Like many peaks in the Stevens Pass area, Baring is known for its brush. Accordingly, the most favorable time to do the trip is when the snow is firm in the spring, for then most of the brush is covered, and brush bashing is kept to a minimum. The northwest ridge provides the simplest and least obstructed route. The slopes are usually snow free by late June; beware of avalanche hazards in the May thaw cycle.

Trailhead Directions: Drive US 2 to Baring General Store. Turn left and cross the railroad tracks. Drive on FS Road 6024 to the end of the road to Barclay Creek Trail 1055. (60 miles, 1.5 hours from Seattle)

Standard Route: Beginning at 2200 feet, walk past the end of the road and do not take the Barclay Creek Trail, but find a climber's trail by a narrow stream. Go less than a mile through trees to a small creek that may be dry in summer. Ascend steeply on the tread, following the creek to the ridge at 4000 feet. Although inconspicuous in places, the tread connects to a boulder basin at 4900 feet. Try to stay on the path as it goes into the basin; it generally trends in a southeastern direction.

From the basin scramble up toward the gully and gap between the north

Baring Mountain (Photo by John Roper)

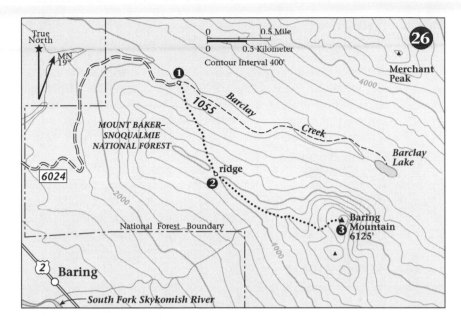

and south peaks at about 5600 feet. The basin is filled with snow through mid-May, with potential avalanche hazard in April or May. At the gap, turn left and ascend roughly north toward the summit. Scramble on the left up a small boulder field beneath the summit block (class 2). A number of steep spots on hard dirt, snow, and rock impede your progress. A hand line may be needed on this trip. After the notch, the way is easy to the summit.

27 LABYRINTH MOUNTAIN

Elevation: 6376 ft (1944 m)

Difficulty: S1/T2

Distance: 7 miles

Elevation gain: 2700 ft

Trip time: 6 hours

Time to summit: 3 hours

Best time of year: May to November

Maps: USGS Labyrinth Mountain; Green Trails Benchmark Mountain 144

Contact: Wenatchee National Forest, Lake Wenatchee Ranger District

GPS WAYPOINT ROUTE
1. Minotaur Lake trailhead: 3800 ft (10U 647094mE 5298810mN)
2. Minotaur Lake: 2.5 miles, 5550 ft (10U 647064mE 5300682mN)
3. Saddle: 3 miles, 5900 ft (10U 646532mE 5300974mN)
4. Labyrinth summit: 3.5 miles, 6376 ft (10U 646488mE 5301603mN)

Labyrinth is a lesser summit located east of the Cascade Crest north of Stevens Pass. Named by A. H. Sylvester for its bewildering map contours, Labyrinth lies in a Grecian setting. Minotaur and Theseus are cherubic lakes occupying high glacial cirques. Heather meadows and alpine firs complete the mythological scene. In autumn the setting is particularly ethereal with purple, magenta, and auburn hues infusing the hillsides. The views from the summit are of mountains west to Stevens Pass, north to Glacier Peak, and eastward beyond Lake Wenatchee. Wander the crests and join the forest gods in this heavenly junction between the earthly and the divine.

Trailhead Directions: Drive US 2 east from Stevens Pass 19 miles to the junction with SR 207 and turn left to Lake Wenatchee. Continue northwest along the shore of the lake. Go left on Little Wenatchee River Road (FS Road 65) and cross the White River. Go left on FS Road 6700 at a junction. Then go right on FS Road 6704. This road can also be reached from the Smith Brook–

Labyrinth Mountain (Photo by Mike Torok)

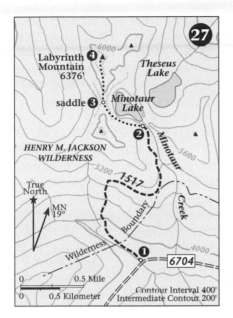

Rainy Pass Road (FS Road 6700) at 5 miles east of Stevens Pass. In 1 mile find Minotaur Lake Trail 1517. (120 miles, 2.5 hours from Seattle)

Standard Route: From Minotaur Lake trailhead at 3800 feet, Trail 1517 switchbacks up the hill, and then evolves into a fishermen's path shooting straight up. There is no formal tread and views are limited. At the end of the dry ascent the trail goes down the valley 0.5 mile losing 100 feet, then turns up Minotaur Creek. The forest gives way to meadows at 3 miles at 5550-foot Minotaur Lake. From the south end of Minotaur Lake, scramble to the saddle at 5900 feet just west of the lake. From there ascend the south ridge to the summit.

Alternate Route: From the south end of Minotaur Lake, gain the ridge on the eastern side of the lake and follow it to the northeast end of the lake. From here head north to 5800 feet. Then turn northwest and continue to the summit.

28 MOUNT MASTIFF AND MOUNT HOWARD

Elevations: 6741 ft (2055 m), 7063 ft (2153 m)

Difficulty: S5/T3

Distance: 13 miles one way

Elevation gain: 5500 ft

Trip time: 10 hours

Time to summit: 4 hours from trailhead to Mastiff; 1 hour from Mastiff to Howard

Best time of year: June to September

Maps: USGS Mount Howard; Green Trails Wenatchee Lake 145

Contact: Wenatchee National Forest, Lake Wenatchee Ranger District

GPS WAYPOINT ROUTE

1. Merritt Lake trailhead: 3100 ft (10U 658488mE 5294969mN)
2. Leave trail: 3.6 miles, 5300 ft (10U 655295mE 5296371mN)
3. Mastiff summit: 5 miles, 6741 ft (10U 654599mE 5297924mN)
4. Howard summit: 6 miles, 7063 ft (10U 653220mE 5297506mN)
5. Crescent Lake: 7 miles, 5440 ft (10U 653369mE 5296497mN)

Mount Mastiff and Mount Howard are neighbors on the crest of Nason Ridge, about midway between Stevens Pass and Lake Wenatchee. Mount Mastiff was named due to the similarity of its outline to the head of a dog. This mountain couple offers enjoyable scrambling with views that begin immediately and do not quit, leading to a full 360-degree circle. Across the valley the bulk of the Chiwaukum Mountains dominates. To the west, the slopes of Arrowhead and Jim Hill Mountain seem to grow greener with every step.

Located east of the Cascade Crest, this trip can be blisteringly hot in late summer. After the snow melts there is little water, and a plethora of flies swarm in the air. But never fear, the scramble also encounters lovely tarns in a tucked-away alpine haven like the promised land near tiny Canaan Lake; these tarns save the trip from the blasting sun.

The twosome is best done with a car shuttle at both ends, to enhance the variety and allow the scrambler to experience the countless switchbacks hiking down the Rock Mountain Trail 1587, rather than climbing up it.

Trailhead Directions: This trip is best done with a car shuttle. Drive US 2 over Stevens Pass to milepost 73; turn left at the sign for Rock Mountain. Leave one car here. Drive to milepost 76 and turn left at FS Road 657. Drive about 2.5 miles on dirt road to the road's end at Merritt Lake Trail 1588. (100 miles, 2.5 hours from Seattle)

Standard Route: From the Merritt Lake trailhead at 3100 feet, hike Trail 1588 to Nason Ridge Trail 1583 (4800 feet) and turn west. Hike about 1 mile to 5300 feet where the trail leaves the ridge and starts a traverse. Then leave the trail and head northwest up the ridge. Follow a boot trail until the ridge turns into a knife-edge. Traverse ledges below the crest on the eastern side about 0.3 mile on exposed but solid rock. Then scramble up the broad ridge to the summit of Mastiff.

Drop to the saddle (6350 feet) where refreshing tarns await. From the saddle ascend the ridge southwesterly, and then westerly to the summit of Howard. Head south off the summit down meadows and through a small cliff band that has several gullies. Then angle westward for the best route to avoid

Mount Howard (Photo by John Roper)

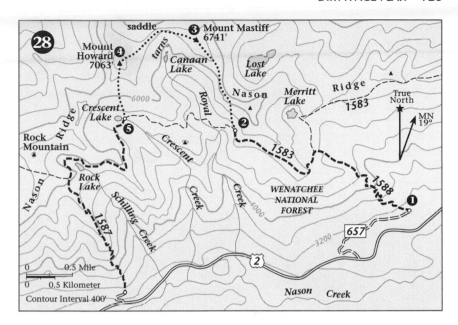

brush to reach Crescent Lake (5440 feet). Follow Nason Ridge Trail 1583 west to Rock Mountain Trail 1587 and the trailhead where you left a second car.

29 DIRTYFACE PEAK

Elevation: 6240 ft (1902 m)

Difficulty: S5/T4

Distance: 13 miles

Elevation gain: 6300 ft

Trip time: 12 hours

Time to summit: 7 hours

Best time of year: June to July

Maps: USGS Lake Wenatchee; Green Trails Wenatchee Lake 145

Contact: Wenatchee National Forest, Lake Wenatchee Ranger District

Special considerations: Moderate rock fall; routefinding around gendarmes near summit

GPS WAYPOINT ROUTE
1. Dirtyface trailhead: 2000 ft (10U 664856mE 5300414mN)
2. Logging road: 1.5 miles, 3500 ft (10U 666273mE 5301785mN)
3. Trail 1500: 2 miles, 3860 ft (10U 666087mE 5301975mN)
4. Lookout: 4.5 miles, 5989 ft (10U 664715mE 5302406mN)
5. Saddle: 5.6 miles, 5700 ft (10U 663636mE 5303442mN)
6. Dirtyface summit: 6.5 miles, 6240 ft (10U 662724mE 5304083mN)

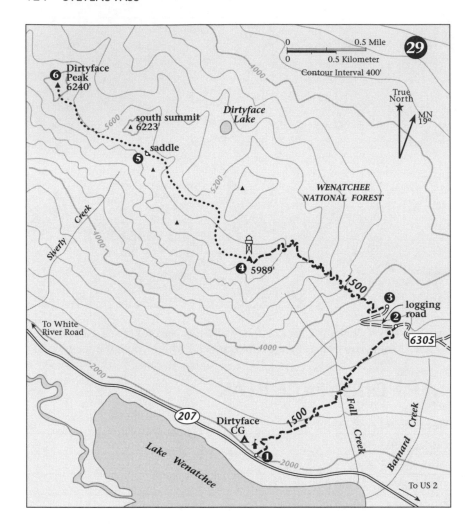

Dirtyface is a colorful name that is reminiscent of the countenance of the wayward scrambler who attempts this dry, arduous journey in full summer without enough water. It also could describe the appearance of the car that takes the hapless trip through back roads in order to avoid some of the exhausting hike up the precipitous slope. But the prize for the labor is the grand aspect west to Nason Ridge, north to Clark Mountain, Chiwawa Ridge, and east to rolling countryside. Below are Fish Lake and shimmering Lake Wenatchee.

The other dividend is the virtuousness of the energetic trek for the scrambler who relishes a good sweat for both punishment and reward. For this is a steep scramble, cruelly hot in sunny and windless weather, to an abandoned lookout site, then on to an airy summit. In early July the rock gardens are brilliant with fresh wildflowers. In late September the upper trail offers blueberries to graze. But Dirtyface is best done in June to take advantage of a few small snow patches and obliging weather.

Trailhead Directions: Drive US 2, 19 miles east of Stevens Pass. Turn left on SR 207 to Lake Wenatchee. Pass the state park road, cross the Wenatchee River Bridge, and stay left another 4.6 miles to the Lake Wenatchee Ranger Station. Turn right behind the station to find Dirtyface Trail 1500. (125 miles, 2.5 hours from Seattle)

Standard Route: The steep 4.5-mile trail begins at the Dirtyface trailhead at 2000 feet and is mostly in good shape. At 1.5 miles intersect an abandoned logging road, follow it westward a scant 0.5 mile to its end, and pick up Trail 1500 again. Continue on the trail to the lookout at Point 5989. Farther on, there are two summits, 0.6 mile apart, on a long ridge crest. The south summit is 6223 feet, but the north summit is higher and the true summit. It is located about 2 miles northwest of the lookout point.

Leave the trail at the lowest point on the ridge and cross to the valley on the north side that provides access to a small pond named Dirtyface Lake. Continue northwest on the ridge to the low point and then head to the saddle between the south summit and the lookout (5700 feet). Because of the many gendarmes on this ridge to the true summit, this way is not a scramble. These technical sections of rock can be avoided by descending and traversing below. Go over the saddle and drop to the south to the 5400-foot level. Contour around the southwest side of the south summit to the ridge between the summits, and follow this ridge around to the base of the north summit. Ascend the highest northern point from the southeast side, scrambling minor gullies through loose rock to the top.

Alternate Routes: A logging road high on the east flank of the mountain reduces the ascent. Reach it from Meadow Creek Road (FS Road 6300) and branch off west on FS Road 6305. The condition of the road is poor so, if you own a car whose paint is valuable, avoid this approach.

For a direct return route from the top, go down the Siverly Creek drainage from the middle summit. The gully gets brushy, but continue dropping 400 feet, then go left and find some timber where the brush is not as thick. Continue down through the trees; easily avoid any cliff bands encountered. To save road walking, leave the car near the White River Road about 1.7 miles northwest of the ranger station. The Siverly Creek route can also be done for the ascent (9 miles, 5000 feet).

Dirtyface Peak (Photo by Mike Torok)

30 MOUNT PILCHUCK

Elevation: 5324 ft (1623 m)

Difficulty: S2/T3

Distance: 10 miles

Elevation gain: 2900 ft

Trip time: 7 hours

Time to summit: 4 hours

Best time of year: April to November

Maps: USGS Verlot; Green Trails Silverton 110, Granite Falls 109

Contact: Mount Baker–Snoqualmie National Forest, Darrington Ranger Station

Special considerations: Ice on blocks possible at summit lookout

GPS WAYPOINT ROUTE
1. Pinnacle Lake trailhead: 2600 ft (10U 594244mE 5323393mN)
2. Pinnacle Lake: 2 miles, 3800 ft (10U 592723mE 5322677mN)
3. Bathtub Lakes: 4 miles, 4800 ft (10U 591172mE 5322979mN)
4. Pilchuck summit: 5 miles, 5324 ft (10U 589681mE 5323235mN)

Mount Pilchuck lookout in winter (Photo by Chris Weidner)

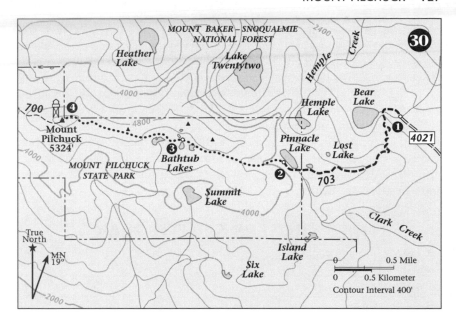

Located on the western edge of the Cascade Crest, Mount Pilchuck is readily apparent when viewed from the lowlands and highways. Its name is derived from the Indian word for the river meaning "red water," perhaps from the hue that wild game and berries gave to the streams when tribes hunted here. Pilchuck offers comprehensive views west to the Olympics and east to the Cascades from Mount Baker to Mount Rainier. From the top the entire gamut of lowland civilization in one direction and mountain wilderness in the other completely fill the view space. Another attraction of this trip's summit is the historic lookout cabin that the Everett Mountaineers restored and established as a museum.

Although the scramble is easy, when the fog rolls in or the trail is covered by snow, visibility is reduced and routefinding becomes imperative: dangerous steep snow sections and treacherous cliffs wait below. In summer, meet the throng of hikers who swarm the lookout from the west like ants at a picnic on a clear weekend. Instead, do this trip in winter to protect the vulnerability of this fragile ecosystem that is sacred to some who wish to protect it from casual trespassers. Scramble Pilchuck in winter when the lookout is lonesome and covered in rime ice and the wintry scene transforms the frozen cabin into an eerie and forbidding ghost of its summer presence.

Trailhead Directions: Drive on I-5 to US 2 in Everett. Go east and turn off on SR 9. Head north on SR 9 to the Granite Falls exit (SR 92) north of Lake Stevens. Continue to the eastern end of Granite Falls and turn north onto Mountain Loop Highway (FS Road 20). At 4.6 miles beyond Verlot, turn south onto Schweitzer Road (FS Road 4020), and at about 2.7 miles turn right onto FS Road 4021. Take this road about 3.3 miles to Pinnacle Lake Trail 703. (48 miles, 1.25 hours from Seattle)

Standard Route: Begin at the Pinnacle Lake trailhead at 2600 feet. Follow the trail to Pinnacle Lake, and then along the southern side of the lake to a large gully bearing east and up about 1000 feet to 4800 feet. Follow a boot track west and pass by Bathtub Lakes. Travel through tarns, on heather and on slabs. Ascend to the summit ridge. On this section the way is also marked with yellow paint on the rocks. For the last 200 feet, cross grass and a dirt gully to the lookout at the summit.

Alternate Route: You can do this scramble as a one-way trip with a car shuttle by leaving a car at the Pilchuck Mountain Trail 700 off of the Mountain Loop Highway shortly after the Verlot Campground. From the lookout, follow the trail to the car.

31 THREE FINGERS SOUTH PEAK

Elevation: 6854 ft (2089 m)	

Difficulty: S4/T5

Distance: 15 miles

Elevation gain: 4200 ft

Trip time: 11 hours

Time to summit: 6 hours

Best time of year: June to September

Maps: USGS Whitehorse Mountain; Green Trails Granite Falls 109, Silverton 110

Contact: Mount Baker–Snoqualmie National Forest, Darrington Ranger Station

Special considerations: Steep, hard snow year-round; bring crampons

GPS WAYPOINT ROUTE
1. Three Fingers trailhead: 3100 ft (10U 591405mE 5338345mN)
2. Saddle Lake: 2.5 miles, 3780 ft (10U 592515mE 5336685mN):
3. Goat Flat: 4.5 miles, 5000 ft (10U 594670mE 5335475mN)
4. Tin Can Gap: 6 miles, 5700 ft (10U 596464mE 5335598mN)
5. Three Fingers South Peak: 7.5 miles, 6854 ft (10U 597665mE 5335813mN)

The Indians called the massif Queest-Alb, but named now for its three peaks, Three Fingers and its western glacier are distinctive sights from the cities lining the Puget Sound Basin

The ladders on Three Fingers
(Photo by Susan Alford)

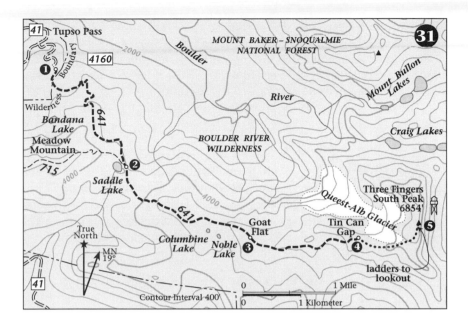

and from many North Cascade summits. The Queest-Alb Glacier hangs below and west of the north peak while a high perennial snowfield nestles in the south peak's southern slope. The middle peak is less distinguished. The east face of Three Fingers is an evil appearing, 2000-foot sheer wall. Although the north peak is a technical climb, the south peak sports a well-known scramble route.

Legend has it that the south peak was the highest by a tiny margin before about 15 feet of its top was blasted away to make space for a lookout cabin. Adding insult to injury, the original summit was never climbed before it was destroyed. But Three Fingers is most famous for the series of creaky ladders installed in the rock to bypass a cliff just below the lookout. For most scramblers, the highlight of the trip is this vertiginous approach to the airy summit. After a visit to the restored lookout cabin, dare to peer over the sheer precipice while your pulse quickens and your palms perspire. A suggestion for the timid: hold on to the rim.

Trailhead Directions: Drive the Mountain Loop Highway from Granite Falls to milepost 7 at the top of the hill. Turn left on FS Road 41 signed "Tupso Pass/Green Mountain." At 0.8 mile the pavement ends at a junction; keep left, passing several side roads. At 11 miles pass the Meadow Mountain Trail. At Tupso Pass, turn right onto FS Road 4160. At 17.3 miles find Three Fingers Trail 641. (65 miles, 2 hours from Seattle)

Standard Route: Begin at the Three Fingers trailhead (3100 feet), and reach Saddle Lake at 2.5 miles. Mud, rock, and tree roots slow down the pace. Continue onward in the meadows of Goat Flat. When nearly to a cliff the trail switchbacks to a minor saddle at 5640 feet. The last water is about 100 feet off-trail to the right. A climber's trail leads to Tin Can Gap (5700 feet). From near the pass, the lookout comes into view.

The trail continues east up the ridge. If there is no snow, follow the trail all the way to the summit. If snow is present, stay high on the ridge on the north side, traversing past two high spots. Then drop sharply about 100 feet down to a saddle. Cross to the south side of the ridge and go around the south buttress, then angle north up to the summit.

The only vague point in the route is near the summit block when the ladder is still out of sight. Stay left on the western side the of the summit rocks until the trail is again obvious. Some steep snow is encountered even in late season and an ice ax and crampons are advisable to prevent a fatal slip. At the final 40-foot rock step, climb up the vertical ladders to the summit. The ladders to the summit are a bit unstable, but they seem safe enough.

Be sure to venture inside the lookout. First read the window opening procedure posted on the outer table. Then go into the lookout through the window on the eastern side for the best views and a break spot.

32 MOUNT PUGH

Elevation: 7224 ft (2202 m)	
Difficulty: S5/T1	
Distance: 11 miles	
Elevation gain: 5500 ft	
Trip time: 11 hours	
Time to summit: 6 hours	
Best time of year: July to September	
Maps: USGS White Chuck Mountain, Mount Pugh; Green Trails Sloan Peak 111	
Contact: Mount Baker–Snoqualmie National Forest, Darrington Ranger Station	
Special considerations: Ice axes recommended	

GPS WAYPOINT ROUTE
1. Mount Pugh trailhead: 1900 ft (10U 617958mE 5333483mN)
2. Lake Metan: 1.5 miles, 3180 ft (10U 619383mE 5332731mN)
3. Stujack Pass: 3.8 miles, 5700 ft (10U 620310mE 5333714mN)
4. Pugh summit: 5.5 miles, 7224 ft (10U 621025mE 5333271mN)

The Indian name for Mount Pugh was *Da Klagwats,* but the present moniker is for John Pugh, who first settled at the base. Stujack Pass, a famous landmark on the mountain, was named for Stuart and Jackson, surveyors who mapped the area more than a century ago.

Part of the trail on Pugh was dynamited into the rock to provide access to an old summit lookout. But lightning destroyed the first cabin, and its replacement was also burned to the ground. Now the lookout has long been deserted but the crude trail remains and has evolved into scrambler's terrain.

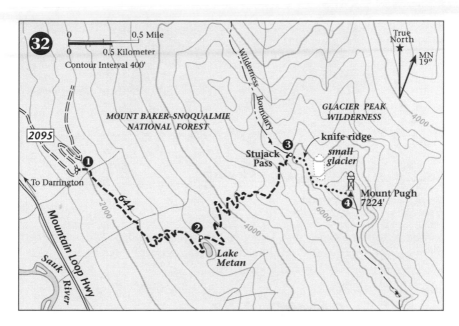

Pugh is strategically positioned far west from the main mountains of the Glacier Peak Wilderness, and therefore appears more imposing due to its detachment. From the summit to the west are lowlands of the Puget Sound Basin. To the north are the Cascades with the serrated majesty of Baker, Eldorado, Dome, and Bonanza. Glacier Peak commands the horizon and forms a broad turret above the White Chuck River. The rhinoceros horn of Sloan, the triple spikes of Three Fingers, the bulk of Whitehorse, and the spires of the Monte Cristo region are immediate and near at hand.

Pugh is further noteworthy for its hefty elevation gain. But the trip is possible in a lengthy day because the route is primarily on an established trail, with the last portion an easy scramble to the old lookout site at the top. For a straightforward trip with no bushwhacking, yet a consuming and rewarding course with an exceptional vantage, choose Pugh.

Trailhead Directions: Drive from Darrington on the Mountain Loop Highway 12.6 miles to Mount Pugh Road (FS Road 2095), which may be signed "095." Turn left and go 1 mile to Mount Pugh Trail 644. There is limited parking, but this is a low use area. (70 miles, 2 hours from Seattle)

Standard Route: Begin at the Mount Pugh trailhead at 1900 feet and climb 1.5 miles to tiny Lake Metan. Ascend switchbacks to meadows at 3 miles. After this point the trail is not maintained. Reach the notch of Stujack Pass at 3.8 miles (5700 feet). Steep snow in early summer requires an ice ax. The abandoned trail climbs abruptly from the pass to a knife-edge rock ridge. Go south along the ridge around the head of a small glacier following the rough scramble trail around the western side when possible. Scramble with some exposure to the summit area (class 2). Steep heather and easy rock slabs provide the final approach to the summit.

Sloan Peak from the summit of Mount Pugh (Photo by Jason Griffith)

Because of the exposed and steep nature over rocky slabs and blocks, this scramble is recommended only for those with competent ice ax arrest skills when snow is present beyond Stujack Pass.

33 DEL CAMPO PEAK

Elevation: 6610 ft (2015 m)

Difficulty: S4/T5

Distance: 12 miles

Elevation gain: 4500 ft

Trip time: 12 hours

Time to summit: 7 hours

Best time of year: July to September

Maps: USGS Bedal, Monte Cristo; Green Trails Sloan Peak 111, Monte Cristo 143

Contact: Mount Baker–Snoqualmie National Forest, Darrington Ranger Station

Special considerations: Frequent rock fall, helmets recommended; exposed summit descent

GPS WAYPOINT ROUTE
1. Monte Cristo Road: 2400 ft (10U 616124mE 5320130mN)
2. Twin Bridge Camp: 1.2 miles, 2300 ft (10U 616219mE 5318454mN)
3. Weeden Creek Trail 724: 1.8 miles, 2500 ft (10U 616268mE 5311328mN)
4. Stream crossing: 4.3 miles, 4000 ft (10U 615384mE 5315708mN)
5. Gothic Basin: 5 miles, 5000 ft (10U 614774mE 5315048mN)
6. Foggy Lake: 5.5 miles, 5280 ft (10U 614626mE 5315494mN)
7. Del Campo summit: 6 miles, 6610 ft (10U 614203mE 5316202mN)

Del Campo Peak is situated in the Monte Cristo area—the region that exemplifies the tug of war between nature and civilization. In the early 1900s, the

Northwest Mining Company poured a fortune into the Monte Cristo Railroad to try to mine the area. But the operation was a bust and the old town of Monte Cristo was deserted. Next, a road was built. But in the 1980s, the South Fork Sauk River flooded the area, and the attempt to restore the region was abandoned.

Del Campo is now named for a mine on its slopes, while the Weeden Creek Trail to the Del Campo Mine is named for the homesteader O. N. Weeden who killed three other settlers during a land feud. The former town of Monte Cristo has been uninhabited for decades, and the bridge to the decayed resort recently washed away. Although a lesser bridge has been reconstructed, the road that once reached for miles into the interior is now closed to vehicles but open to mountain bicycles or to those traveling on foot.

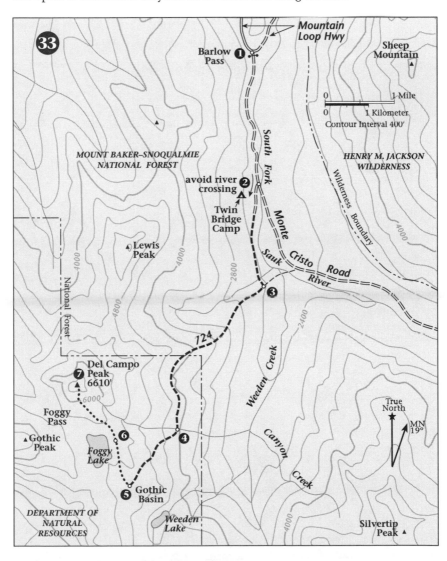

The steepest flank of Del Campo is on the north, but this pinnacle presents a rugged appearance from all perspectives. It is blessed with sound rock. Nevertheless, the way near the summit is covered with diminutive ledges, and the trajectory is nearly vertical. Several fatalities have occurred here, and it can only be surmised that at some point the footing is treacherous on tiny downsloping features. Be very careful, particularly on the descent of the south face. For Del Campo, the party needs to be small, experienced, and courageous. Keep together when doing this peak—helmets are recommended.

Trailhead Directions: Drive the Mountain Loop Highway to Barlow Pass and the gated Monte Cristo Road. You can drive the Mountain Loop Highway 20 miles on gravel road from Darrington, or 30.5 miles on paved road from Granite Falls. (62 miles, 2 hours from Seattle via Darrington)

Scrambling Del Campo Peak (Photo by Susan Alford)

Standard Route: Begin at 2400 feet on the Monte Cristo Road. At Twin Bridge Camp, 1.2 miles from Barlow Pass, look for the unmarked trail by the outhouse and head southwest. This route avoids a river crossing farther along the Monte Cristo Road and connects with Weeden Creek Trail 724 in a little over 0.5 mile.

At about 3000 feet, turn sharply uphill (right) and use a path on the right side of the stream or travel a rib 300 feet higher. Cross a significant stream at about 4000 feet. Continue to Gothic Basin. An ascent west over a minor ridge leads to Foggy Lake (5280 feet) in Gothic Basin. The lake is frozen much of the year. Talus and snow lead to Foggy Pass, which separates Del Campo and Gothic Peaks.

The summit of Del Campo lies 0.5 mile to the north-northwest of Foggy Lake. From the east side of the lake ascend to the shoulder north of the lake, and then climb northwesterly until just left of the gully leading to a notch east of the Del Campo summit. Climb ledges, staying to the left of the gully. When just above the notch, turn left toward the summit. On the upper face climb mixed heather and rock. The best route ascends almost to the high notch of the southeast buttress. From a rocky gully, keep left below a small notch and bypass a 30-foot step. When just above the notch, scramble rock to the summit, trending slightly west of due north (class 3).

Alternate Route: Another variation for reaching the rock of the upper south face is to climb from Foggy Pass at 5480 feet, bearing over onto the face. Del Campo is sometimes combined with a scramble of Gothic into a 2-day trip, with camping at Foggy Lake.

34 SPERRY PEAK AND VESPER PEAK

Elevations: 6000 ft (1829 m), 6214 ft (1894 m)

Difficulty: S5/T4

Distance: 9 miles

Elevation gain: 5800 ft

Trip time: 10 hours

Time to summit: 5 hours from Sunrise Mine trailhead to Sperry; 2 hours from Sperry to Vesper

Best time of year: June to October

Maps: USGS Bedal, Silverton; Green Trails Sloan Peak 111, Silverton 110

Contact: Mount Baker–Snoqualmie National Forest, Darrington Ranger Station

Special considerations: Avalanche hazard on new or unstable snow; ice axes recommended for Headlee Pass

GPS WAYPOINT ROUTE
1. Sunrise Mine trailhead: 2100 ft (10U 613578mE 5319989mN)
2. Headlee Pass: 2.5 miles, 4700 ft (10U 612073mE 5318028mN)

3. Vesper Creek: 2.8 miles, 4700 ft (10U 611629mE 5318299mN)
4. Sperry summit: 4 miles, 6000 ft (10U 611784mE 5318937mN)
5. Basin ridge: 4.5 miles, 5300 ft (10U 611326mE 5319034mN)
6. Vesper summit: 5 miles, 6214 ft (10U 610641mE 5318593mN)

In bygone days, miners quickly roughed out the trail to reach the Sunrise Mine at the base of Sperry and Vesper Peaks. The crude, steep path slices through Headlee Pass, a thin cut in the ridge separating the road from the old mine. Headlee Pass is notorious for its crumbling edges where the steep trail in the slot gully, eroded by hikers who do not follow the switchbacks, has to be remade every summer by volunteers. Headlee Pass is also the gateway to the Sperry-Vesper divide and scrambles there.

This region is close to population centers but still gives the feeling of rugged and wild terrain. Sperry is connected to Vesper by a saddle above tiny Vesper Lake, a lovely place to stop for a rest. Sperry is a rocky pyramid on most sides and is moderate only on its southern slope. Yet even here scrub conifers are often needed as "vegetable belays" and for handholds. Vesper is likewise an asymmetrical peak with a sheer north face that offers excellent technical climbing. But the eastern slopes are milder and provide a scramble route to the summit.

Since nearly its inception, the mine in the vicinity has been abandoned, but not the scrambles revealed through Headlee Pass. Sperry and Vesper are considered by some to be the most popular scramble peaks in the Monte Cristo area.

Trailhead Directions: Drive the Mountain Loop Highway east 17.8 miles from the Verlot Public Service Center toward, but not all the way to, Barlow Pass. Turn right on Sunrise Mine Road (FS Road 4065) and go 2.3 miles to the

Mount Rainier from Vesper Peak (Photo by Jason Griffith)

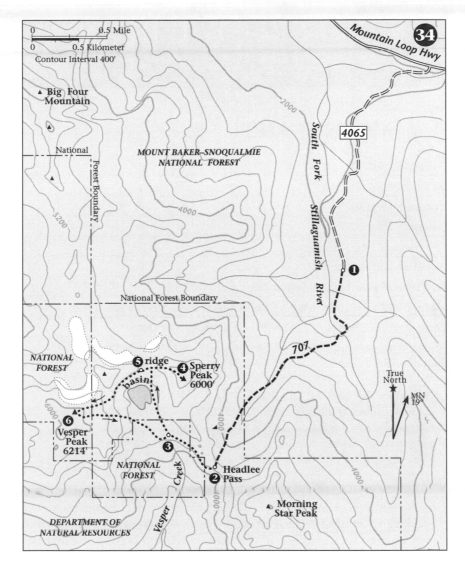

end of the road to find Sunrise Mine Trail 707. The final 0.5 mile may be blocked by a rockslide. (58 miles, 2 hours from Seattle)

Standard Route: For Sperry, hike from the Sunrise Mine trailhead at 2100 feet to Headlee Pass at 4700 feet. Continue past a huge rockslide to a small lake in upper Vesper Creek basin. Pass it to the east and scramble rock to Sperry's west shoulder. Then use scrub pines for handholds on the slope and continue to the summit (class 2). A boot path is present when the snow is gone.

For Vesper, traverse to the basin or stay on the ridge between Sperry and Vesper. Climb west up the snow slope on Vesper's gentle eastern ridge. The path fades into tree clumps at about 5500 feet. Ascend on moderately steep rock slabs to a level spot on the southeast ridge (6050 feet). Find a faint track among boulders to the summit (class 2).

35 MOUNT DANIEL

Elevation: 7960+ ft (2426+ m)

Difficulty: S5/T4

Distance: 16 miles

Elevation gain: 5200 ft

Trip time: 12 hours; 1-2 days

Time to summit: 7 hours

Best time of year: June to September

Maps: USGS The Cradle, Mount Daniel; Green Trails Stevens Pass 176

Contact: Wenatchee National Forest, Cle Elum Ranger District

Special considerations: Bring crampons for icy conditions; wilderness use permit required

GPS WAYPOINT ROUTE
1. Cathedral Rock trailhead 1345: 3400 ft (10U 643249mE 5267047mN)
2. Cathedral Pass: 4.5 miles, 5500 ft (10U 640759mE 5267919mN)
3. Peggys Pond: 5.5 miles, 5540 ft (10U 639836mE 5268397mN)
4. Circle Lake ridge: 6.5 miles, 6860 ft (10U 638287mE 5268411mN)
5. Daniel summit: 8 miles, 7960+ ft (10U 636945mE 5269341mN)

A mammoth hulk of volcanic rock, Mount Daniel presents a gargantuan expanse of glossy snow sliced by lines of dark saw teeth. From most perspectives Daniel appears as a tripartite cap of which the western point is the highest, but there are actually five high points. The named summit is Point 7899 on the USGS Mount Daniel map, but the true summit is the unnamed one to the west (7986 feet).

The Lynch Glacier is the second largest in the area. Extending from high on the northwest slope of Daniel to Pea Soup Lake at 6220 feet, the upper portion of the glacier is still active. The Lynch is connected to a nearly separate glacier on the northeast slope, called the Daniel Glacier. This ice field is losing mass, but still generates crevasses. Other glaciers or remnants include the Hyas Creek Glacier, West Lynch Glacier, and Lower Foss Glacier. Alpine pools whose waters drain to Waptus Lake adorn the less rugged southern flanks. The most striking examples are the combinations of Venus and Spade Lakes, and of Circle and Deep Lakes.

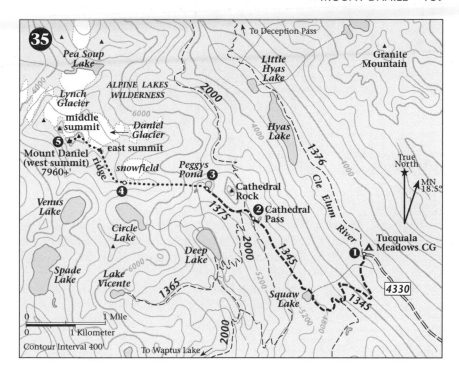

Daniel can be climbed from the glaciers, but a scramble route also leads to this lofty and supremely scenic destination. Daniel is one of the rugged aristocrats of the region. A forthright approach brings the scrambler into the majestic domain of the true alpine realm.

Trailhead Directions: Drive I-90 to the Salmon la Sac–Roslyn exit (no. 80) and proceed on SR 903 beside Cle Elum Lake through Roslyn and Ronald. At 16 miles from Roslyn reach Salmon la Sac. Continue 12.5 miles on FS Road 4330 to a Y nearly at the road's end. (The car ford of Scatter Creek can be a problem during periods of high runoff.) Take the left spur a few dozen yards to Cathedral Rock Trail 1345. (110 miles, 2.5 hours from Seattle)

Standard Route: From the Cathedral Rock trailhead at 3400 feet, follow Cathedral Rock Trail 1345 for 4.5 miles to Cathedral Pass (5500 feet). At the end of a switchback, while descending toward Deep Lake on Pacific Crest Trail 2000, find a good climber's trail (no. 1375) leading northwest toward Peggys Pond. The path traverses under Cathedral Rock.

After the snow has melted, a way trail leads from Peggys Pond to Mount Daniel along the southeast between Circle Lake and a permanent snowfield. Follow the south ridge to the saddle below the 7899-foot east summit. Follow a traverse across the south slope of the east peak—a steep sidehill with treacherous footing. Stay close to the top until the saddle (7600 feet) between the east and middle summit.

From here the middle summit is a walk up a talus slope. If the middle summit is not ascended, follow a plateau just to its south to reach the true

Mount Daniel (Photo by John Roper)

west summit. Or, from the middle summit, follow the southeast ridge of the west summit to the base of the summit block. Ascend the scramble route on the south side. Crampons should be taken on this trip due to icy conditions common near the summit.

Note that this trip can be done as an overnight with a camp near Peggys Pond; however, the mosquitoes can be ferocious in late July and early August.

36 GRANITE MOUNTAIN AND TRICO MOUNTAIN

Elevations: 7144 ft (2178 m), 6640 ft (2024 m)

Difficulty: S4/T3

Distance: 19 miles

Elevation gain: 4400 ft

Trip time: 13 hours; 1 strenuous day

Time to summit: 7 hours trailhead to Granite; 2 hours from Granite to Trico

Best time of year: June to October

Maps: USGS Mount Daniel, The Cradle; Green Trails Stevens Pass 176

Contact: Wenatchee National Forest, Cle Elum Ranger District

Special considerations: Loose rock, exposure; wilderness use permit required

GPS WAYPOINT ROUTE
1. Deception Pass trailhead: 3400 ft (10U 643246mE 5267244mN)
2. Hyas Lake: 2 miles, 3448 ft (10U 641704mE 5269741mN)
3. Robin Lakes Trail 1376.1: 4.5 miles, 4200 ft (10U 640303mE 5272016mN)
4. Tuck Lake: 6.5 miles, 5300 ft (10U 641408mE 5272001mN)
5. Robin Lakes: 7.5 miles, 6178 ft (10U 642783mE 5271814mN)
6. Saddle: 6700 ft (10U 643336mE 5271350mN)
7. Granite summit: 9 miles, 7144 ft (10U 643678mE 5271280mN)
8. Trico summit: 10.5 miles, 6640 ft (10U 641910mE 5273055mN)

Granite Mountain is just southeast of Tuck and Robin Lakes while Trico Mountain, its name derived from the three-county junction, is situated to the northwest. The twosome borders the exquisite ice-polished nooks and crannies that comprise the "Mini-Enchantments." Tuck and Robin Lakes and their surroundings provide a stunning setting of a glacier scoured haven dotted with tarns and lakelets set like jewels in austere stone.

In our age of urban sprawl and wilderness overpopulation there's no keeping a secret. This land is nearly as popular as the Enchantment Lakes of even greater fame. In years past, the granite sanctuary has been plagued with more

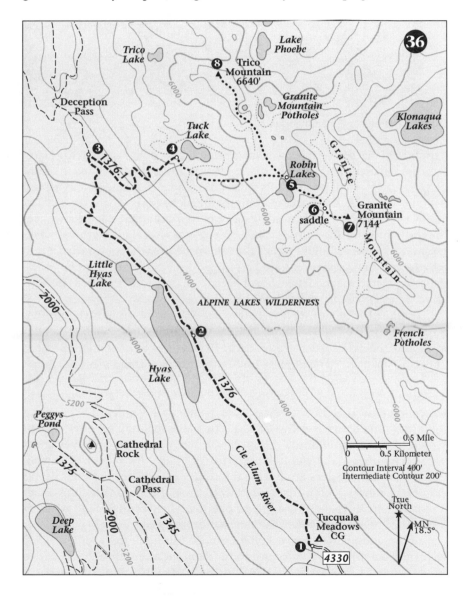

Granite Mountain (Photo by John Roper)

people than marmots. The new management goal is not to conceal the place, which is impossible, but to keep it from being pounded and polluted to death. Now a permit system protects this outstanding, open parkland. Though entry is limited, day hikers can still overrun the fragile region.

Attempt this outing as a single day trip, but note that the distances are long with unremitting altitude gain and loss. Stay overnight here only when essential. Campers absolutely must not initiate new patches of bare dirt. Carry a stove, and find privacy in nooks on ridges or in basins. Be mindful of the delicate vegetation, and where possible walk on bare rock. Preserve and conserve the phenomenal charm for others.

Trailhead Directions: Drive I-90 to the Salmon la Sac–Roslyn exit (no. 80). Follow signs on SR 903 through Roslyn to the Cle Elum River. At Salmon la Sac take the right branch of FS Road 4330 and drive to its end. Just past the Tucquala Meadows Campground, find Deception Pass Trail 1376. (110 miles, 2.5 hours from Seattle)

Standard Route: From the Deception Pass trailhead at 3400 feet, hike on Deception Pass Trail 1376 to Hyas Lake. At about 4.5 miles (4200 feet) go right (east) on Robin Lakes Trail 1376.1. The trail is maintained, obvious, and signed. The trail contours to the southeast about 0.5 mile, and then turns abruptly northeast and climbs steeply to Tuck Lake (5300 feet). Follow an inconspicuous boot track around the right side of Tuck Lake and then ascend east up the ridge to Robin Lakes (6178 feet). Cross the stream dividing Upper and Lower Robin Lakes. If needed, an overnight stay can be made at Upper Robin Lake on the bare patches of established campsites.

At the south end of Upper Robin Lake, go southeast to a saddle at 6700 feet. From the saddle, scramble east to the summit. Alternatively, you can go from the saddle to a col on the north ridge (more difficult scrambling). Go south on the north ridge to the summit (class 2).

For Trico, return to Granite Mountain Potholes at 6280 feet. Trico is 0.3 mile northwest of the upper pothole. Ascend the easy southeast spur to the summit.

37 GRINDSTONE MOUNTAIN

Elevation: 7533 ft (2296 m)

Difficulty: S5/T3

Distance: 10 miles

Elevation gain: 5100 ft

Trip time: 9 hours

Time to summit: 6 hours

Best time of year: July to September

Maps: USGS Chiwaukum Mountains, Jack Ridge; Green Trails Chiwaukum Mountains 177

Contact: Wenatchee National Forest, Leavenworth Ranger District

Special considerations: Slippery rocks in snow; wilderness use permit required

GPS WAYPOINT ROUTE

1. Chatter Creek trailhead: 3000 ft (10U 658674mE 5275190mN)
2. Leave trail: 4 miles, 6200 ft (10U 657615mE 5278261mN)
3. North ridge: 4.4 miles, 7000 ft (10U 657104mE 5278429mN)
4. Bench: 4.8 miles, 7400 ft (10U 656987mE 5277955mN)
5. Grindstone summit: 5 miles, 7533 ft (10U 656860mE 5277821mN)

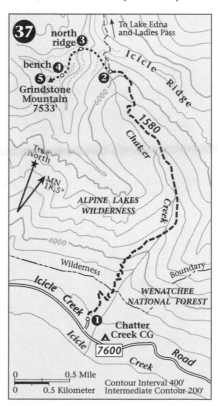

Grindstone Mountain lies in the Wenatchee Mountains south of Icicle Ridge, which provides the southern high route on the Chatter Creek Trail to Ladies Pass. This entrance is a thoroughfare to the much-beloved alpine realm of "Mormon Ladies Lakes," named by legend for the many wives of Brigham Young. The milieu is a country of contrasting lush meadows, ice-polished buttresses, and austerely stunning lakes.

A spectacular highland traverse from the foot of Grindstone leads to Lake Edna, the loneliest, most barren, and perhaps the prettiest of the ladies. Relish the high tableau from Cashmere and Stuart to Monte Cristo and from Glacier Peak to Index and Baring. Across the range is the supreme green of Snowgrass Mountain with tundra ridges, lakes, and basins. But overlooking the portal to Ladies Lakes, the summit of Grindstone provides even more astonishing outlooks into this ravishing, magical realm.

Trailhead Directions: Drive to Leavenworth and turn on Icicle Creek Road (FS Road 7600). Drive the Icicle Creek Road for 16 miles, pass Chatter Creek Campground, and then take the next road to the right. Continue to ~Chatter Creek Trail 1580. (145 miles, 3.5 hours from Seattle)

Standard Route: Chatter Creek Trail 1580 starts at 3000 feet on an old road through a brushy clear-cut. In 100 yards go right at a junction. In 0.3 mile the road ends. The trail climbs beyond a hunter's camp through the forest along Chatter Creek. Cross the creek, rounding a corner to enter the upper valley. In 0.5 mile enter an open basin. Near timberline at 2.5 miles

(5300 feet), rest at a scenic spot for a food break. Gaze over the Icicle River valley to Trout Creek and Eightmile Mountain, and over to Blackjack Ridge and Bootjack Mountain.

After leaving the trail at 6200 feet and just after traversing above the basin, cross the drainage and then ascend the open slope, heading for a saddle on the north ridge of Grindstone. When 100 feet below the saddle, head left toward a broad gully and a bench on the ridge (7400 feet). Travel west and descend about 70 feet to traverse a boulder field, which can be slippery and treacherous under snow cover. Gain the minor summit just before Grindstone, and then drop about 50 feet from the minor summit to a basin. From here ascend readily to the summit. Note that running the ridge from the bench at 7400 feet is not a scramble due to more difficult climbing.

Scrambling on the ridge
(Photo by Chris Weidner)

38 CASHMERE MOUNTAIN

Elevation: 8501 ft (2951 m)

Difficulty: S5/T3

Distance: 17 miles

Elevation gain: 5700 ft

Trip time: 11 hours; 1-2 days

Time to summit: 6 hours

Best time of year: May to September

Maps: USGS Cashmere Mountain; Green Trails Chiwaukum Mountains 177

Contact: Wenatchee National Forest, Leavenworth Ranger District

Special considerations: Avalanche hazard and loose rock in gullies, helmets advised; wilderness use permit required

GPS WAYPOINT ROUTE

1. Eightmile Creek trailhead: 3300 ft (10U 664563mE 5266827mN)
2. Little Caroline Lake: 5 miles, 6300 ft (10U 660280mE 5267773mN)
3. Leave trail: 6 miles, 6740 ft (10U 660495mE 5268443mN)
4. Saddle: 8 miles, 8000 ft (10U 661691mE 5269307mN)
5. North ridge: 8.2 miles, 8240 ft (10U 662072mE 5269394mN)
6. Cashmere summit: 8.5 miles, 8501 ft (10U 662042mE 5269283mN)

The tallest and huskiest in the Wenatchee Mountains except for the major Stuart Range peaks, Cashmere Mountain is a lonely giant just north of the Enchantment Lakes. Cashmere is situated in the Alpine Lakes Wilderness, a picturesque region of sharp-sculpted pinnacles and glacier-scoured valleys speckled with sparkling tarns and cirques. Since this district is located near the Cascade Crest, there are places on the eastern slopes where any day of the year a person has an excellent chance of sunburn, while on the western side a person has as good a chance of getting drenched.

The north-facing slopes of Cashmere hold a cornucopia of deep-walled valleys. The western shoulder is a craggy rock basin with lovely scalloped meadows. Because the west and south sides are moderate, Cashmere offers a natural site for spring scrambling and can make a fine early season trip.

Cashmere can be done as a day trip, somewhat strenuous because of the mileage, or as an overnight journey. A high camp lends time to appreciate Little Caroline Lake, a high, tree-ringed pool amidst meadows, sparkling under a wealth of cliffs. From here the awesome spectacle of the illustrious north face of Mount Stuart is seen closely enough to distinguish crevasses in the convoluted glaciers.

Cashmere can be scrambled from almost any direction, but the easiest way is to use the high trail to Windy Pass. Due to heavy usage, a permit system for day use as well as camping is now in place to manage the wilderness. You should check with the Leavenworth Ranger Station to ascertain current requirements.

Trailhead Directions: Drive to Leavenworth on US 2. At the western out-skirts of town, turn on Icicle Creek Road (FS Road 7600). Drive the Icicle Creek Road 8.5 miles south and turn left across a bridge on FS Road 7601 up Eightmile Creek, past the Bridge Creek Campground. Continue steeply about 3.2 miles to Eightmile Creek Trail 1552 on the uphill side of FS Road 7601. (130 miles, 3 hours from Seattle)

Standard Route: Begin at the Eightmile Creek trailhead (3300 feet) and follow Eightmile Creek to Little Eightmile Lake. At the junction continue on the right fork of Eightmile–Trout Creek Trail 1554, climbing switchbacks from the valley. At 5 miles find the alpine basin of Lake Caroline (6190 feet). The best campsites are 0.5 mile farther and 200 feet higher at Little Caroline Lake.

The 2-mile hike to 7200-foot Windy Pass, on a good trail amid flowers and larches, is worth the extra time. But a shorter route is to leave the trail at a switchback at about 6700 feet above the meadow. Head northeast on a rising traverse to gain a ridge off a minor peak west of Cashmere. Follow this

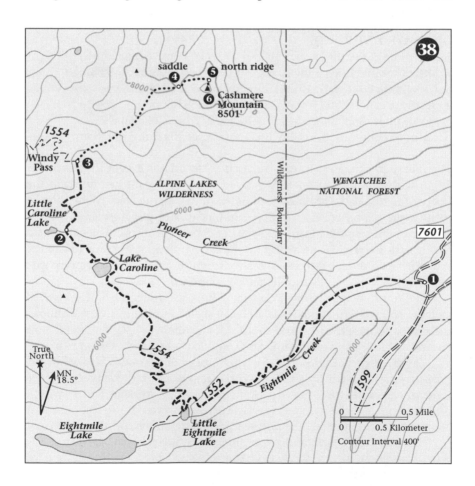

Cashmere Mountain from Icicle Ridge (Photo by John Roper)

ridge until it intersects with the west ridge of Cashmere, and then drop to the saddle at about 8000 feet. Avoid taking the most obvious path up, which is a more difficult scramble route. Follow the lower path to the north ridge by taking the most easterly gully that is directly north of the summit. Ascend that gully to the summit.

Return by descending the gully, keeping the party close together to minimize rock fall danger. Follow on the same lower route you ascended on. The party may choose to go down the gully from the saddle and travel cross-country to join the trail just north of Little Caroline Lake or stay high on the ridge back to Windy Pass.

Alternate Route: Hike the trail to Windy Pass and follow the ridge toward Cashmere. Then follow the standard route after reaching the 8000-foot saddle, adding about 1.5 miles and 250 feet.

39 WEDGE MOUNTAIN

Elevation: 6885 ft (2099 m)

Difficulty: S2/T2

Distance: 5 miles

Elevation gain: 2600 ft

Trip time: 6 hours

Time to summit: 4 hours

Best time of year: May to July

Maps: USGS Leavenworth, Blewett; Green Trails Leavenworth 178, Liberty 210

Contact: Wenatchee National Forest, Leavenworth Ranger District

GPS WAYPOINT ROUTE
1. FS Road 7305: 2400 ft (10U 675451mE 5264633mN)
2. Left fork: 3700 ft (10U 675152mE 5263576mN)

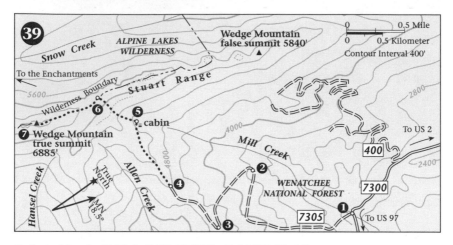

3. Switchback: 4100 ft (10U 674879mE 5262867mN)
4. Road end: 4600 ft (10U 674148mE 5262992mN)
5. Cabin: 0.5 mile, 5400 ft (10U 672561mE 5262494mN)
6. Ridge: 1 mile, 6160 ft (10U 672052mE 5262627mN)
7. Wedge true summit: 2.5 miles, 6885 ft (10U 671900mE 5261737mN)

Wedge Mountain is a simple tour, yet the trip is exceptional for stunning views into the Cashmere Crags, a region of myriad outcrops and pinnacles in the Alpine Lakes Wilderness. Located just outside the eastern boundary of the wilderness, Wedge is the unrivaled vantage point of the entire Enchantments, a legendary group of lakes in rock basins and one of the most famous places in the Cascade mountains. Wedge is also the ideal viewpoint for the emperor Mount Stuart, Cashmere Mountain, and the serrated length of Icicle Ridge.

Maps show the summit of Wedge at about 5840 feet lying midway between Icicle Creek and Nada Lake. But logic dictates the choice of the true summit to be the 6885-foot peak positioned between the heads of Allen and Hansel Creeks 2 miles southwest on the same crest at the terminus of the Stuart Range. Because it is gentle, Wedge is a commendable winter or spring trip.

From the summit unfolds the unprecedented scope of Snow Lakes, Temple Ridge, McClellan Peak, Little Annapurna, and the rest of the Enchantments. These cathedral-like masses of granite spires are awe inspiring any time of year, but if the clouds are forgiving, the entire horizon of the jagged landscape comprises a divine encounter with this extraordinary realm. The reaction on the top of Wedge is humility, as the scale of human effort is miniscule in comparison with such imperial mammoths. But immersed in the expansive tableau, the imagination and spirit can soar. This is the place for dreams of the exquisite adventures that the highland promises.

Trailhead Directions: The eastern slope of Wedge Mountain is intersected with roads that climb upslope. Driving to the trailhead is a headache, and the

Snow Lakes and the Enchantments from Wedge Mountain (Photo by John Roper)

crux of the trip is finding the start. But take heart; just about any route up the hill to the summit ridge will suffice. However, roads higher than 4500 feet may not always be drivable, and gates often present obstacles. Both the Hansel and Allen Creek branch roads can be used as starting points for easy cross-country routes to the summit of Wedge via the north ridge crest. Many way trails create a labyrinth not on maps and several paths lead nearly to the ridge.

For this scramble, drive I-90 to US 97 and drive north over Blewett Pass. About 5 miles south of Peshastin, turn left (west) on FS Road 7300, also called Mountain Home Road. At 2 miles (just before the crossing of Mill Creek), turn left (south) on FS Road 7305. Follow the most used road, which usually requires left turns. At 3700 feet, the road takes a sharp turn left. At 4100 feet the road makes a switchback to the wooded ridge between Mill and Allen creeks. Follow this branch to the parking area. The last section is drivable but quite narrow and brushy; low-clearance vehicles will drag bottom. (135 miles, 3 hours from Seattle)

Standard Route: From the end of FS Road 7305 at 4600 feet, follow the path uphill until it becomes a trail. Continue on the trail to about 5200 feet in a cleared area with a campsite. The trail to the left leads to a cabin; follow this trail through the campsite and up the ridge. Break into an open, burned area. Travel up and toward the left to the ridge top. Follow the crest proximal to the apex; drop to the left (east) of the ridge as required to bypass difficulties. Scramble the final gully to the true summit. Farther along the ridge is another unnamed but highter peak at 6977 feet.

 COLCHUCK PEAK

Elevation: 8705 ft (2653 m)

Difficulty: S5/T5

Distance: 13 miles

Elevation gain: 5100 ft

Trip time: 11 hours; 1-2 days

Time to summit: 7 hours

Best time of year: May to June

Maps: USGS Enchantment Lakes; Green Trails The Enchantments 209S

Contact: Wenatchee National Forest, Leavenworth Ranger District

Special considerations: Crampons necessary for ice after June; wilderness use permit required

GPS WAYPOINT ROUTE
1. Stuart Lake trailhead: 3400 ft (10U 664149mE 5265908mN)
2. Colchuck Lake Trail 1599A: 2.5 miles, 4500 ft (10U 662734mE 5263342mN)
3. Colchuck Lake: 4 miles, 5570 ft (10U 663173mE 5262426mN)

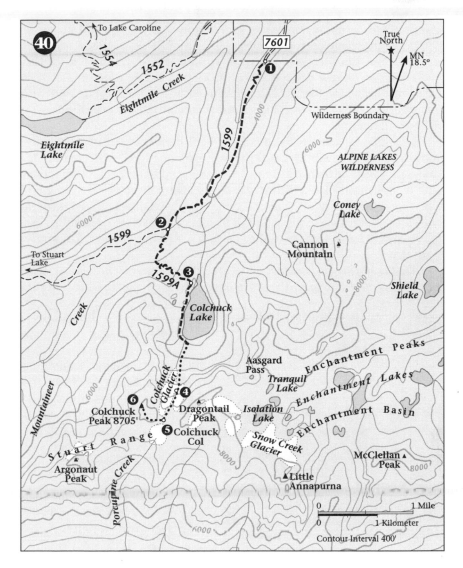

4. Snowfield: 6 miles, 7300 ft (10U 662965mE 5260464mN)
5. Colchuck Col: 6.2 miles, 8040 ft (10U 662793mE 5260112mN)
6. Colchuck summit: 6.5 miles, 8705 ft (10U 662351mE 5260366mN)

Colchuck Peak is one of the stately granite czars constituting the rim of the Enchantment Lakes. At its base, the Colchuck Glacier fills the cirque between Colchuck and Dragontail Peaks. The glacial ice, which has shrunken considerably in modern times, is now largely broken into two lobes, but still extends nearly to Colchuck Lake. Colchuck Peak is quite rocky and steep everywhere except on the south. The western summit is the highest of several points. From the summit of Colchuck the monster monarch Mount Stuart dominates the scene, while the exquisite Enchantments Lakes and the Lost Plateau reside below. This vicinity at the eastern end of the Stuart Range is a haven for climbers, but scramblers too can derive joy from the top of the spires.

Colchuck can be accomplished as an energetic day trip. A party with more time can include an overnight camp by the emerald waters of Colchuck Lake amid subalpine forests under granite cliffs. But if it is peace and quiet you want, don't come here at all, because this is the most heavily used area in the Enchantments.

Be additionally aware that this trip is a scramble only late in spring when snow covers permanent ice along the way. Do not attempt the ascent to the Colchuck Col later than mid-June, or be prepared to be entirely competent with crampons on a steep incline. Avoid significant danger by traveling only when snow blankets the Colchuck Glacier, and by keeping to the edges of the snowfield. Nevertheless, the ascent of Colchuck is relatively straightforward for the scrambler seeking the exalted reaches of a distinguished Enchantment sovereign.

Trailhead Directions: Drive US 2 east to Leavenworth. Drive on the Icicle Creek Road past the Snow Creek trailhead, the large parking lot along the

paved road. To reach Stuart Lake trailhead, continue up the paved road to Bridge Creek Campground. Turn left onto Eightmile Road (FS Road 7601) and drive about 4 miles to its end at Stuart Lake Trail 1599. (145 miles, 3.5 hours from Seattle)

Standard Route: Begin at the Stuart Lake trailhead (3400 feet) and follow Stuart Lake Trail 1599 as it parallels Mountaineer Creek on a constant upward grade for a mile. The trail then switchbacks up the valley to a junction at 2.5 miles (4500 feet). Take the left fork, Colchuck Lake Trail 1599A, which crosses Mountaineer Creek and ascends with many switchbacks along East Mountaineer Creek. During the final 0.3 mile, the way leaves the creek and comes to Colchuck Lake at 4 miles (5570 feet). Camping is available all the way around the lake; the best campsite for this scramble is at the south end of the lake below the Colchuck Glacier.

Colchuck Peak (Photo by John Roper)

From Colchuck Lake, climb up talus and snow slopes on the left of the small pocket glacier to the Colchuck Col 0.8 mile south of the lakeshore (8040 feet). From the col, turn right and continue to the summit, keeping just south of the crest. This route is a moderate rock scramble. (4 hours from the lake)

Alternate Routes: For the south route, take Ingalls Creek Trail 1215 about 9 miles to Porcupine Creek (4160 feet). Be certain you are west of Dragontail Ridge. Follow the drainage to about 7000 feet, and then keep on Dragontail's western side on polished slabs for a direct ascent to the Colchuck summit. Alternatively, at 7600 feet where the valley splits, bear right to Colchuck Col (8040 feet). From the col, proceed to the summit. (5 hours from Ingalls Creek)

DRAGONTAIL PEAK

Elevation: 8840 ft (2695 m)

Difficulty: S5/T5

Distance: 14 miles

Elevation gain: 5600 ft

Trip time: 13 hours; 1-2 days

Time to summit: 7 hours from trailhead; 2 hours from upper Enchantment Basin

Best time of year: July to September

Maps: USGS Enchantment Lakes; Green Trails The Enchantments 209S

Contact: Wenatchee National Forest, Leavenworth Ranger District

Special considerations: Crampons advised for hard, icy snow travel; wilderness use permit required

GPS WAYPOINT ROUTE
1. Stuart Lake trailhead: 3400 ft (10U 664149mE 5265908mN)
2. Colchuck Lake Trail 1599A: 2.5 miles, 4500 ft (10U 662734mE 5263342mN)
3. Colchuck Lake: 4 miles, 5570 ft (10U 663173mE 5262426mN)
4. Aasgard Pass: 6.2 miles 7800 ft (10U 664146mE 5260684mN)
5. Dragontail ridge: 6.7 miles, 8490 ft (10U 663500mE 5260344mN)
6. Dragontail summit: 7 miles, 8840 ft (10U 663354mE 5260453mN)

Dragontail's name originated from the miniature rock needles on the thin "tail" of the crest southwest of the summit. The second-highest peak in the Stuart Range, its Serpentine Arete is one of the most famous climbs in the Cascades. Popular with climbers because of its accessibility, good rock, and impressive appearance, Dragontail is also remarkable for a nontechnical approach, without ropes and protection, to the same aerial vistas. While the north face is noteworthy on the approach, the northeast face is less noticeable because of its orientation toward the broad couloirs leading to Aasgard Pass. It is from the east that the scramble route is achieved, but only after reaching the plateau of the Enchantment Lakes basin.

Dragontail can be scrambled in a single day as an ultra-strenuous marathon if you are traveling light and fast over Aasgard Pass. But to savor the full, exalted experience, take 2 days and camp in the upper Enchantment Basin, or take several days and bask in the divine ambiance of this exquisite area. On a more leisurely trip, the approach to the Enchantments can be made from Snow Lakes. Some scramblers complain about the Snow Creek Trail—too many miles to accomplish the elevation and when you get to the eastern basin there are too many people. Aasgard Pass is a shortcut to the Enchantments: notorious not only for cliffs and slick boulders, but also for sudden summer storms that can dump snow any time of year. Finally, when you get to the Enchantments, the people are everywhere anyway. Yet Aasgard Pass is the

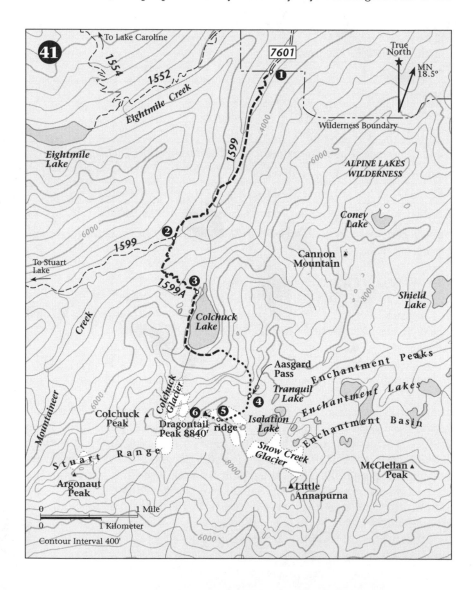

shortest distance into the Enchantments, and the only feasible route for a single day scramble.

If you plan to camp overnight, be sure to plan several months in advance to get an overnight camping permit. A wilderness permit for day use is also required. Because day use permits are more plentiful, the single day method requires less planning; but it also requires considerably more stamina.

Trailhead Directions: Drive US 2 east to Leavenworth. Drive on the Icicle Creek Road past the Snow Creek trailhead, the large parking lot along the paved road. Continue up the paved road to Bridge Creek Campground beyond Mountaineer Creek. Then turn left onto Eightmile Road (FS Road 7601) and drive about 4 miles to its end at Stuart Lake Trail 1599. (145 miles, 3.5 hours from Seattle)

Standard Route: Begin at Stuart Lake trailhead (3400 feet) and drop left off Stuart Lake Trail 1599 at about 2.5 miles and cross Mountaineer Creek. Ascend Colchuck Lake Trail 1599A to Colchuck Lake between Dragontail and Colchuck Peaks. Round the shore to the right, to a camping area where the formal trail ends and boulder hopping begins.

Dragontail Peak
(Photo by Chris Weidner)

Follow a boot path below the Colchuck Glacier on the side of Colchuck Peak, and over talus to the slopes below Aasgard Pass. From the lake, the ascent is nearly vertical, gaining 2200 feet in less than a mile. Watch for cairns placed by the Forest Service, a practice generally unacceptable in the wilderness but necessary here to keep neophytes from straying into the cliffs. About two-thirds of the way to the pass, cross to the right under a knot of trees and rocks and follow cairns over a small stream and snowfield to Aasgard Pass (7800 feet).

For the east scramble route of Dragontail, from near Aasgard Pass bear southwest and ascend over snow through the saddle to the ridge crest above. Here a gentle rock spur with ice on its north side leads to the summit rocks about 300 feet above. The highest point is a small bedrock bump that drops on the north. This is a class 2 scramble, but bring crampons because the snow ascent from the Enchantment Basin can be steep and icy.

ENCHANTMENT PEAK

Elevation: 8520 ft (2597 m)	
Difficulty: S5/T2	
Distance: 24 miles	
Elevation gain: 7500 ft	
Trip time: 2-3 days	
Time to summit: 11 hours from trailhead; 2 hours from Lake Viviane	
Best time of year: July to October	
Maps: USGS Enchantment Lakes; Green Trails The Enchantments 209S	
Contact: Wenatchee National Forest, Leavenworth Ranger District	

Special considerations: Wilderness use permit required; plan several months in advance

GPS WAYPOINT ROUTE
1. Snow Creek trailhead: 1300 ft (10U 672473mE 5267972mN)
2. Enchantment Lakes: 10 miles, 7100 ft (10U 666203mE 5261034mN)
3. Prusik Pass: 11 miles, 7400 ft (10U666532mE 5261497mN)
4. Enchantment summit: 12 miles, 8520 ft (10U 665615mE 5261662mN)

The Enchantments are a renowned group of rock basin lakes nestled amid the Cashmere Crags of the Stuart Range, and they are one of the most celebrated domains in the Cascade mountains. Dazzling ponds and diminutive tarns punctuate huge slabs of ice-polished stone. In the intensity of the summer sun, the color of the granite blazes pink at sunset. But swirling winds give shape to the gnarled and twisted trees and stir the desolate waterfalls, snowfields, and glaciers. This is a land of extremes—from warm, luxuriant beauty to stunning, austere grandeur.

The Enchantment Lakes bear mythological and fanciful names such as Viviane, Valkyrie, Leprechaun, Lorelei, Pixie, Gnome, Brynhild, and Sprite. On the ridge above the Snow Lakes, fuzzy needles of larches stand out boldly on the crests. The Cashmere Crags contain formations rich in description: the Rat Creek group, Three Musketeers ridge, The Temple, Yellowjacket Tower, Monkeys Head, The Mole, Black Pyramid, The High Priest, The Chessmen, and Prusik Peak.

On the uplands, cross-country travel is marvelously unconstrained. This "Lost Plateau" of the Stuart Range, with its wryly imaginative names, has become a haven for the hiker, rock climber, and scrambler. Enchantment Peak is an unobtrusive but altitudinous spot west of Prusik Pass. A northwest face sports a steep rock wall that contains gullies, snow, and ice patches. Nevertheless, the northeast summit is merely a miniature rock pyramid. Hence Enchantment Peak is a gentle outcropping amongst the rugged pinnacles. The approach is otherworldly, open, and free in a magic land.

Trailhead Directions: Drive US 2 east to Leavenworth. Drive on the Icicle Creek Road to Snow Creek Trail 1553 at a large parking lot along the paved road. (130 miles, 3 hours from Seattle)

Standard Route:

Day 1: From Snow Creek trailhead at 1300 feet, Trail 1553 crosses the river and immediately starts to climb with views toward Snow Creek Wall. At 5.5 miles is Nada Lake (5000 feet). At 6.6 miles the trail passes between the two Snow Lakes (5415 feet). To the north rises The Temple (8928 feet) and to the south McClellan Peak (8364 feet). Cross the low dam between the two lakes and continue on the trail along the south shore. At the southern end, cross the stream at the inlet and proceed up Snow Creek. At 10 miles reach Lake Viviane (6785 feet). Camp at an established site at Enchantment Lakes and follow all the backcountry rules; this is fragile country and deserves respect.

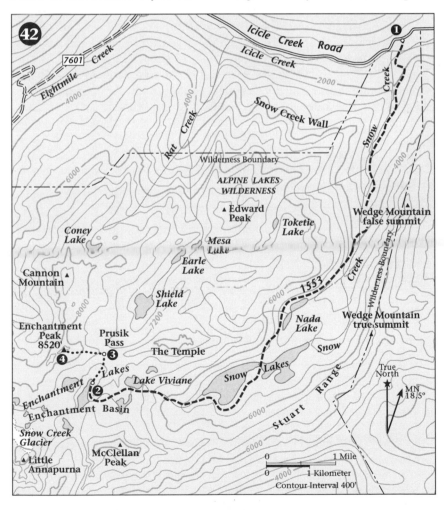

Enchantment Peak (Photo by John Roper)

Day 2: To attain the summit of Enchantment, hike west from Prusik Pass on the broad talus ridge. The northeast summit is a scramble on its south side; the southwest summit is not a scramble. The span between the summits is composed of broken bedrock blocks; keep east of the crest to avoid the obstacles.

Alternate Route: The Enchantment Basin can also be approached from Aasgard Pass. If traveling from Aasgard Pass, scramble northward to attain the summit.

43 LITTLE ANNAPURNA

Elevation: 8440 ft (2573 m)

Difficulty: S4/T1

Distance: 16 miles

Elevation gain: 5500 ft

Trip time: 2-3 days

Time to summit: 9 hours from trailhead; 1 hour from camp

Best time of year: July to October

Maps: USGS Enchantment Lakes, Cashmere Mountain; Green Trails The Enchantments 209S

Contact: Wenatchee National Forest, Leavenworth Ranger District

Special considerations: Wilderness use permit required; plan several months in advance

GPS WAYPOINT ROUTE
1. Stuart Lake trailhead: 3400 ft (10U 664149mE 5265908mN)
2. Colchuck Lake Trail 1599A: 2.5 miles, 4500 ft (10U 662734mE 5263342mN)

3. Colchuck Lake: 4 miles, 5570 ft (10U 663173mE 5262426mN)
4. Aasgard Pass: 6.2 miles 7800 ft (10U 664146mE 5260684mN)
5. Enchantment Basin: 7 miles, 7500 ft (10U 665342mE 5260395mN)
6. Little Annapurna summit: 8 miles, 8440 feet (10U 664770mE 5259292mN)

A pyramidal peak with a steep south face, Little Annapurna was named for its resemblance to its namesake in the Himalayas. The summit is a prominent feature on the south rim of the Enchantments, situated amongst the jagged spires that comprise some of the best climbing in the region. While working as a topographer for the U.S. Geological Survey, A.H. Sylvester named the

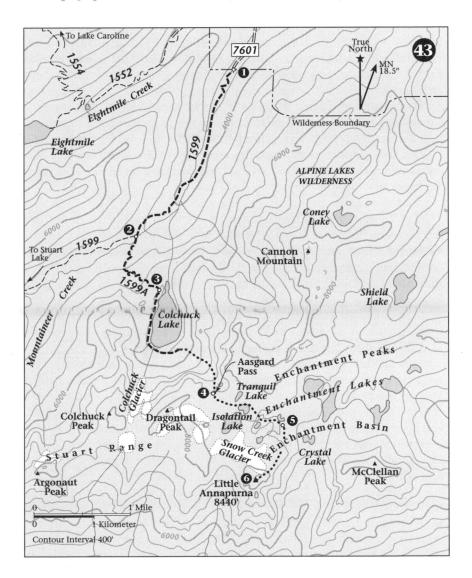

locale. "Enchantment" expressed his reaction—and that of all who have followed into this magical realm. In early season, the northeast snowfields of Little Annapurna offer commendable glissading. But later the route from the plateau is merely a walk-up from the upper basin lakes.

Despite the remote locale, this is not a trip for hermits. Because the Forest Service limits entry permits, the scene is no longer mobbed but is always busy. Be prepared to obey a strict Leave No Trace ethic. No fires or dogs are allowed. Camp only on bare ground at established sites, use toilets where provided, and walk on rock or snow and not on plants. Limit the party size. If you can't live with all that, do without this trip.

Even with the mass of rules and the difficulty in obtaining a permit, the journey is well worth the elbow grease. Visit in summer for brilliant flowers or in late September for the dazzling golden larch. This is a picturesque and radiant land any time of year, a high, lost plateau sheltered from the pedestrian world below, resplendent with awe-inspiring towers and endless heavenly wandering.

Trailhead Directions: Drive US 2 east to Leavenworth. Take the Icicle Creek Road past the Snow Creek trailhead, the large parking lot along the paved road. To reach the Stuart Lake trailhead, continue up the paved road to Bridge Creek Campground at 8.6 miles, turn left onto Eightmile Road (FS Road 7601), and drive about 4 miles to its end at Stuart Lake Trail 1599. (145 miles, 3.5 hours from Seattle)

Standard Route:

Day 1: Begin at Stuart Lake trailhead at 3400 feet. At about 2.5 miles, turn left onto Colchuck Lake Trail 1599A and cross Mountaineer Creek. Continue to Colchuck Lake. To ascend Aasgard Pass, follow the path around the lake to a route marked by rockslide on the southeast corner of the stream dropping from a gully under the pass. There are several routes upslope; the safest strategy is to keep left into a basin, and then continue southeast up rock and heather to northeast of Aasgard Pass. From the pass, a gentle talus or snow descent leads into the Enchantment Basin. Camp at an established site and avoid any activity that disturbs the soil or fragile alpine plant life.

Day 2: The actual scramble of Little Annapurna is simple. Ice axes may be needed in early season, but by October there is little snow. From a camp at Enchantment Lakes, the plateau trail can be followed past Isolation Lake to the level tableland below. From there travel easily cross-country to the northeast spur of Little Annapurna and ascend to the summit. Climbers' tracks are everywhere. On the descent, go down the ridge to the northwest, toward Dragontail. From the saddle that is the low point of the ridge, descend north and northeast back to the level floor of the plateau.

Alternate Routes: The Enchantment Basin may be approached from Aasgard Pass or from Snow Creek Trail 1553. The Aasgard Pass route is preferred because the trip can then be done in 2 days. However, Aasgard Pass represents a 5000-foot approach and is therefore rigorous with an overnight pack. Little Annapurna can also be done in 3 days, as a one-way partial loop

Little Annapurna (Photo by John Roper)

going in via Aasgard Pass and out via Snow Lakes and Snow Creek Trail. This itinerary is highly recommended to enhance the enjoyment of this beautiful area. The 6000-foot descent on the final day of the trip is meaty, but with an early start the way down the Snow Creek Trail is not as painful as feared.

44 KALEETAN PEAK

Elevation: 6259 ft (1908 m)

Difficulty: S4/T4

Distance: 12 miles

Elevation gain: 4000 ft

Trip time: 9 hours

Time to summit: 6 hours

Best time of year: July to September

Maps: USGS Snoqualmie Pass; Green Trails Snoqualmie Pass 207

Contact: Mount Baker–Snoqualmie National Forest, North Bend Office

Special considerations: Beware of rock fall in gullies; wilderness use permit required

GPS WAYPOINT ROUTE
1. Denny Creek trailhead: 2300 ft (10U 617536mE 5252264mN)
2. Melakwa Lake: 4.5 miles, 4500 ft (10U 615492mE 5255994mN)
3. Summit ridge: 5 miles, 5600 ft (10U 614926mE 5257030mN)
4. Kaleetan summit: 6 miles, 6259 ft (10U 614791mE 5257476mN)

In former days, Kaleetan Peak was known as "The Matterhorn." But now it is named for the Indian word for "arrow," a more fitting description for the eye-catching triangular peak that juts up from the Denny Creek valley.

Kaleetan is a moderately challenging pinnacle with a rugged and impos-ing face. Still, several scramble routes lead to the top. For those that reach the objective the prize is the choice landscape of the nearby Snoqualmie sum-mits: Roosevelt, Chair, Bryant, Denny, and The Tooth. But the recompense is from the passage as much as from the final destination. Whilst on the jour-ney, pass Keekwulee and Snowshoe Falls that splash and flume with delight-ful energy. At Melakwa Lake, luxuriate in views of rocks, snowfields, and cliffs falling precipitously from the summits of Kaleetan and Chair. The basin is pounded with use, but here you can still enjoy the respite and anticipate the exalted exploration above.

Trailhead Directions: Drive I-90 to Exit 47 at Denny Creek. Turn left over the freeway, and then right on Denny Creek Road (FS Road 58). Just past Denny Creek Campground and about 3 miles from the freeway, turn left and cross the South Fork Snoqualmie River on FS Road 5830. Follow this road for 0.2 mile, passing private homes, to the end of the road and Denny Creek Trail 1014. Parking is limited. (50 miles, 1 hour from Seattle)

Standard Route: From the Denny Creek trailhead at 2300 feet, follow Trail 1014 to Melakwa Lake. Then follow the boot path around the upper

Kaleetan Peak (Photo by Susan Alford)

lake. Ascend north along the creek. Before you get to Melakwa Pass, turn northwest beyond a stand of trees and ascend white ledges to the skyline. At the summit ridge, turn north to the summit gully; beware of loose rock on ledges and in the gully. The return is via the ridge route back to Melakwa Lake.

Alternate Routes: Before reaching the stand of trees near Melakwa Pass, notice a broad gully that splits in two. Ascend the right (north) gully on loose, steep rock and dirt. The final 50 feet narrows considerably into more stable rock scrambling.

Alternatively, from the stream outlet of Melakwa Lake, follow a boot tread until the final 120 feet (class 3). This route follows the ridge crest and not the white ledges or the gully. It provides good return passage, but remember to stay high on the ridge and do not drop into the basin on the eastern side.

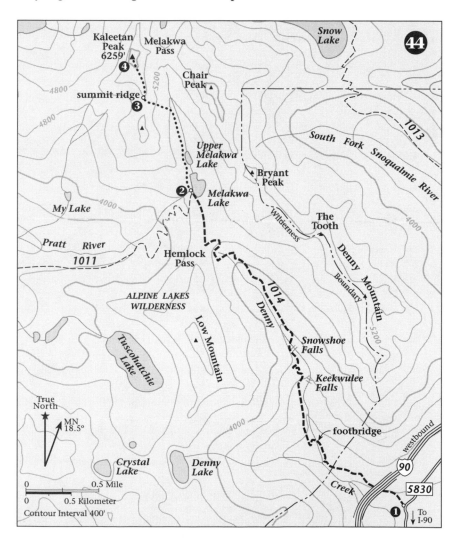

45 MOUNT ROOSEVELT

Elevation: 5835 ft (1779 m)

Difficulty: S4/T5

Distance: 14 miles

Elevation gain: 3500 ft

Trip time: 9 hours

Time to summit: 5 hours

Best time of year: June to October

Maps: USGS Snoqualmie Pass; Green Trails Snoqualmie Pass 207, Bandera 206

Contact: Mount Baker–Snoqualmie National Forest, North Bend Office

Special considerations: Bring hand line for summit gully; ice axes advised; wilderness use permit required

GPS WAYPOINT ROUTE
1. Snow Lake trailhead: 3100 ft (10U 618965mE 5255674mN)
2. Snow Lake: 3.5 miles, 4016 ft (10U 617066mE 5258025mN)
3. Gem Lake: 4.5 miles, 4857 ft (10U 615741mE 5258991mN)
4. Roosevelt summit: 7 miles, 5835 ft (10U 614847mE 5258282mN)

Mount Roosevelt (Photo by John Roper)

Located between Snow and Kaleetan Lakes, Mount Roosevelt is the small, rocky outcrop north of the more notable Kaleetan Peak. The usual approach to Roosevelt is past Snow Lake, more than a mile long and the largest alpine lake in this region. On one side of Snow Lake jagged cliffs rise to Chair Peak, while on the other side the terrain falls abruptly toward the deep gulf of the Middle Fork Snoqualmie River.

Most scramblers move quickly past Snow Lake, since the trail and lake shore are often overrun by hikers and picnickers on hot summer weekends. Roosevelt is notorious for the steep, exposed heather gully near the summit. Even though there is now a distinct boot track, the small ravine is very slippery when wet, and each scrambler should carry an ice ax to use on the heather, even if snow is not present. Otherwise, be prepared to place a hand line on the descent for anyone uncomfortable with its intimidating angle.

Trailhead Directions: Drive I-90 east and take the first Snoqualmie Pass exit (no. 52). Turn left from the off-ramp on the Alpental Road (FS Road 9040) and drive to the Alpental ski area (The Summit) and park at the Snow Lake trailhead. (50 miles, 1 hour from Seattle)

Standard Route: From 3100 feet, follow Snow Lake Trail 1013 in heather

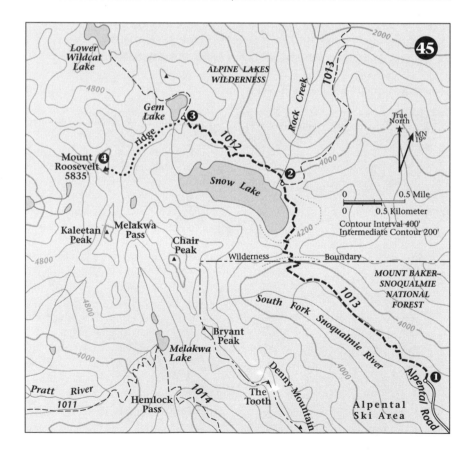

and parkland to a saddle at 3 miles (4400 feet) where the Alpine Lakes Wilderness is entered. The trail drops sharply 0.5 mile from the saddle to the meadow shores of Snow Lake at 3.5 miles (4016 feet). Continue on the trail to Gem Lake, cross the outlet, and climb to the lightly wooded ridge running southwest from the lake.

Stay high and follow the ridge to a scree slope at 5400 feet. Make a leftward traverse several hundred feet on a scree bench above a small set of cliffs. A distinct boot tread leads upward from Gem Lake to this area. Continue upward for about 100 feet, and then traverse to the base of the summit block (5500 feet) at a relatively flat spot. At the southeast base of the summit rocks, ascend west up a steep gully about 200 feet on a foot tread through the heather (class 3). The middle section of the gully is steep and exposed and slippery when wet. It may be desirable to put in a hand line for safety, even if the party has ice axes. From here scramble north to the summit.

Alternate Route: Consider a longer loop trip and return by Chair Lake and over Melakwa Pass to the Denny Creek trailhead. Remember to leave a car there for the return.

46 SNOQUALMIE MOUNTAIN AND GUYE PEAK

Elevations: 6278 ft (1914 m), 5168 ft (1575 m)

Difficulty: S3/T3

Distance: 7 miles

Elevation gain: 4200 ft

Travel time: 8 hours

Time to summit: 4 hours from Snow Lake trailhead to Snoqualmie; 2 hours from Snoqualmie to Guye

Best time of year: May to November

Maps: USGS Snoqualmie Pass; Green Trails Snoqualmie Pass 207

Contact: Mount Baker–Snoqualmie National Forest, North Bend Office

Special considerations: Avalanche hazard in early season

GPS WAYPOINT ROUTE
1. Snow Lake trailhead: 3100 ft (10U 618965mE 5255674mN)
2. Snoqualmie summit: 2 miles, 6278 ft (10U 619459mE 5257167mN)
3. Guye-Snoqualmie basin: 3 miles, 4800 ft (10U 619802mE 5256089mN)
4. Guye summit: 3.5 miles, 5168 ft (10U 620085mE 5255299mN)

Directly north of Snoqualmie Pass, Snoqualmie Mountain is the stout, amorphous hulk and Guye Peak is the prominent thimble-shaped rock. Snoqualmie's summit is rounded and stands above a steep hidden face, while Guye's pyramid

is craggy and nearly vertical, thus forming technical climbs on generally brittle and crumbling rock. Snoqualmie is much mellower than Guye, but Guye too has a scramble route that leads to the same summit as its dicier, technical climbs. Both mountains are conspicuous from Snoqualmie Pass and are favorites for exploring any time of year.

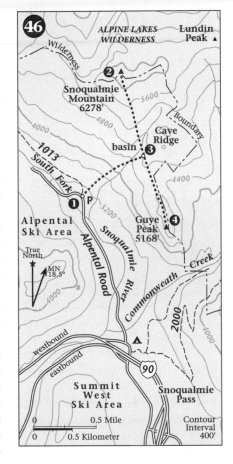

Located just at the border of the Alpine Lakes Wilderness, they are often scrambled together. The duo makes for a trip that is best done when snow is present, because the many footpaths make a later-season journey little more than a hike. But beware, in winter and spring the Forest Service sets off blasts for avalanche control on the large slide path on the southwestern slopes of Snoqualmie Mountain. During the ski season check with the ranger station at North Bend or the ski patrol at Alpental ski area (The Summit) for an avalanche update. Nonetheless, at any time of year exploit this mountain couple for as close to a wilderness experience as is possible in a domain touching the buzzing interstate highway.

Trailhead Directions: Drive I-90 east and take the first Snoqualmie Pass exit (no. 52). Turn left from the off-ramp on the Alpental Road (FS Road 9040) and drive to the Alpental ski area and park at the Snow Lake trailhead. (50 miles, 1 hour from Seattle)

Standard Route: About 50 feet to the right of the 3100-foot Snow Lake trailhead, find a boot tread that leads to the base of Snoqualmie and Guye. For Snoqualmie, follow the footpath staying left at all intersections until reaching the basin below Cave Ridge (4800 feet). Go left to gain the southern ridge of Snoqualmie and follow it to the summit. For Guye, return to the basin and go south to the Guye-Snoqualmie saddle. From there circle south and ascend through trees to small knobs and the north summit (class 2).

Alternate Route: In the springtime, approach the peaks from the south from Alpental Road or the Crest Trail. This route avoids hard snow in the morning and is less avalanche-prone during the afternoon sun.

Near the summit of Snoqualmie Mountain (Photo by Jason Griffith)

47 RED MOUNTAIN

Elevation: 5890 ft (1795 m)

Difficulty: S3/T3

Distance: 10 miles

Elevation gain: 2900 ft

Trip time: 7 hours

Time to summit: 4 hours

Best time of year: June to October

Maps: USGS Snoqualmie Pass; Green Trails Snoqualmie Pass 207

Contact: Mount Baker–Snoqualmie National Forest, North Bend Office

Special considerations: Avalanche and rock fall hazards; wilderness use permit required

GPS WAYPOINT ROUTE
1. Pacific Crest Trail trailhead: 3000 ft (10U 619766mE 5253695mN)
2. Commonwealth Creek Trail 1033: 3 miles, 3900 ft (10U 620959mE 5255054mN)
3. Red Pond: 4.5 miles, 4900 ft (10U 621116mE 5256943mN)
4. Red summit: 5 miles, 5890 ft (10U 621531mE 5256892mN)

Red Mountain is a rounded chunk of loose, maroon rock, with the typical name given to a peak of such color. It sits as a sentinel with Snoqualmie, Lundin, and Guye as protectors of Commonwealth Basin below. In the Snoqualmie

Indian paintbrush (Photo by Chris Weidner)

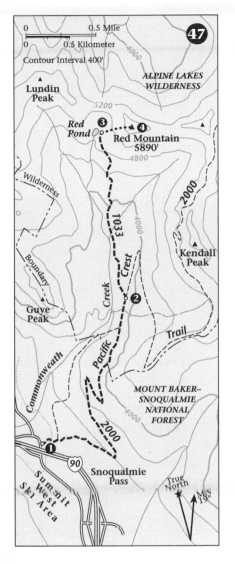

Pass vicinity this valley represents a near-at-hand refuge for those who seek tranquil pleasure in the natural environment. The peaceful subalpine forest, the pure and rippling creeks, and the whistling marmots are reminders of the "olden days" before the crunch of population hit Puget Sound.

Be warned that Red Mountain, like many other scrambles near Snoqualmie Pass, is rather popular. Nevertheless, Red gives a feeling of a throwback to the past, of another era when the air was quiet and clean. On the edge of the broad cirque, look over the bowl toward the rimming peaks and south to Mount Rainier. The scene is glorified by the Middle Fork Snoqualmie valley, the sharp tower of Mount Thompson, the rugged Chikamin Ridge and distant horizons.

Trailhead Directions: Drive I-90 east to Exit 52 at Snoqualmie Pass. Follow the Alpental Road for several hundred feet to Pacific Crest Trail 2000. (50 miles, 1 hour from Seattle)

Standard Route: From the trailhead at 3000 feet, hike on the Pacific Crest Trail and enter the Alpine Lakes Wilderness at 2.3 miles. Shortly afterward, go left on Commonwealth Creek Trail 1033. The trail drops, and then turns upstream 1 mile to the valley head and ascends the crest of an open-forested spur. After many switchbacks, the way flattens out in heather and trees in a cirque basin at the foot of Red Mountain. Red Pond at 4.5 miles (4900 feet) can be located on a short side trail.

Ascend the prominent spur on Red's southwest slope above Red Pond that bears toward the summit at a constant slope of about 40 degrees. This hillside holds snow poorly and is prone to avalanche and rock fall. Be cautious: more than a few serious injuries have occurred here. Keep the southwest face on the right and rock cliffs on the left. Follow a climber's trail near the summit to achieve the summit block.

48 KENDALL PEAK

Elevation: 5784 ft (1763 m)

Difficulty: S2/T2

Distance: 10 Miles

Elevation gain: 2800 ft

Trip time: 7 hours

Time to summit: 4 hours

Best time of year: June to October

Maps: USGS Snoqualmie Pass, Chikamin Peak; Green Trails Snoqualmie Pass 207

Contact: Mount Baker–Snoqualmie National Forest, North Bend Office

Special considerations: Wilderness use permit required

GPS WAYPOINT ROUTE

1. Pacific Crest Trail trailhead: 3000 ft (10U 619766mE 5253695mN)
2. Leave trail: 4.8 miles, 5200 ft (10U 621679mE 5255516mN)
3. Kendall summit: 5 miles, 5784 ft (10U 621885mE 5255455mN)
4. Kendall Katwalk: 5.5 miles, 5400 ft (10U 622262mE 5256251mN)

Kendall Peak is not a particularly outstanding peak, but its location near one of the most breathtaking parts of the Pacific Crest Trail, the Kendall Katwalk,

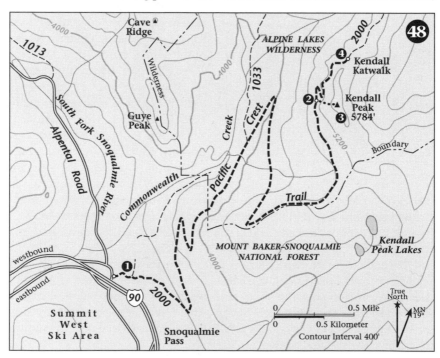

Descending Kendall Peak (Photo by Susan Alford)

makes it a commendable journey. Kendall Peak is 2 miles northeast of Snoqualmie Pass and simple to come within reach of on the new section of the
Pacific Crest Trail. Kendall has four petite and nearly equal rocky summits on
the rim above the three Kendall Peak Lakes that are located in the basin to the
southeast. The true summit is about a mile north of the most western lake.

On the return trip, a visit to the Kendall Katwalk farther along the Pacific
Crest Trail is mandatory—superlatives are not enough. The Katwalk is aptly
named for its delicate character as a minimal ledge blasted across a cliff in
solid granite. When snow free, it's safe enough. When snowy, think twice. This
portion of the Pacific Crest Trail is airy with a sizable drop on one side, yet
nothing compared to scrambling off the trail here when the slopes are frosty.

Trailhead Directions: Drive I-90 east to Exit 52. Follow the Alpental
Road several hundred feet to the trailhead parking lot for Pacific Crest Trail
2000. (50 miles, 1 hour from Seattle)

Standard Route: From the trailhead at 3000 feet, hike the Pacific Crest
Trail to the last switchbacks on the rising traverse across the boulder field
(about 0.5 mile directly downslope from the steepening of the slope at the
Kendall Katwalk). Leave the trail at 5200 feet. Ascend to the right of the rock
rib in the middle of the steep meadow. You can reach the ridge in about 15
minutes. Follow boot paths or rocky ramps that lead to the right (south) to
the summit. Be careful about rock fall as loose rocks can easily reach the busy
trail. After a summit break, a side trip to the Katwalk is recommended to
enjoy this striking perch above the chasm below.

49 ALTA MOUNTAIN

Elevation:	6250 ft (1905 m)
Difficulty:	S4/T1
Distance:	12 miles
Elevation gain:	4000 ft
Trip time:	9 hours
Time to summit:	5 hours
Best time of year:	June to September
Maps:	USGS Chikamin Peak, Stampede Pass; Green Trails Snoqualmie Pass 207
Contact:	Wenatchee National Forest, Cle Elum Ranger District

Special considerations: Dangerous cornice conditions in early season; wilderness use permit required

GPS WAYPOINT ROUTE
1. Rachel Lake trailhead: 2800 ft (10U 629574mE 5250956mN)
2. Rachel Lake: 4 miles, 4700 ft (10U 626146mE 5253301mN)

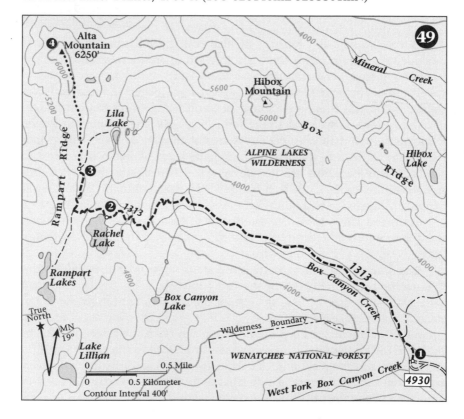

3. Rampart Ridge: 4.5 miles, 5140 ft (10U
625745mE 5253432mN)
4. Alta summit: 6 miles, 6250 ft (10U
625862mE 5255329mN)

Alta Mountain is the extended and amiable crest between Box Ridge and Gold Creek. The access to Alta is through the Rampart Ridge district, famous for sublime alpine roaming. Rachel Lake is the site of parkland gardens speckled with delicate tarns superlative in their abundance and appeal. Here the scrambler can luxuriate in the vista downhill to Gold Creek, west to Snoqualmie Pass, north to Three Queens and Chimney Rock, east to Stuart, and south to Rainier and Adams.

As one of the most fashionable destinations in the Snoqualmie Pass sector, on a clear summer weekend the idyllic scene attracts hundreds of hikers who throng to Rachel Lake, where goats and humans have produced a labyrinth of footpaths. Unfortunately, this is now an ill-fated haven where the land has been loved nearly to death. Alta is more appropriate in early season when snow covers the terrain, not only to create

Alta Mountain
(Photo by John Roper)

a more challenging scramble, but also to protect the fragile alpine growth. Yet the area is so lovely when the lakes are thawed that the temptation is to enjoy the spot at the peak of the season. Just obey the principles of wilderness conservation—use only the paths that are already beaten into existence, step on stones and not flowers, and savor this trip only once in a long while.

Trailhead Directions: Drive I-90 east from Snoqualmie Pass 12.5 miles to Kachess Lake Exit 62. Follow the signs 5 miles to Kachess Lake Campground. Turn left onto Box Canyon Road (FS Road 4930) and drive 4.2 miles to Rachel Lake Trail 1313. (70 miles, 1.5 hours from Seattle)

Standard Route: From the Rachel Lake trailhead at 2800 feet, Trail 1313 ascends moderately for 1 mile. Then the trail levels out along the creek for 1.5 miles, at which point Hibox Mountain can be discerned. At 2.5 miles the valley ends in an abrupt headwall laced with waterfalls. At 4 miles is Rachel Lake (4700 feet). Turn right at the shore on a boot path, climbing above the cirque, with views down to the lake.

Gain Rampart Ridge at a junction at 5100 feet: to the right is Lila Lake, to the left are Rampart Lakes, and ahead is Rampart Ridge, with about 1.5 miles of scrambling to the summit of Alta. Be cautious: in early season cornices on both sides of the long summit ridge create dangerous conditions. In summer only a minor portion of the trip is off trail.

50 HIBOX MOUNTAIN

Elevation: 6560 ft (2000 m)	
Difficulty: S4/T4	
Distance: 10 miles	
Elevation gain: 3900 ft	
Trip time: 9 hours	
Time to summit: 5 hours	
Best time of year: June to November	
Maps: USGS Chikamin Peak; Green Trails Snoqualmie Pass 207	
Contact: Wenatchee National Forest, Cle Elum Ranger District	

Special considerations: Moderate rock fall; exposure at the summit block; wilderness use permit required

GPS WAYPOINT ROUTE
1. Rachel Lake trailhead: 2800 ft (10U 629574mE 5250956mN)
2. Leave trail: 2.5 miles, 3300 ft (10U 627643mE 5252938mN)
3. Southeast ridge: 4.7 miles, 6000 ft (10U 628429mE 5254190mN)
4. Hibox summit: 5 miles, 6560 ft (10U 628247mE 5254337mN)

Box Ridge trends northwest for more than 4 miles between Box Canyon and Mineral Creek in the Snoqualmie Pass region. At the apogee, find Hibox Mountain, an engaging alpine scramble that tests the mettle of the avid scrambler. The upper west and east faces are jagged and precipitous with extensive scree beneath.

Hibox has three distinct major points: the southeast peak is somewhat higher than the northwest peak, but the middle peak is the highest of all. Hibox is a classic rock scramble in an enchanting setting. Skillful routefinding is needed to avoid heavy brush and abrupt cliff bands down low and dangerous climbing on the summit block. The

Hibox Mountain summit
(Photo by Susan Alford)

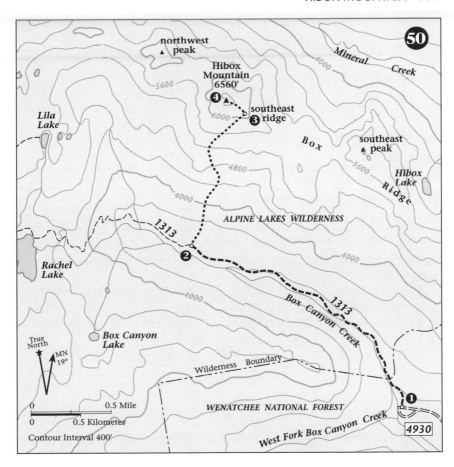

apex is a delicate scramble in the sky creating a zestful challenge for those who seek it.

Trailhead Directions: Drive I-90 east from Snoqualmie Pass 12.5 miles to Kachess Lake Exit 62, and follow signs 5 miles to Kachess Lake Campground. Turn left onto Box Canyon Road (FS Road 4930) and drive 4.2 miles to Rachel Lake Trail 1313. (70 miles, 1.5 hours from Seattle)

Standard Route: From Rachel Lake trailhead at 2800 feet, hike for about 2.5 miles. After the second major clearing (3300 feet) leave the trail on a definite boot path in the forest on the north side of the trail.

Follow the path directly up and northeast through open forest followed by gullies, to the right of a large rocky buttress. The route ascends, steeply at times, through open slopes of heather and grass. Ascend over rock fields and talus to the top of the southeast ridge to the east of the summit. Finish with a short but exposed rock scramble to the small summit area. This route avoids the expansive, but loose, gully that leads directly to the summit.

Alternate Route: From Rachel Lake Trail 1313 at 1 mile, follow the stream northeast to the area of the 5200-foot saddle between the southeast and the middle peaks. Scramble the southeast ridge to the middle summit of Hibox.

 SILVER PEAK

Elevation: 5605 ft (1708 m)

Difficulty: S3/T3

Distance: 9 miles

Elevation gain: 3800 ft

Trip time: 7 hours

Time to summit: 4 hours

Best time of year: May to November

Maps: USGS Snoqualmie Pass, Lost Lake; Green Trails Snoqualmie Pass 207

Contact: Mount Baker–Snoqualmie National Forest, North Bend Office

Special considerations: In early season beware of cornices and frequent avalanches.

GPS WAYPOINT ROUTE
1. Annette Lake trailhead: 1900 ft (10U 615269mE 5249747mN)
2. Iron Horse Trail: 0.7 mile, 2400 ft (10U 615482mE 5248814mN)
3. Annette Lake: 3.5 miles, 3600 ft (10U 615120mE 5246325mN)
4. Silver summit: 4.5 miles, 5605 ft (10U 616281mE 5246292mN)

Summit of Silver Peak (Photo by John Roper)

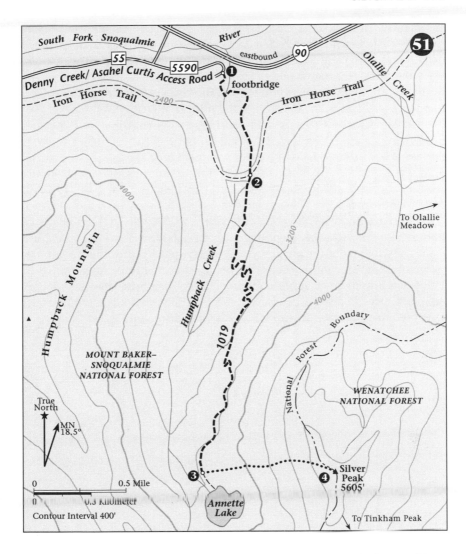

Silver Peak, an all-time beloved summit, is located 4.5 miles southwest of Snoqualmie Pass and is visible from the freeway. The terrain is largely subalpine, but open meadow slopes transition to exposed rock near the apex. Silver is a favorite winter jaunt when skis or snowshoes are the means of travel. The peak also provides a popular spring trip, when the high snow-locked crags are not yet accessible to scramblers chafing at the bit to get the season rolling.

Trailhead Directions: Drive I-90 east to Snoqualmie Pass Exit 47, signed "Denny Creek/Asahel Curtis Picnic Area." Leave the freeway, turn right at 0.1 mile, then left on FS Road 55 and go 0.4 mile to the parking lot at Annette Lake Trail 1019. (50 miles, 1 hour from Seattle)

Standard Route: From the Annette Lake trailhead at 1900 feet, hike Trail 1019 for 0.7 mile to where the route crosses the Iron Horse Trail, the abandoned

Milwaukee Railroad Grade. Gain 1200 feet in 2 miles to reach Annette Lake, ringed by talus from Abiel Peak above. Just before the lake, head eastward (left) up the slope and follow the trees, avoiding potential avalanche areas. Gain the ridge and follow it south. Stay on the western (right) side of the north ridge to avoid cornices and cliffs. If the ridge is free of snow, look for a faint boot trail just below the crest of the ridge that facilitates the traverse of steep loose rock near the summit. This trip is best when the snow is stable.

When you are descending, it may appear to be an easy, straight shot from the summit or from the saddle between Silver and Abiel down to Lake Annette. But do not be deceived: moderate brush and dangerous cliffs just above the lake await you. If attempting this descent route, stay to the north to avoid unpleasant surprises.

Alternate Routes: Follow Annette Lake Trail 1019 to 3200 feet. Just past the last major switchback, go uphill to about 4800 feet, leave the forest and reach the shoulder of the north ridge. Proceed up the north ridge to join the standard route, staying on the western side when the ridge runs into cliffs. This route attains the ridge at a lower point to maximize the time to view Rainier. Silver can also be approached from the Silver-Tinkham saddle on its south spur from the Pacific Crest Trail via Olallie Meadow.

TEANAWAY

52 MOUNT SKOOKUM AND JOLLY MOUNTAIN

Elevations: 6394 ft (1949 m), 6443 ft (1964 m)

Difficulty: S4/T2

Distance: 9 miles

Elevation gain: 2400 ft

Trip time: 7 hours; 11 hours with car shuttle

Time to summit: 5 hours to Skookum; 3 hours from Skookum to Jolly

Best time of year: May to October

Maps: USGS Davis Peak, Mount Stuart; Green Trails Kachess Lake 208, Mount Stuart 209

Contact: Wenatchee National Forest, Cle Elum Ranger District

Special considerations: To do both mountains as a loop trip requires a fast pace.

GPS WAYPOINT ROUTE
1. Sasse Ridge: 5400 ft (10U 646723mE 5249739mN)
2. West Fork Trail 1353: 1 mile, 5480 ft (10U 648735mE 5250227mN)
3. Jolly saddle: 1.5 miles, 6000 ft (10U 649422mE 5250338mN)
4. Boot tread: 2.5 miles, 5400 ft (10U 649839mE 5250908mN)
5. Skookum summit: 3.4 miles, 6394 ft (10U 650978mE 5252238mN)
6. Jolly summit: 6.5 miles, 6443 ft (10U 649453mE 5249478mN)

Just another long trail trip to an abandoned lookout site in summer, Jolly Mountain is a righteous early season conditioner when covered in soft deep snow. Mount Skookum is the unofficial name of Point 6394 about 2 miles northeast of Jolly. The combined scramble is a spirited outing. Skookum is a zealous diversion for a trip that otherwise might be too tame: it is meant for the peakbagger who is not fully content unless run hard and put away wet.

These eastern outposts of Cle Elum Lake burrowed between the two lobes of the Alpine Lakes Wilderness give a 360-degree panorama from Mount Stuart, Mount Daniel, and the Dutch Miller Gap peaks to Mount Rainier. A magnificent time for the trip is June, when the path meanders through fields of glacier lilies and other blooming wildflowers. The route over the old Sasse Mountain sheep divide takes the least toll by foot, but is the roughest on a vehicle.

Trailhead Directions: Drive east on I-90 to the Salmon la Sac–Roslyn exit (no. 80). Exit right and turn left over the freeway. Follow the road through the towns of Roslyn and Ronald past a cafe called "The Last Resort." Continue along Salmon la Sac Road (SR 903) to turn right on FS Road 4315, just before the Salmon la Sac Ranger Station. Drive 8 miles to the end of the road, steep and rough for the last 2 miles. Depending on the time of year, you may find a locked gate at 3350 feet, adding 2.5 miles to the trip. (100 miles, 2.5 hours from Seattle)

Standard Route: Begin at about 5400 feet on a way trail in a recent clearcut with a sign to Sasse Ridge and Sasse Mountain Trail 1340. Hike upslope to meet the trail and follow it north about 0.5 mile to the main Jolly Mountain Trail 1307 (5600 feet). In about 0.4 mile, Trail 1353 branches south to the right along the West Fork Teanaway River.

Continue 0.6 mile on the main trail to the saddle in front of Jolly Mountain. The Jolly Mountain Trail continues south to the summit. However, continue for 0.5 mile on what appears to be the continuation of the trail, but is now Jolly Creek Trail 1355 toward Jolly Creek basin. Do not continue all the way down to the basin, but stay on the lower ridge at 5300 feet and keep as high as possible above a major gully and rockslide; keep high on the ridge but do not climb every high point. A faint boot tread may be encountered. Skookum can be seen in the distance at times, appearing rugged and rocky.

At about 5600 feet, ascend steep grass and talus toward Skookum (Point 6394). Enter the rocks to follow the safest route. Some exposure is encountered on the false summit. The true summit is at the end of the block of rocks. To avoid loose scree on the left, drop down to the right, go around the scree, and then climb back up the slab. The Skookum summit is exposed, but scramblers

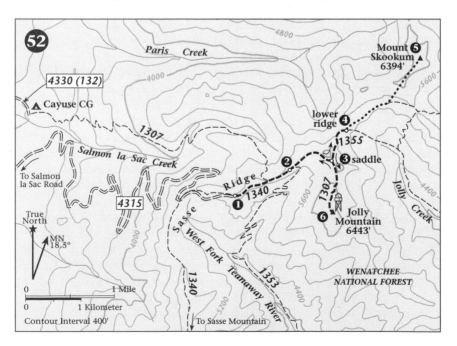

Jolly Mountain (Photo by John Roper)

can climb up one at a time and each touch the top. Retrace the route back to the Jolly saddle, and then follow Jolly Mountain Trail 1307 south to the summit of Jolly.

Alternate Route: If transportation can be arranged, a good trip can be made by going up from the end of FS Road 4315 and going out via Jolly Mountain Trail 1307 to finish at Cayuse Campground near a corral. Leave a car at the campground, taking FS Road 4330 (132) from just south of the Salmon la Sac Ranger Station. This trip is only for the super-speedy on a race against time, as it adds 4.2 miles and 3000 feet of descent.

INGALLS SOUTH PEAK

Elevation: 7640 ft (2329 m)

Difficulty: S4/T3

Distance: 11 miles

Elevation gain: 3600 ft

Trip time: 9 hours

Time to summit: 5 hours

Best time of year: June to October

Maps: USGS Mount Stuart; Green Trails Mount Stuart 209

Contact: Wenatchee National Forest, Cle Elum Ranger District

Special considerations: Moderate rock fall; exposed and hot; bring adequate water; wilderness use permit required

GPS WAYPOINT ROUTE

1. Ingalls Lake trailhead: 4200 ft (10U 655666mE 5255574mN)
2. Longs Pass Trail 1229: 2.4 miles, 5400 ft (10U 656492mE 5256978mN)
3. Ingalls Pass: 3 miles, 6500 ft (10U 655723mE 5258076mN)
4. Ingalls Lake: 4.5 miles, 6463 ft (10U 655369mE 5259143mN)
5. North and South Peaks saddle: 5 miles, 7300 ft (10U 654766mE 5259390mN)
6. Ingalls South summit: 5.5 miles, 7640 ft (10U 654607mE 5259170mN)

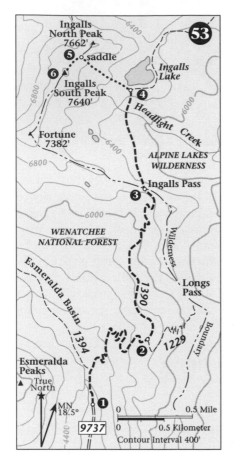

Located on the western fringe of the mighty Stuart Range of the Alpine Lakes Wilderness, Ingalls Peak is a little brother to 9415-foot Mount Stuart, the highest point between Glacier Peak and Mount Rainier. Also in the Stuart Range are some of the "big boys," the peaks above 8300 feet that comprise the most rugged and lofty in the state. In contrast to the white granite of Stuart, Ingalls presents huge red cliffs on high, glaciated surfaces, while nearby ridges display a startling blend of gray and rusty-brown rocks.

Ingalls has a triple-summit: The north main peak is the highest and is more precipitous than the south peak, while the east peak has a horn shape. The north peak is a technical climb, but the south peak is a scramble. The way to Ingalls is mostly free of snow in late June when slopes to the north are still frosty.

To the south beyond Esmeralda Peaks appear Mount Adams, the Goat Rocks, and Mount Rainier. The view of the Dutch Miller Gap peaks and Mount Stuart is exceptional. But the most refreshing premium of this scramble is the passage by Ingalls Lake (Lake Ingalls on USGS map), a rock-basin tarn at the foot of Ingalls Peak. Set in an alp-like, glacier-scoured basin, the mix of azure lakes, alabaster snowfields, and polished slabs of brown rock is startling. The combination of lush green meadows, a glory of flowers, and groves of larch is ambrosial. Scramble to Ingalls South Peak, this little kinsman of imperial Stuart. Stare into Stuart's immense face to bring chills to your senses from the massive blank snowfields, deep wounds from hanging glaciers, and sterile clean granite ridges. Be happy for the exhilarating journey.

Trailhead Directions: Drive I-90 east to Exit 85, East Cle Elum. On the north side of the freeway, follow SR 970 east to the Teanaway River Road. Follow the Teanaway River Road north to the North Fork Teanaway River Road (FS Road 9737) and take it 23 miles to the end at Ingalls Lake Trail 1390. (120 miles, 2.75 hours from Seattle)

Standard Route: Begin at the Ingalls Lake trailhead (4200 feet). This is also the trailhead for Esmeralda Basin. Hike 0.4 mile to a junction and turn right on the trail signed for Longs Pass and Ingalls Lake. Carry a full water bottle or two; the climb can be hot and is often without a water source.

At 5400 feet and the junction with Longs Pass Trail 1229, go left, swinging around the mountainside into a small valley where the route joins an older trail. In 3 miles, the final stretch switchbacks up to Ingalls Pass (6500 feet) with a grand view of Mount Stuart.

Contour left on a slope above Headlight Creek basin toward Ingalls Lake and the trail's end. The way down to the shore is easy, but getting around the west (left-hand) side of the outlet requires a scramble up and down slabs and boulders. Do not try the right-hand side that is more of a climbing route. The lake basin is so heavily pounded it must be a day-use zone only; no overnight camping. If doing this scramble as a 2-day trip, camp either in Headlight Creek basin or below the lake in the meadow headwaters of Ingalls Creek.

From Ingalls Lake, ascend slabs, talus, and boulders to the notch between Ingalls North and South Peaks. A small spire, often called "the dogtooth," sits in the saddle; aim for the left of it. Steep snow may be just below the saddle. Then drop onto the western side of the ridge about 50 feet and continue back up one of several gullies that lead up to the summit ridge 100 feet.

The most difficult part of the scramble is just above the saddle (class 2). Follow the ridge to the summit on snow and rock. Caution: expect rock fall from talus especially on the eastern side and while negotiating gullies on the western side of the ridge. Navigating the slabs on the eastern side may lead to some confusion on the way. Do not try to descend directly down the broad east shoulder of Ingalls South, as it abruptly terminates in cliffs.

Alternate Routes: From the saddle, the party can cross steep slabs and attain the broad east shoulder with a subsequent easy walk to the summit.

Make an interesting loop by continuing down the south ridge of Ingalls to Fortune (Point 7382), and then down Fortune's west ridge to Trail 1394, which enters Esmeralda Basin. Hike on the trail to the south, and intersect Trail 1390 about 1 mile north of the trail-head (12 miles round trip).

Scrambling on granite in the Alpine Lakes Wilderness
(Photo by Susan Alford)

54 ESMERALDA PEAKS

Elevation: 6765 ft (1975 m)

Difficulty: S3/T3

Distance: 8 miles

Elevation gain: 3000 ft

Trip time: 7 hours

Time to summit: 4 hours

Best time of year: June to October

Maps: USGS Mount Stuart; Green Trails Mount Stuart 209

Contact: Wenatchee National Forest, Cle Elum Ranger District

GPS WAYPOINT ROUTE
1. Boulder–DeRoux trailhead: 3800 ft (10U 655616mE 5253488mN)
2. Leave trail: 3 miles, 5500 ft (10U 652738mE 5255332mN)
3. Esmeralda summit: 4 miles, 6765 ft (10U 653297mE 5255935mN)

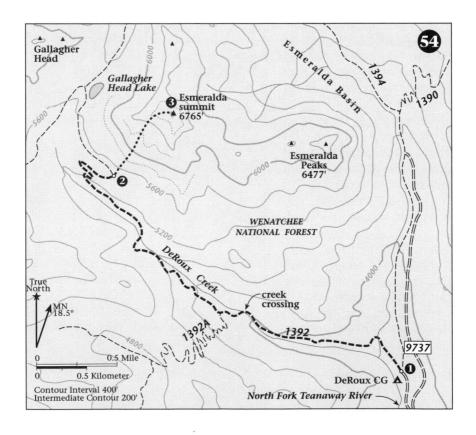

Located east of Hawkins Mountain in the angle between DeRoux Creek and the upper North Fork Teanaway River, Esmeralda Peaks has four high points with two principal summits, the highest of which is the farthest western peak. The approach to Esmeralda is along the Boulder–DeRoux Trail, heavily traveled by horses. The valley exposes a ridge of orange cliffs and a view south to Koppen Peak.

From the eastern perspective, Esmeralda Peaks appear jagged and rutted with gullies. But, as for most of the peaks in the Teanaway, the scrambling from the south is quite moderate and unencumbered. For Esmeralda the situation is even more accentuated, as the true summit at 6765 feet is less rigorous than the lower 6477-foot point that is named on the map to the east. Moreover, the weather is lovely most of the year except in the most blasting heat of summer. The best time for this scramble is in June when the atmospheric conditions are unsettled and cool to the west, but the sun is still bright east of the Cascade Crest.

Trailhead Directions: Drive I-90 east to Exit 85, East Cle Elum. On the north side of I-90, follow SR 970 east to the Teanaway River Road. Follow the Teanaway River Road north to the North Fork Teanaway River Road (FS Road 9737). Drive on this road to 29 Pines Campground where the pavement ends. Continue about 9 miles on the gravel road to DeRoux Campground and Boulder–DeRoux Trail 1392. (115 miles, 2.75 hours from Seattle)

Standard Route: From the Boulder–DeRoux trailhead at 3800 feet, hike Trail 1392 to about 5500 feet at the last switchback before arriving at the left-hand turn along the main trail that heads to Gallagher Head Lake. Leave the trail and

head uphill, with easy scrambling, to the summit. The true summit of 6765 feet is west of the summit identified on the map as 6477 feet.

Note that the beginning of the trail is somewhat obscured by way trails. Make sure that you are traveling in the right direction before going too far.

Alternate Route: Hike the Boulder–DeRoux Trail to the first crossing of DeRoux Creek (4000 feet). Here head north to gain the ridge on Esmeralda's west peak. Follow the ridge, dropping off to the left to avoid the technical sections, to the true summit (Point 6765).

Esmeralda Peaks and
Gallagher Head Lake
(Photo by John Roper)

55 BILL PEAK, BEAN PEAK, AND VOLCANIC NECK

Elevations: 6917 ft (2108 m), 6743 ft (2056 m), 6600 ft (2012 m)

Difficulty: S4/T5

Distance: 11 miles

Elevation gain: 4900 ft

Trip time: 11 hours

Time to summit: 5 hours from trailhead to Bill; 1.5 hours from Bill to Bean; 1.5 hours from Bean to Volcanic Neck

Best time of year: May to October

Maps: USGS Enchantment Lakes, Mount Stuart; Green Trails Mount Stuart 209

Contact: Wenatchee National Forest, Cle Elum Ranger District

Special considerations: Loose rock, exposed route at Volcanic Neck summit

GPS WAYPOINT ROUTE
1. Beverly-Turnpike trailhead: 3600 ft (10U 660680mE 5250428mN)
2. Fourth Creek Trail 1218: 3 miles, 5200 ft (10U 659434mE 5253738mN)
3. Saddle: 3.6 miles, 5500 ft (10U 659644mE 5254126mN)
4. Bill summit: 4 miles, 6917 ft (10U 659089mE 5254643mN)
5. Bean summit: 6 miles, 6743 ft (10U 661399mE 5253914mN)
6. Volcanic Neck summit: 6.6 miles, 6600 ft (10U 661559mE 5254562mN)
7. Bean Creek basin: 8 miles, 5200 ft (10U 661843mE 5255231mN)

Bucolic and picturesque, the approach to the Teanaway region is rolling farmland in the shadow of 9415-foot Mount Stuart, the second-highest nonvolcanic mountain in the state. These Teanaway peaks are superb, ridge crest strolls in a relatively dry land. When fog is rolling though the Cascades, and rain is dumping in the convergence zones, the Teanaway provides a nearly always sunny respite from gray, gloomy, and soggy weather elsewhere.

Part of the attraction of the landscape in this region is the weird, desertlike serpentine barrens for which the area is famous. Views can be had of Mount Stuart and the Columbia Plateau by climbing above Bean Creek basin to the ridge tops. From there, scrutinize the boundary of the Alpine Lakes Wilderness with the Stuart Range right in your face. Bill, Bean, and Volcanic Neck provide a sweet diversion, with lush, flower-filled basins, easy rambling, and some moderate scrambling to boot.

These peaks are unnamed on the maps, and only Bean Peak with an elevation of 6743 feet is designated on the USGS Enchantment Lakes Quadrangle. The peaks lie within 2 miles of one another. From all directions a multitude of trails intersect the land, and thus the trio can be combined in innumerable ways. Yet this trip is best done in a large loop that allows for the

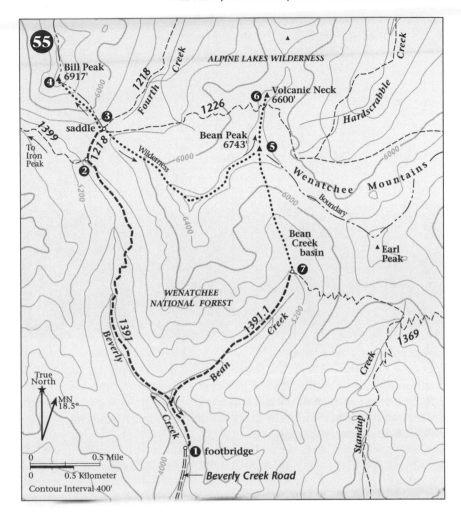

premium variety of adventures on the unenclosed and boundless terrain.

Trailhead Directions: Drive I-90 east to Exit 85, East Cle Elum. On the north side of the interstate, follow SR 970 east to the Teanaway River Road. Follow the Teanaway River Road north to the North Fork Teanaway River Road (FS Road 9737). Drive on this road to 29 Pines Campground where the pavement ends. Continue north 4 miles to the Beverly Creek Road and drive to its end at Beverly-Turnpike Trail 1391. (110 miles, 2.5 hours from Seattle)

Standard Route: Begin at the Beverly-Turnpike trailhead at 3600 feet. To attain Bill Peak first, follow Trail 1391 past the intersection with Bean Creek Trail 1391.1 to the junction with Fourth Creek Trail 1218 at 3 miles (5200 feet). Follow Trail 1218 to a saddle at 5500 feet. Go directly northwest uphill on a grassy slope, and then traverse across the scree to the trees. Stay left of the wide ridge from the saddle aiming toward the true summit (the left-most point on the skyline). Stay left of a rock rib and a notch leading to a false

Bill Peak (Photo by John Roper)

summit. Ascend amongst trees and boulders, following an open gully to the right just below the summit block. Traverse left toward the summit. The first gully is steep, but an easier gully to the south provides better access.

For Bean, most people hike east on Trail 1226 to the saddle just south of Volcanic Neck, then scramble up Bean on the north ridge. But for more adventure, travel southeast on the ridge from Bill to the 6670-foot summit (called Mary Peak), then northeast to Bean.

For Volcanic Neck, traverse over Bean, dropping 300 feet on the north ridge to the saddle intersecting with County Line Trail 1226. Traverse around Volcanic Neck on the southeast side, dropping and then gaining the saddle to the northeast. At the saddle ascend the gully to the right. Continue on ledges and gullies to the summit ridge and on to the summit. Beware of loose rock in the gully on Volcanic Neck where the summit block is steep and exposed. Keep the party together while watching for loose rock. Due to the distances involved, a car camp at Beverly Campground is suggested for the night before.

Alternate Routes: To approach Bean Peak first in the sequence, hike Beverly-Turnpike Trail 1391 to the first junction (1.2 miles) and take the right branch, continuing northeast on Bean Creek Trail 1391.1. Leave the trail at the second creek crossing (5100 feet), and continue into Bean Creek basin. Several routes can be done to attain Bean. The easiest one is to scramble upward and approach the summit from the left (west). Approaching from the Earl-Bean ridge involves good rock scrambling (class 2).

56 KOPPEN MOUNTAIN AND IRON PEAK

Elevations: 6031 ft (1839 m), 6519 ft (1988 m)

Difficulty: S4/T2

Distance: 14 miles

Elevation gain: 5000 ft

Trip time: 2 days

Time to summit: 4 hours from campground to Koppen; 4 hours from campground to Iron

Best time of year: May to October

Maps: USGS Mount Stuart; Green Trails Mount Stuart 209

Contact: Wenatchee National Forest, Cle Elum Ranger District

GPS WAYPOINT ROUTE

1. DeRoux Campground: 3800 ft (10U 655636mE 5253361mN)
2. Trail 1392A: 1.6 miles, 4180 ft (10U 653820mE 5254033mN)
3. Pass: 2.6 miles, 5000 ft (10U 653439mE 5253549mN)
4. Koppen summit: 3.5 miles, 6031 ft (10U 654067mE 5252217mN)
5. Leave Iron Peak Trail: 3 miles (from campground), 6100 ft (10U 658039mE 5253984mN)
6. Iron summit: 3.5 miles, 6519 ft (10U 658483mE 5253225mN)

The Teanaway region is lovable any time of year, but it is prime in spring when higher, more rugged peaks are inaccessible due to road closures, avalanche hazard, and rime ice. In the summer when the snow is gone, Iron Peak

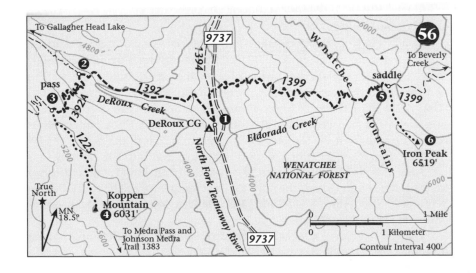

Iron Peak (Photo by Mike Torok)

and Koppen Mountain are almost too easy, for a trail leads to the summit of Koppen and nearly to the top of Iron. Nevertheless, the Teanaway terrain is more open and inviting than the terrain of the northern or western Cascades. The peaks are small, yet the zone near the top of the surrounding ridges is above timberline and graced with expansive skies.

As an overnight trip, Koppen and Iron can be combined on 2 separate days with the same car camp for a weekend of rambling and exercise. The extended junket yields leisurely scrambling to hone early-season ice ax skills and an opportunity just to enjoy a spring weekend in the mountains.

Trailhead Directions: Drive I-90 east to Exit 85, East Cle Elum. On the north side of the freeway, follow SR 970 east to the Teanaway River Road. Follow the Teanaway River Road north to the North Fork Teanaway River Road (FS Road 9737). Drive on this road to 29 Pines Campground where the pavement ends. Continue about 9 miles on the gravel road to DeRoux Campground. (115 miles, 2.5 hours from Seattle)

Standard Route:

Day 1: For Koppen Mountain, find Boulder-DeRoux Trail 1392 in the DeRoux Campground. Begin at 3800 feet and go west for 1.6 miles. Then take the left branch (Trail 1392A), which leaves the creek. Follow the trail up switchbacks to the pass (5040 feet), and then turn left and follow an old trail (Trail 1225) along the ridge to the summit. The tread is hard to follow.

Day 2: For Iron Peak, hike east on Iron Peak Trail 1399, which begins across the road from the DeRoux Campground. Take it to the saddle at 6100 feet, and then leave the trail and follow the ridge south to the summit.

Alternate Routes: For Koppen Mountain, the trip could start at Johnson Medra Trail 1383 and follow the ridge to the summit from Medra Pass (10 miles, 3000 feet). The return is via Trail 1383. DeRoux Peak (Point 6260) can be done for a bonus summit.

For Iron Peak, leave a car at Beverly Turnpike Trail 1391 (Scramble 55) and descend to that trailhead.

57 FIRST MOTHER MOUNTAIN AND CASTLE PEAK

Elevations: 6480 ft (1994 m), 6110 ft (1862 m)

Difficulty: S2/T3

Distance: 5 miles

Elevation gain: 2400 ft

Trip time: 6 hours

Time to summit: 2 hours to First Mother; 2 hours from First Mother to Castle

Best time of year: July to October

Maps: USGS Mowich Lake; Green Trails Mount Rainier West 269

Contact: Mount Rainier National Park

GPS WAYPOINT ROUTE
1. Rangers Cabin: 4900 ft (10U 586670mE 5198323mN)
2. Knapsack Pass: 1 mile, 6200 ft (10U 588184mE 5198378mN)
3. First Mother summit: 1.3 miles, 6480 ft (10U 588234mE 5198790mN)

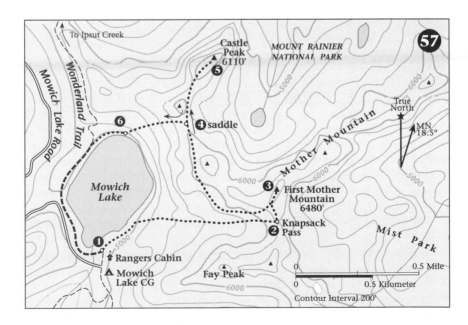

4. Saddle: 2.5 miles, 5800 ft (10U 587622mE 5199164mN)
5. Castle summit: 3 miles, 6110 ft (10U 587659mE 5199861mN)
6. Mowich Lake: 4 miles, 4929 ft (10U 586824mE 5199205mN)

Mother Mountain is the long subrange east of Mowich Lake containing three principal summits. The massif is named for the resemblance of the outline of the northeastern summit to a female figure. The western and highest point is First Mother Mountain. Second and Third Mother lie farther east on the crest. The entire formation was built from successive lava flows erupting from low volcanoes. Castle Peak is an ancillary, flat-topped spur coming northwest off Mother Mountain to the northeast of Mowich Lake.

The combined scramble of First Mother Mountain and Castle Peak is a pretty, casual stroll, done best in fall when the colors are luminous and the party requires a stress-free day. Mowich Lake is a handsome sight at this time, but beware: on clear weekends the area is bustling and parking is limited. Try to visit these gems during midweek if at all possible to avoid the crowds at the lake. Nonetheless, when scrambling higher elevations off the trail, the way is still pristine and open, with nary a human to mar the splendid panorama with Mount Rainier in the background.

Trailhead Directions: Drive to Enumclaw via SR 164 or SR 169, and then take SR 410 west to Buckley. Alternatively, drive SR 167 to Sumner, and then take SR 410 east to Buckley. From Buckley, drive south on SR 165 to Wilkeson and then to Carbonado. Mowich Lake Road (SR 165) branches from the Carbon River Road 3 miles south of Carbonado, and then extends 17 miles to Mowich Lake. The last few miles of the road are seldom open before mid-July. (75 miles, 2 hours from Seattle)

Standard Route: From the Rangers Cabin at Mowich Lake, find a climber's path at 4900 feet that follows the lake edge at first and then trends east. The path is well defined, but unmaintained. The tread generally heads to a saddle between First Mother and Fay Peak, called Knapsack Pass (6200 feet). First Mother is the easternmost point before a deeper cleft to the east within the Mother Mountain formation. From the pass head northeast following a climber's tread to the summit.

From the summit of First Mother head back down the ridge toward Knapsack

Castle Peak (Photo by Mike Torok)

Pass but do not descend to the pass. Instead, pick up the ridge running northwest. Stay on top of the ridge as much as possible, dropping to the west while losing as little elevation as necessary to avoid gendarmes. Eventually reach a broad saddle at 5800 feet between Castle and First Mother where another climber's path trends to the right around this false summit of Castle. Stay just at the base of the rocky formation. After one airy step along the way, attain a path that leads to the summit region. Climb to the top of the block, and then drop off the backside about 50 feet to regain Castle's true summit. Note that the true summit is farther along the ridge than the highest rocky point.

The return is via the saddle. From there, travel westward, dropping to contour toward the north end of Mowich Lake. To complete the loop, hike back along the northwest side of the lake to reach the Wonderland Trail and the parking area.

Note that the road into Mowich Lake usually does not open until mid-July. Also, early season presents moderately steep snow up to Knapsack Pass and down from First Mother to the saddle and Castle.

Alternate Route: In early season, before the Mowich Lake Road opens, this trip can be done via Ipsut Creek and Ipsut Pass adding 11 miles and 2600 feet.

58 FAY PEAK, MOUNT PLEASANT, AND HESSONG ROCK

Elevations: 6492 ft (1979 m), 6454 ft (1967 m), 6385 ft (1948 m)	
Difficulty: S2/T2	
Distance: 6 miles	
Elevation gain: 3000 ft	
Trip time: 5 hours	
Time to summit: 1.5 hours to Fay; 1 hour from Fay to Pleasant; 1 hour from Pleasant to Hessong	
Best time of year: July to October	
Maps: USGS Mowich Lake; Green Trails Mount Rainier West 269	
Contact: Mount Rainier National Park	
Special considerations: Moderate rock fall	

GPS WAYPOINT ROUTE
1. Rangers Cabin: 4900 ft (10U 586670mE 5198323mN)
2. Knapsack Pass: 1 mile, 6200 ft (10U 588184mE 5198378mN)
3. Fay summit: 1.5 miles, 6492 ft (10U 587737mE 5198054mN)
4. Pleasant summit: 2.1 miles, 6454 ft (10U 588508mE 5197561mN)
5. Hessong summit: 2.5 miles, 6385 ft (10U 588003mE 5197122mN)
6. Spray Park Trail: 3 miles, 5700 ft (10U 588638mE 5196939mN)

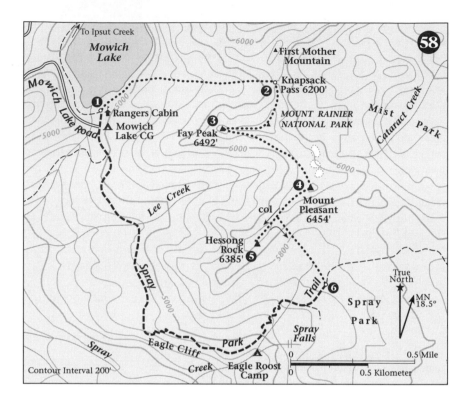

Fay Peak is named for Fay Fuller, the first woman to ascend Mount Rainier. Mount Pleasant is undoubtedly named for the sensation it evokes. Hessong Rock was summited early in the exploration of Mount Rainier. Located close to Mowich Lake, the trio offer majestic views of Mount Rainier and its northern and western glaciers.

The area between Fay, Pleasant, and Hessong is often done on a single-day traverse, with easy scrambling and spectacular vistas from each vantage point. The way is rocky near the summits, and in early season steeper patches of snow present obstacles. But the total distance of the trip is minimal and the exertion mild. Nevertheless, the payoff in panorama is immense.

For a breathtaking side trip, return via Spray Park—a supreme flower garden with few rivals. Even when Mount Rainier is shrouded in fog, in early season the sea of avalanche lilies, or later in summer the riot of wildflower color, are well worth the visit. Make a loop trip, and return to Mowich Lake via the Spray Park Trail, stopping at Eagle Cliff, a fine spot to sit for a long look at Mount Rainier and especially the Mowich Glacier. Return to glittering Mowich Lake, where you will be saturated and sated at nearly every turn with the spectacle of the giant volcano.

Trailhead Directions: Drive to Enumclaw via SR 164 or SR 169, and then take SR 410 west to Buckley. Alternatively, drive SR 167 to Sumner, and then take SR 410 east to Buckley. From Buckley, drive south on SR 165 to Wilkeson and then to Carbonado. Mowich Lake Road (SR 165) branches from the

Carbon River Road at 3 miles south of Carbonado, and then extends 17 miles to Mowich Lake. The last few miles are seldom open before mid-July. (75 miles, 2 hours from Seattle)

Standard Route: From the Rangers Cabin at 4900 feet, find a well-defined but unmaintained climber's path that trends east. The tread generally heads to a saddle between First Mother and Fay called Knapsack Pass (6200 feet). In early season, expect steep snow to Knapsack Pass. In late season, expect loose rock on traverses to the summits.

About 200 feet before the pass, head west to attain the ridge at 6400 feet at a small saddle between Fay and a false summit. Avoid the false summit. From Fay's eastern ridge scramble easily to the summit by going west on a climber's path. From Fay, traverse southeast to Mount Pleasant.

For Hessong, descend to the col between Hessong and Pleasant and then ascend to the summit via the northwest ridge. From here, a side trip to Spray Park can be accomplished by descending the slope between Hessong and Pleasant southward to an area of small ponds at 5700 feet. Return to the cars via the Spray Park Trail.

Alternate Routes: Gullies on the south side of Hessong Rock offer steeper but more direct routes; a chimney route, distinguished by a tall slender tree at its top, is perhaps the standard class 2 route from Hessong Rock to Spray Park.

Scramblers on Hessong Rock (Photo by Susan Alford)

If the Mowich Lake Road is closed, approach the trip from Ipsut Creek and Ipsut Pass adding 2500 feet and 11 miles. For an extended, athletic scramble, the journey can be combined with First Mother and Castle (Scramble 57).

59 ECHO ROCK AND OBSERVATION ROCK

Elevations: 7870 ft (2399 m), 8364 ft (2549 m)	
Difficulty: S4/T4	
Distance: 11 miles	
Elevation gain: 3800 ft	
Trip time: 10 hours	
Time to summit: 5 hours to Echo Rock; 1 hour from Echo to Observation	
Best time of year: July to September	
Maps: USGS Mowich Lake; Green Trails Mount Rainier West 269	
Contact: Mount Rainier National Park	

Special considerations: Serious rock fall on Echo, wear helmets; crampons needed for steep and icy snow

GPS WAYPOINT ROUTE
1. Rangers Cabin: 4900 ft (10U 586670mE 5198323mN)
2. Knapsack Pass: 1 mile, 6200 ft (10U 588184mE 5198378mN)
3. Spray Park: 2.5 miles, 6060 ft (10U 589621mE 5196295mN)
4. Col: 4 miles, 7600 ft (10U 591085mE 5195062mN)
5. Echo summit: 4.2 miles, 7870 ft (10U 591445mE 5195305mN)
6. Observation summit: 4.6 miles, 8364 ft (10U 590989mE 5194718mN)

Echo and Observation Rocks are conspicuous pyramids that punctuate the terrain on the northeastern fringe of lower Ptarmigan Ridge. Directly ahead and in view are Liberty Ridge, the Willis Wall, and Liberty Cap. Echo Rock is a craggy outcrop nearly surrounded by the Russell Glacier, while Observation Rock has a more temperate form with merely a short cliff facing east. Both Echo and Observation are remnants of two satellite cones that erupted after Mount Rainier was nearly full grown. These flows slapped up against the older lava of Ptarmigan Ridge and formed the plateau of Spray Park.

A trip to Echo and Observation renders a reach-out-and-touch-me experience of Rainier that only scramblers and climbers experience. The blanket of snow is enormous, persistent, and reminiscent of the monumental glaciers above. Yet the approach to the points in this scramble lacks crevasses that would require ropes and rescue skills. On a fine summer day, Echo and Observation render a skyscraping locale to scrutinize the polarity between the sheets of frosty alabaster and the spikes of shaggy and crumbling volcanic debris.

This divergence underscores the violent persona of the giant volcano, leading to reflection on the merciless power of nature.

Trailhead Directions: Drive to Enumclaw via SR 164 or SR 169, and then take SR 410 west to Buckley. Alternatively, drive SR 167 to Sumner, and then SR 410 east to Buckley. From Buckley, drive south on SR 165 to Wilkeson and then to Carbonado. Mowich Lake Road (SR 165) branches from the Carbon River Road at 3 miles south of Carbonado, and then extends 17 miles to Mowich Lake. The last few miles are seldom open before mid-July. (75 miles, 2 hours from Seattle)

Standard Route: From the Rangers Cabin at Mowich Lake at 4900 feet, find a climber's path that heads generally east to 6200-foot Knapsack Pass between First Mother Mountain and Fay Peak. Descend into a basin and climb the shoulder of Mount Pleasant, crossing it at about 6000 feet. Cross over the Spray Park Trail while traveling southeast into Spray Park. Continue southeast across open lobes of subalpine landscape, crossing the broad ridge and snowfields next to the foot of the west tongue of Flett Glacier.

For Echo Peak, ascend easy snow and pumice to the broad col between Echo and Observation Rocks (7600 feet). Scramble left and keep near the farthest

Echo Rock and Observation Rock (Photo by Mike Torok)

western side of the crag. Hands may be needed, ascending on loose volcanic debris. Find a boot path in the pumice on the south side of Echo. The path climbs counterclockwise but stays on the south side as it swings back to the final, crumbling summit block. Beware of rock fall; keep the party together and wear helmets.

For Observation Rock, return to the col between Echo and Observation. Traverse southwest and climb snow slopes to the ridge just southeast of the easy rocky grade to the Observation's summit. The party can return to Spray Park by descending Observation via the easy south or southwest side, and then cross snowfields on the western side of Observation to pick up the Spray Park Trail back to Mowich Lake.

Note that remarkably loose rock on Echo creates serious rock fall hazard. Crampons should be brought on this trip any time of year to ensure a safe crossing of the snowfields. Crampons are required in late season because of the steep and icy snow especially treacherous on Observation Rock and in other areas along the way.

Alternate Route: Both the approach and the return can be done from Spray Park Trail.

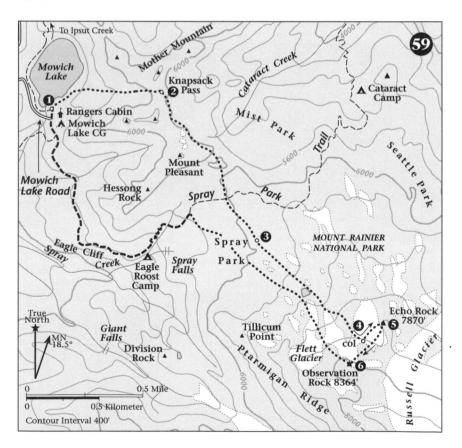

60 THE PALISADES AND MARCUS PEAK

Elevations: 7070 ft (2155 m), 6962 ft (2122 m)

Difficulty: S3/T3

Distance: 10 miles

Elevation gain: 3400 ft

Trip time: 8 hours

Time to summit: 4 hours

Best time of year: July to October

Maps: USGS White River Park; Green Trails Mount Rainier East 270

Contact: Mount Rainier National Park

Special considerations: Be cautious of rock fall on Marcus. In early October the road to Sunrise closes at 5 p.m.; road closes completely in mid-October.

GPS WAYPOINT ROUTE
1. Palisades Lakes trailhead: 6100 ft (10U 607603mE 5196786mN)
2. Clover Lake: 1.5 miles, 5732 ft (10U 607004mE 5198096mN)
3. Hidden Lake: 2.5 miles, 5915 ft (10U 606483mE 5199429mN)
4. The Palisades summit: 4 miles, 7070 ft (10U 606275mE 5200099mN)
5. Marcus summit: 5 miles, 6962 ft (10U 606038mE 5199002mN)

The Palisades and Marcus Peak are two unassuming landmarks in the northeast of Mount Rainier National Park on the dry side of the mountain. Unlike most other scrambles in the national park, there are no views of Mount Rainier. Yet the area is attractive in part for the trip past Palisades Lakes, a series of at least seven tarns along the trail.

The Palisades are an interesting cliff formation and the major destination. Marcus Peak is a subsidiary peak that borders the lakes to the south. There are many ways to scramble the two, but a loop is the most entertaining and aesthetic. On warm days, allow extra time to cool off with a swim in the sparkling chain of lakes. This trip yields supreme high alpine roaming in lush, green, fresh air country, providing a satisfying ramble in a tucked away corner of Mount Rainier National Park.

Trailhead Directions: Drive SR 169 or SR 164 to Enumclaw. Continue on SR 410 for 38 miles to the White River Entrance to Mount Rainier National Park. Drive 10.5 miles on Sunrise Road to the parking area at Sunrise Point and find the Palisades Lakes Trail. (115 miles, 2.5 hours from Seattle)

Standard Route: At the north end of the horseshoe bend in the road, cross the highway at Sunrise Point to the Palisades Lakes trailhead on the north side of the road (6100 feet). Follow the trail down the ridge, and then up switchbacks toward Sunrise Lake. At a junction at 0.5 mile, take the right fork. In 1.5 miles from the road the path skirts Clover Lake, largest of the

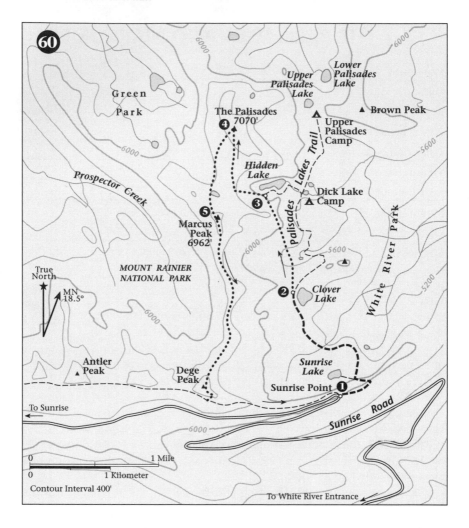

Palisades Lakes. Follow the trail to the saddle above Clover Lake. From here, you may choose to leave the trail to go cross-country north to Hidden Lake and the saddle between Marcus and The Palisades.

Alternatively, at Clover Lake stay on the main Palisades Lakes Trail (easier than going cross-country) to Dick Lake Camp, and from there, take a spur west to Hidden Lake. From the saddle above Hidden Lake, pick a route up the broad south slope of The Palisades. Aim northwest of the summit block and then back to the ridge to avoid the thick trees below the summit.

To attain Marcus Peak, return to the saddle above Hidden Lake. Ascend directly to the northeast ridge where loose rock is encountered. Alternatively ascend the vegetated rib to the right of the broad rock and sand gully as seen from the saddle to gain the northwest ridge. Be careful of persistent loose rock on the summit block of Marcus. From Marcus the choice of return is to

The Palisades (Photo by John Roper)

retrace the steps to Hidden Lake, to travel east directly to attain the trail, or to continue south cross-country to Dege Peak.

Alternate Routes: If only doing Marcus, consider taking the trail to Dege Peak and follow the ridge over to Marcus. This is a slower route with more rock scrambling.

Taking the trail to Upper Palisades Lake and scrambling to the northeast ridge is an alternate approach to The Palisades. Continue up the right side of the northeast ridge or cross a bowl and scramble up the north ridge to the summit. A party can descend westward into Green Park and then past Hidden Lake back to the main trail.

GOAT ISLAND MOUNTAIN

Elevation: 7288 ft (2221 m)	
Difficulty: S3/T3	
Distance: 12 miles	
Elevation gain: 4000 ft	
Trip time: 11 hours	
Time to summit: 6 hours	
Best time of year: June to September	
Maps: USGS Mount Rainier East, White River Park, Sunrise; Green Trails Mount Rainier East 270	
Contact: Mount Rainier National Park	
Special considerations: Difficult stream crossings	

GPS WAYPOINT ROUTE
1. Wonderland Trail trailhead: 3800 ft (10U 605906mE 5193494mN)
2. Fryingpan Creek footbridge: 4 miles, 5200 ft (10U 602709mE 5191354mN)

3. Point 7218: 5 miles, 7218 ft (10U 602155mE 5192527mN)
4. Goat Island summit: 6 miles, 7288 ft (10U 603146mE 5192997mN)

An enormous, rounded mound located between White River and Fryingpan Creek, Goat Island Mountain stands right in the middle of mammoth views toward two huge glaciers: the Fryingpan and the Emmons. Mount Rainier and Little Tahoma Peak, the highest and third highest mountains in the state, tower above the Fryingpan Glacier and dominate the scene. To the southeast lie the Sarvant Glaciers, and plugs from old volcanic eruptions, the Cowlitz Chimneys. To the south is Panhandle Gap, the highest and most barren section of the Wonderland Trail. Backcountry skiers and snowboarders are often seen swooshing along Meany Crest. The return trip through Summer Land leads to broad alpine meadows that bridge the gap between civilization and the desolate moraines and ice above.

Trailhead Directions: Drive SR 169 or SR 164 to Enumclaw. Continue on SR 410 east through Greenwater to the White River Entrance to Mount Rainier National Park. On the White River Road at 3 miles past the park entrance and just beyond the Fryingpan Creek Bridge, find the trail to Summer Land, on part of the Wonderland Trail. (110 miles, 2.5 hours from Seattle)

Standard Route: Begin at 3800 feet on the Wonderland Trail. After crossing

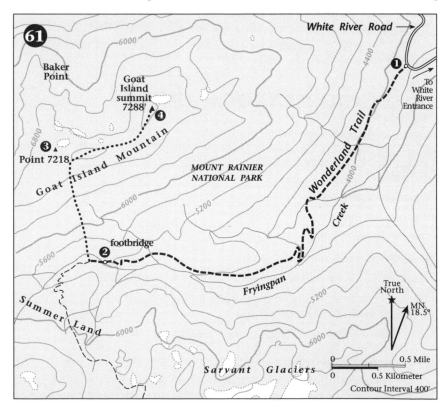

Camping on Goat Island Mountain (Photo by Chris Weidner)

the footbridge over Fryingpan Creek, leave the trail just before the switchbacks. Follow the most rightward of the creeks, crossing as far up the slope as possible and head for the saddle east of Point 7218. Then follow the ridge trending northeast to the Goat Island summit. For a loop trip, return from the summit back toward the Wonderland Trail.

There are many ways to approach the peak—this route is the easiest and the longest, and it avoids most of the brush on the lower portion on the ascent. Note however that in the high country on the slopes of Goat Island Mountain, rushing water from snowmelt can create difficult stream crossings. Crossing a tributary of Fryingpan Creek on a frail snow bridge can be dangerous. Therefore, the trip is best done when ample snow is present in early season, or when the water level is low in late season.

NACHES PEAK AND YAKIMA PEAK

Elevations: 6452 ft (1967 m), 6226 ft (1898 m)

Difficulty: S1/T4

Distance: 5 miles

Elevation gain: 1600 ft

Trip time: 4 hours

Time to summit: 1 hour to Naches; 2 hours from Naches to Yakima

Best time of year: July to October

Maps: USGS Chinook Pass; Green Trails Mount Rainier East 270

Contact: Mount Rainier National Park; Wenatchee National Forest, Naches Ranger District

GPS WAYPOINT ROUTE
1. Chinook Pass: 5400 ft (10U 613207mE 5191809mN)
2. Naches summit: 0.8 miles, 6452 ft (10U 613840mE 5191347mN)
3. Yakima summit: 1.6 miles, 6226 ft (10U 612684mE 5191961mN)

Both mountains within a stone's throw from Chinook Pass, Naches Peak is an excellent point for a Mount Rainier panorama, while Yakima Peak is a popular meadow ridge ramble. This charming little circle around Chinook Pass creates an intimate experience of flower fields and ponds, yet at the same time yields big views of Mount Rainier. The way to these knolls winds to high meadows and in a tiny distance offers as nice a combination of flowers and mountains as one can find anywhere. Flowers are at their peak roughly from late July to early August. But this trip is best done in late September for ripe blueberries and the fiery hues of autumn.

Trailhead Directions: Drive SR 169 or SR 164 to Enumclaw. Continue on SR 410 east and then south to Cayuse Pass, and then east to Chinook Pass. Park on either the north or south side of the highway and begin at the Pacific Crest Trail 2000 trailhead. (110 miles, 2.5 hours from Seattle)

Standard Route: For Naches Peak, start at 5400-foot Chinook Pass and take the Pacific Crest Trail over SR 410 on the wooden overpass. Find a boot path that ascends the ridge, staying on the southwest slope of Naches. This path eventually leads to the south ridge crest near the summit block. A tricky, big step down on the apex of the crest just before the summit is treacherous if the rock is wet or icy.

For Yakima Peak, return to Chinook Pass, hike up easy, grass slopes and ascend a gully on the eastern side. Turn left at the top to follow the ridge to the summit.

Alternate Routes: Due to its diminutive nature, a trip to Naches and Yakima is often combined with a scramble of Seymour Peak. A party could also start at Tipsoo Lake and take the Tipsoo Lake Trail north to the Pacific Crest Trail to create more distance, elevation gain, and enjoyment.

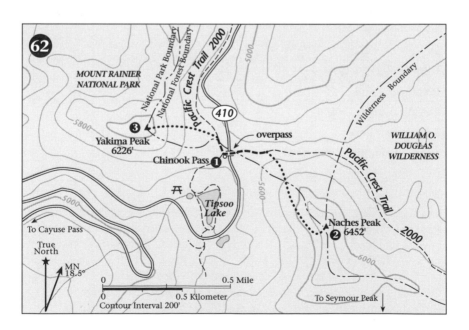

Yakima Peak (Photo by John Roper)

63 GOVERNORS RIDGE AND BARRIER PEAK

Elevations: 6620 ft (2017 m), 6521 ft (1988 m)

Difficulty: S4/T5

Distance: 11 miles

Elevation gain: 3800 ft

Trip time: 9 hours

Time to summit: 5 hours

Best time of year: July to September

Maps: USGS White River Park, Chinook Pass; Green Trails Mount Rainier East 270

Contact: Mount Rainier National Park

Special considerations: Dangerous rock fall in gullies, wear helmets

GPS WAYPOINT ROUTE
1. Owyhigh Lakes trailhead: 3700 ft (10U 606984mE 5193757mN)
2. Owyhigh Lakes: 4.6 miles, 5300 ft (10U 607940mE 5191294mN)
3. Saddle: 5 miles, 6100 ft (10U 608636mE 5190551mN)
4. Governors Peak: 5.4 miles, 6620 ft (10U 608847mE 5190915mN)
5. Barrier summit: 6 miles, 6521 ft (10U 608563mE 5190333mN)

Governors Ridge is the north-south trending crest of jagged points between Cayuse Pass and Owyhigh Lakes. The most obvious features are two spires a few hundred feet apart named Governors Needle and Governors Peak. Governors Needle, a technical climb, is the slender pinnacle that is to the south of Governors Peak. Higher than the Needle, Governors Peak is the craggy pyramid and the one that is usually scrambled. Achieving the summit requires some delicate class 3 moves. In contrast, Barrier Peak is a rounded structure at

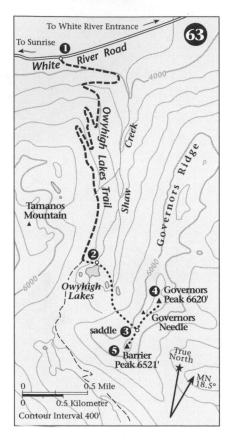

the south end of the ridge crest that is average in difficulty.

Named for Chief Owyhigh, a Yakama Indian leader, Owyhigh Lakes enhance the scenic foreground beneath the ragged edge of Governors Ridge. Here, as for many scrambles in the national park, grassy parkland slopes are dotted with crumbling, tattered needles and cliffs. The journey transitions from a strolling of serene lakes to a scaling of steep, exposed, friable rock, thus creating a challenging trip for advanced scramblers.

Trailhead Directions: Drive SR 169 or SR 164 to Enumclaw. Continue on SR 410 to the White River Entrance of Mount Rainier National Park. At 2 miles from the park entrance and 1 mile beyond Shaw Creek, find the Owyhigh Lakes trailhead. (110 miles, 2.5 hours from Seattle)

Standard Route: Start at 3700 feet and hike to Owyhigh Lakes (5300 feet). Ascend toward the saddle north of Barrier Peak. Drop over to the eastern side of the ridge between Barrier Peak and Governors Ridge, and traverse north toward Governors Ridge past three buttresses. Ascend 300 feet in a gully, and then ascend and traverse north and scramble to the highest point on the ridge, which is Governors Peak (6620 feet). Return to the saddle and ascend south to the summit of Barrier. From the summit, descend the west ridge to the lowest saddle. Scramble down a short gully to return to Owyhigh Lakes.

Barrier Peak and Governors Ridge (Photo by John Roper)

64 TATOOSH RANGE TRAVERSE
Pinnacle Peak, Plummer Peak, Denman Peak, Lane Peak,
Wahpenayo Peak, Chutla Peak, Eagle Peak

Elevations: 6562 ft (2000 m), 6370 ft (1942 m), 6006 ft (1831 m), 6012 ft (1833 m), 6231 ft (1899 m), 6000 ft (1829 m), 5958 ft (1816 m)

Difficulty: S5/T5

Distance: 10 miles one way

Elevation gain: 5000 ft

Trip time: 12 hours

Time to summit: 1-2 hours between each peak

Best time of year: July to August

Maps: USGS Mount Rainier East, Mount Rainier West, Wahpenayo Peak; Green Trails Mount Rainier East 270, Mount Rainier West 269, Randle 301

Contact: Mount Rainier National Park

Special considerations: Extreme rock fall on Pinnacle and Lane, wear helmets; bring hand line for Eagle

GPS WAYPOINT ROUTE
1. Pinnacle Peak trailhead: 4900 ft (10U 596941mE 5180006mN)
2. Pinnacle summit: 1.5 miles, 6562 ft (10U 596882mE 5178840mN)
3. Plummer summit: 2.5 miles, 6370 ft (10U 596359mE 5178323mN)
4. Denman summit: 3 miles, 6006 ft (10U 596057mE 5178759mN)
5. Lane summit: 3.5 miles, 6012 ft (10U 595349mE 5178811mN)
6. Wahpenayo summit: 5 miles, 6231 ft (10U 594298mE 5177575mN)
7. Chutla summit: 6 miles, 6000 ft (10U 593672mE 5178213mN)
8. Eagle summit: 6.5 miles, 5958 ft (10U 593350mE 5178534mN)

A high traverse along the Tatoosh Range, the prominent string of mountains located near the southern boundary of Mount Rainier National Park, is one of the ultimate scrambling experiences that Rainier has to offer. Individually the summits are popular because of their quick accessibility and their intimate perspective of The Mountain. But the combination of all peaks in a single day is a scrambling classic.

The Tatoosh peaks can be done separately as decent, true scrambles. But for the advanced, super-ambitious overachiever, the entire line can be completed in a fast-paced, fun-filled day of frolicking in the park. There are many variations of the Tatoosh traverse with numerous combinations of peaks. But for the entire chain, the classic way is to start early with a small party, travel light, wear helmets, and go when the days are long.

Completing the Tatoosh traverse gives the scrambler a solid feeling of accomplishment and pride. If you are into the numbers, peak hopping and peak bagging are seldom, if ever, this good.

Trailhead Directions: Drive SR 169 or 164 to Enumclaw. Continue on SR 410 past Cayuse Pass to the Stevens Canyon Entrance to Mount Rainier National Park. Drive west on the Stevens Canyon Road about 17.5 miles or east 1.5 miles from the Nisqually-Paradise Road to the Reflection Lakes parking area. The Pinnacle Peak trailhead is on the southern side of the road (130 miles, 3 hours from Seattle). Arrange for a car shuttle at the west end of the Tatoosh Range at the Eagle Peak trailhead at the Longmire parking area.

Standard Route: Begin from the Pinnacle Peak trailhead (4900 feet) and hike the Pinnacle Peak Trail to the Pinnacle-Plummer saddle at 6000 feet. Cross to the southern side and ascend the ridge northeast to Pinnacle's summit with friable, loose rock in places. Return to the saddle and take easy slopes west past a tree to the summit of Plummer.

Return to the Pinnacle-Plummer saddle and find a boot path traverse on the southern side of the ridge heading west past tarns. Descend 200 feet to pick up the ridge and head northwest to the wooded summit of Denman. Descend 600 feet to a saddle between Denman and Lane. Travel west to the first prominent peak below the summit block of Lane.

Scramble up a steep gully, with good handholds but many loose blocks. At the top of the gully turn left to the summit of Lane. Caution: extreme rock fall potential on Pinnacle and Lane requires the use of helmets. The party size must therefore be limited. In wet years on Lane, loose rock covered with thick moss in the vertical gully has made scrambling too hazardous to attempt.

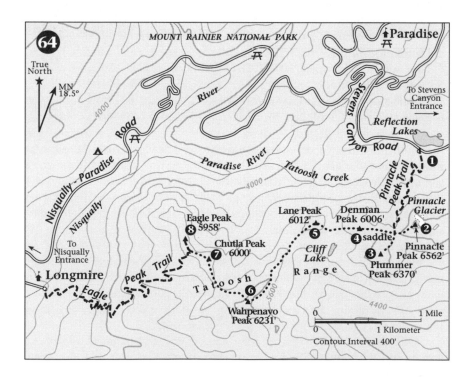

Tatoosh Range traverse (Photo by Mike Torok)

From Lane, descend easy slopes southwest to 5100 feet at the level of a small tarn. Scramble southwest ascending talus and scree to a 5800-foot saddle between Wahpenayo and an unnamed satellite peak. Cross the ridge and traverse over to the western ridge of Wahpenayo. Find a goat trail leading to the summit. Near the summit turn northeast for the final rocky scramble to the top. Note that early in the season, dangerous snow cornices form on the summit ridge of Wahpenayo.

Descend and continue west to the Chutla-Wahpenayo saddle. Traverse west around the base of buttresses and begin the ascent of Chutla. In early season do not go all the way to the saddle but head up open snow slopes. The final summit ridge is best approached from the north.

For Eagle, descend to the saddle between Eagle and Chutla. From the saddle a boot path leads northwest through brush toward Eagle's summit block. A rocky ledge presents a challenging and exposed big step; use extreme caution. A hand line for the descent is appropriate if the rock is wet. Return on the Eagle Peak Trail to Longmire.

Alternate Route: Reversing the route to start at Longmire and end at Reflection Lakes yields 2000 feet more elevation gain.

65 MOUNT WOW

Elevation: 6040 ft (1841 m)	
Difficulty: S4/T3	
Distance: 9 miles	
Elevation gain: 4400 ft	
Trip time: 10 hours	
Time to summit: 6 hours	
Best time of year: May to October	
Maps: USGS Mount Wow, Sawtooth Ridge; Green Trails Randle 301, Mount Rainier West 269	
Contact: Mount Rainier National Park	
Special considerations: Bring a hand line.	

GPS WAYPOINT ROUTE

1. Nisqually Ranger Station: 2100 ft (10U 582898mE 5176787mN)
2. Leave Boundary Trail: 1.5 miles, 4200 ft (10U 582754mE 5179028mN)
3. Point 5614: 2.5 miles, 5614 ft (10U 584243mE 5179283mN)
4. Wow summit: 3.5 miles, 6040 ft (10U 584190mE 5180303mN)
5. Lake Allen: 4.7 miles, 4577 ft (10U 584745mE 5179464mN)
6. Westside Road: 6.7 miles, 2500 ft (10U 585603mE 5178824mN)

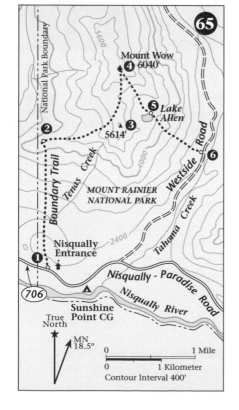

"Wow" expresses the breathtaking sight of Mount Rainier that suddenly pops into view while scrambling to this knoll at the southwestern edge of the national park. The approach to Wow uses well-defined but unmaintained trails. Because of its location in an area that appears to be accessible only by cross-country travel, the peak sees few visitors. Yet the scramble is one where there is little brush and the navigation is relatively simple.

Mount Wow provides a marvelous vantage to spy Mount Rainier, and it is well worth the minimal strain to find the Boundary Trail, the

Mount Wow (Photo by John Roper)

path in the forest that leads north along the western park boundary. On a clear day the expanse of Rainier stands majestically in the distance, with wondrous details of Sunset Ridge, the Amphitheater, the Tahoma Glacier, and many more commanding features. An energetic loop trip can be accomplished by continuing past Lake Allen to the Westside Road, now closed to automobile traffic.

Trailhead Directions: Drive SR 161 south through Eatonville. At SR 7 turn left and continue to Elbe, and then take SR 706 to the Nisqually Entrance of Mount Rainier National Park. Park cars off the road just outside the park near the Gateway Cafe. Find the start of the Boundary Trail north of the entrance. (90 miles, 2 hours from Seattle)

Standard Route: Find the unmaintained Boundary Trail on the north side of the park's Nisqually Entrance, just past the rangers' residence near the ranger station. From 2100 feet, take this trail that heads north along the park boundary to its high point of 4200 feet, where it crosses the ridge that leads to Mount Wow. Leave the trail and head east, staying on top of the ridge as it crosses several rocky knobs which can be slippery in bad weather.

At 5200 feet, approaching the false summit of Wow (5614 feet), leave the ridge and traverse north across a steep open slope. Be careful at the "big step," which is an exposed break in the rocks on the way. Under wet conditions, a hand line for the big step down could be necessary.

The ridge levels out before it again encounters steep rock. Drop left and down about 100 feet from a grassy saddle and once again find a climber's trail that traverses in trees around a big bowl. When the trail disappears ascend toward the open slope. Ascend on the right side in the trees, and contour right at the top to a saddle between the false and true summits. Then scramble the south ridge to the summit.

Alternate Route: From 1.5 miles up the Westside Road (2500 feet), take a 2-mile trail to Lake Allen and from there follow a rudimentary trail about 1 mile to the top of Wow.

SOUTH CASCADES

66 MOUNT CURTIS GILBERT

Elevation: 8184 ft (2496 m)

Difficulty: S4/T4

Distance: 18 miles

Elevation gain: 4500 ft

Trip time: 2 days

Time to summit: 9 hours; 4 hours from Warm Lake

Best time of year: June to October

Maps: USGS Pinegrass Ridge, Jennie's Butte, Walupt Lake; Green Trails White Pass 303, Walupt Lake 335

Contact: Wenatchee National Forest, Naches Ranger District

Special considerations: Loose rock and moderate rock fall

GPS WAYPOINT ROUTE
1. South Fork Tieton River trailhead: 4100 ft (10U 631817mE 5151609mN)
2. Tieton Peak Trail junction: 1.5 miles, 4100 ft (10U 630039mE 5150261mN)

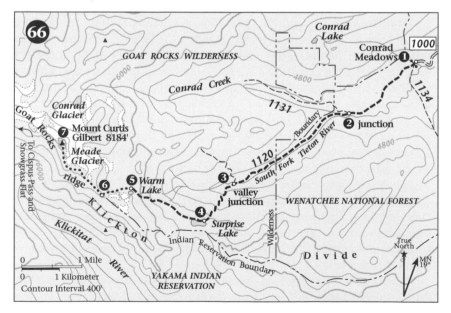

3. Valley junction: 4 miles, 4300 ft (10U 627006mE 5148413mN)
4. Surprise Lake: 6 miles, 5255 ft (10U 625965mE 5147331mN)
5. Warm Lake: 7 miles, 6340 ft (10U 624211mE 5148025mN)
6. Klickton Divide: 7.5 miles, 6800 ft (10U 623718mE 5147755mN)
7. Curtis Gilbert summit: 9 miles, 8184 ft (10U 622305mE 5149354mN)

The highest point in the Goat Rocks is Mount Curtis Gilbert, also known as Gilbert Peak and Goat Rocks. Curtis Gilbert is situated on the Klickton Divide with the Meade Glacier to the southeast and the Conrad Glacier to the north. At the base of the melting glacier is a small tarn called Cold Lake that floats small icebergs from the melting glacier. Farther south, Warm Lake is usually frozen until August. The mountain is moderate on the west, but a crumbly sheer eastern face forms a cut in the lobes of the fast disappearing ice fields below. The true summit is the most northwestern of a series of high points along the ridge.

Curtis Gilbert can be approached from Snowgrass Flat, Cispus Pass, or Conrad Meadows. But the best entry is through scenic Conrad Meadows, the largest subalpine valley in the Cascades. The territory is dry and more open than the brushy slopes of the North Cascades. Horse traffic is widespread, and mountain goats are often seen traversing the snowfields. Gray, brown, yellow, and maroon rock creates a patchwork quilt of colors covering neighboring Tieton Peak and the Devils Horn.

This trip follows the South Fork Tieton River's broad, even valley from Conrad Meadows to the river's source amid alpine cirques and disintegrating ice fields. The feeling from the top is of a barren and desolate, glacier-destroyed landscape, austerely beautiful in contrast to the profuse and exuberant meadows below.

Trailhead Directions: Drive SR 169 or 164 to Enumclaw. Continue on SR 410 to Cayuse Pass. Continue south on SR 123 and follow it to US 12. Turn east on US 12 and follow the road over White Pass. Continue past Rimrock Lake to just west of Hause Creek Campground and the intersection with South Fork Tieton River Road (FS Road 12). Turn south and go to FS Road 1000 (signed "Conrad Meadows") and drive 14 miles to a gate at the edge of private property. Park here at the start of South Fork Tieton River Trail 1120. (150 miles, 3.5 hours from Seattle)

Standard Route:

Day 1: From the South Fork Tieton River trailhead at 4100 feet, pass though a gate, and ford Short and Long Creeks. At a junction, Ten Day Trail 1134 goes to the left. Continue on the right fork of Trail 1120 to Conrad Meadows. Beware of misleading paths in the meadows that confuse the route; the crux of the trip may be finding the appropriate start of the trail to Warm Lake.

At 1.5 miles the trail crosses a gated logging road and continues on an old road. At a junction with Tieton Peak Trail 1131, continue left on the South Fork Tieton River Trail. At about 4 miles (4300 feet) at another fork, the new trail goes left to a bridge over the South Fork Tieton River, and then switchbacks to Surprise Lake at 6 miles. To get to Warm Lake, continue on the trail to Upper Surprise Camp (one could also gain Klickton Divide from here). Follow

Mount Curtis Gilbert (Photo by Mike Torok)

the trail until just before a stream crossing. Exit left (west) up the old trail. Follow the steep track upward until it fades away. Then travel northwest to arrive at Warm Lake and set up camp.

Day 2: For the summit of Curtis Gilbert, from Warm Lake head southwest through a patch of green to the Klickton Divide. Turn right and, staying sometimes on the left and sometimes on the right, follow the divide northwest to the summit block. At the summit block, stay on the west (left) side and remain close to the buttress. Scramble upward through loose rock, particularly near the summit block, to the true summit. The map indicates that the top is 8184 feet, while the USGS benchmark says it is 8201 feet.

 MOUNT ADAMS

Elevation: 12,276 ft (3742 m)	
Difficulty: S5/T4	
Distance: 12 miles	
Elevation gain: 6800 ft	
Trip time: 13 hours; 1-2 days	
Time to summit: 8 hours	
Best time of year: July to September	
Maps: USGS Mount Adams East; Green Trails Mount Adams 367S	
Contact: Gifford Pinchot National Forest, Mount Adams Ranger District	
Special considerations: Wear crampons above 11,000 feet; altitude sickness possible; volatile weather conditions; Cascades Volcano Pass required	

GPS WAYPOINT ROUTE
1. South Climb Trail 183: 5600 ft (10U 616386mE 5110001mN)
2. Lunch Counter: 3 miles, 9400 ft (10U 616871mE 5114925mN)

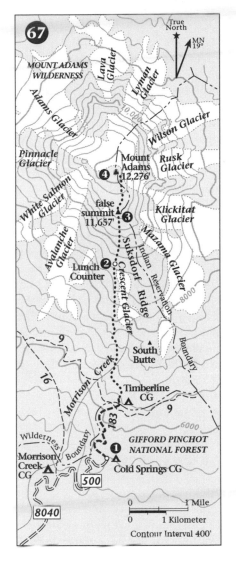

3. False summit: 4.5 miles, 11,657 ft (10U 616840mE 5116626mN)
4. Adams summit: 6 miles, 12,276 ft (10U 616526mE 5117442mN)

To the Klickitat Indians, majestic Mount Adams was the mythical warrior called *Pah-to,* son of the Great Spirit, who fought his brother *Wyeast* (Mount Hood) in the courtship of *Loo-wit* (Mount Saint Helens). Ever the handsome prince, Adams still towers over the terrain north of the Columbia River and dwarfs the now misshapen dome of Saint Helens.

Mount Adams is a vast mountain in all respects. The second highest peak in the state, the volcano compares closely with Mount Rainier in total volume of extruded material. Ten principal glaciers cover the slopes, ranging from 1 to 2 miles in length. The greatest cliffs and ice fields are on the eastern side, which creates one of the wildest appearances in the Cascades. Nonetheless, the south route is safe, facile, and well within the skills of the average scrambler. The grade is so moderate that a lookout cabin was built on the summit in 1921 and was occupied for several years. A trail was forged to the top to service a sulfur mine claim, and at the height of activity in the 1930s mule pack trains were taken to the summit.

Today Mount Adams is a designated wilderness area that is popular with the peakbagger. The south spur route is known as the Suksdorf Ridge, named for pioneer German botanist Wilhelm N. Suksdorf, who began his local visits and studies in 1877. This route demands more physical effort than it does technical skill; those in physically fit condition will find this a relatively easy journey. Due to its modest ascent, dramatic nature, and popular appeal, on a clear summer weekend the south spur is jammed with a never-ending stream of pilgrims marching inexorably to the top. At the summit, the views are distant and spacious, and to some might constitute a disappointment. In spite of that and the crowds, pick good weather to do this trip, and do not expect solitude, but still enjoy the parade and circus of fellow travelers to this apogee of Washington State scrambles.

Trailhead Directions: Drive I-5 south to Chehalis, then go east on US 12 for 48 miles to Randle. Turn south on FS Road 23, continuing east for 56 miles to Trout Lake. Alternatively, drive south on I-5 to I-205 at the Washington-Oregon border. Cross the Columbia River and drive into Oregon. Continue east on I-84 to Hood River. Go north, cross the Columbia and take SR 141 to Trout Lake. At 0.5 mile west of Trout Lake is the ranger station to register for the climb. From Trout Lake drive north on the road signed "Mt. Adams Recreation Hwy." At 1.3 miles, pass FS Road 23, which enters from the left. At 2 miles turn left on FS Road 80, signed "South Climb." Turn right on FS Road 8040 to Morrison Creek Campground at 6 miles, and then go right again on FS Road 500 to the end of the road, Cold Springs Campground, and South Climb Trail 183. Note that the 3-mile section of the road beyond Morrison Creek Campground is extremely rough and narrow. Trout Lake to Cold Springs Campground is 14 miles and takes about 1 hour to drive. (220 miles, 4 hours from Seattle)

Standard Route: Start at 5600 feet and follow South Climb Trail 183 on an old roadway across the intersection with Round-the-Mountain Trail 9. The common springtime route is more direct and ascends between South Butte and the Crescent Glacier. For the normal summer route, enter and cross a basin to the left. South Butte is the same elevation as Crescent Glacier, and the summer route goes well west of South Butte. Bear to the left of Crescent Glacier and continue on the main south spur of snow.

Continue the ascent to the top of the Crescent Glacier at 8600 feet. At 9400 feet find the "Lunch Counter," a broad shoulder suitable for a rest break or overnight camp. Bear to the right to Suksdorf Ridge. When the route steepens at about 9700 feet, ascend due north up snow or talus to the 11,657-foot false summit of Adams. Cross the plateau to the true (middle) summit, the last pull being on pumice or snow.

The route is largely a hike on a well-defined path, but be prepared for icy conditions and carry crampons. Looking back occasionally on your way from timberline to the summit helps minimize route confusion on your way down. Do not follow the ridge all the way down on your descent—the trail leaves

Mount Adams from Ives (Photo by John Roper)

the ridge and turns southeast just below Crescent Glacier.

Many climbers begin their ascent on the first day, and then spend the night at higher elevation in order to adjust to the altitude. On an overnight trip, most parties camp at the Lunch Counter at 9400 feet. Crowds can be avoided by camping at about 9050 feet, to the left of the snowfield, where there is a water source. Another choice is to camp lower at Timberline Campground below the Crescent Glacier in the Morrison Creek drainage.

Cautions: Perhaps the greatest danger of scrambling Mount Adams is getting caught in a whiteout. Inexperienced scramblers should prepare for rapidly changing weather and poor visibility. Crampons are needed for icy conditions above 11,000 feet. Occasionally "step ladders" in the snow made by other parties make crampons optional, but do not count on these conditions.

Be aware that altitude sickness can pose a real threat; nearly everyone who scrambles Adams will be affected to some extent by the change in altitude. Symptoms include headache, dizziness, and nausea. If you experience these symptoms, descend to lower elevations immediately.

Permits: You must purchase a Cascades Volcano Pass to climb Mount Adams. This annual pass is good for multiple climbs on Adams and Mount Saint Helens. A Cascades Volcano Pass is available by mail or in person from the Mount Adams Ranger Station in Trout Lake (see Appendix D). Day passes are available from the self-issuing fee stations at this ranger station and at the Killen Creek Trail 113. Human-waste bags are available at the Mount Adams Ranger Station.

MOUNT SAINT HELENS

Elevation: 8365 ft (2549 m)

Difficulty: S5/T4

Distance: 12 miles

Elevation gain: 5700 ft

Trip time: 12 hours; 1-2 days

Time to summit: 7 hours

Best time of year: May to June

Maps: USGS Mount Saint Helens; Green Trails Mount Saint Helens NW 364S

Contact: Gifford Pinchot National Forest, Mount Saint Helens National Volcanic Monument

Special considerations: Avalanche hazard; permits required May 15 to October 31

GPS WAYPOINT ROUTE
1. Swift Creek Ski Trail 244B: 2600 ft (10U 564007mE 5108491mN)
2. Above timberline camp: 3 miles, 4100 ft (10U 563594mE 5112395mN)
3. Monitor Ridge: 5 miles, 7600 ft (10U 562650mE 5114757mN)
4. Saint Helens summit: 6 miles, 8365 ft (10U 562283mE 5115397mN)

To the Klickitat Indians, Mount Saint Helens of ancient times was *Loo-wit-lat-Kla,* a fair maiden who was transformed into a mountain. But her graceful symmetry was indicative of youth and activity; the perfect cone had not yet formed when prehistoric glaciers carved Mount Adams.

Despite its mystic and ice-clad splendor, the seemingly angelic volcano was a time bomb. The apocalyptic eruption on May 18, 1980, resulted in an immense rockslide-avalanche. Pulverized rock mixed with melted glacier ice raced down the two forks of the Toutle River killing motorists and destroying everything in its path. The upper plume drifted eastward, inundating nearby cities and settling as far away as Montana. Some ash drifts were up to three feet thick and in places immersed the land in 100 tons per acre. The eruption blasted out an enormous semicircular crater more than 2 miles long, 1.5 miles wide, and 2100 feet deep. The highest remaining point on the peak was a paltry 8365 feet in altitude, a mere shadow of the south rim. No longer was

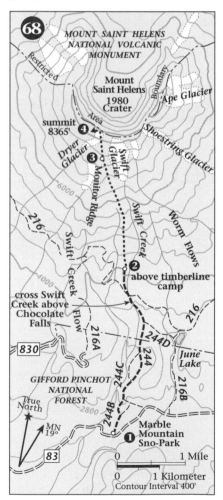

the mountain a beautiful maiden, but was left diminished and gnarled.

Nature is resilient and the plants and animals of the sector are on the way to recovery. But for an eerie and unearthly experience, scramble in the snow to the vast caldera's edge, peer in over the cornices, and imagine the specter of this entry to Hades' domain. Be properly awed and somewhat spooked, visualizing what it would have been like to be here that catastrophic day. Imagine giant mudflows, trees laid flat by hurricane winds, and timber roasted by superheated air.

Do the trip in early season while ample snow covers the route, for the volcanic ash and pumice are a stinging punishment for those who choose the journey when the snow is gone. To fully appreciate the cataclysm of the volcanic eruption, there is no substitute for scrambling to the top of what is left of Mount Saint Helens, marveling that it used to be known as the most symmetrical volcano in the West.

Trailhead Directions: Drive I-5 south to Exit 21, Woodland, and take SR 503 east to Jack's Restaurant and

Mount Saint Helens (Photo by John Roper)

Store. Follow FS Road 81 to Cougar Sno-Park and continue on FS Road 83 for 18 miles to Marble Mountain Sno-Park and the Worm Flows route, which begins at Swift Creek Ski Trail 244B. (200 miles, 4 hours from Seattle)

Standard Route: The Worm Flows route up Mount Saint Helens is the best early season route. From the Marble Mountain Sno-Park at 2600 feet, follow Swift Creek Ski Trail 244B north to Trail 244 (still called Swift Creek Trail) and from there go about 2.5 miles to timberline. Above timberline, cross Swift Creek immediately upstream from Chocolate Falls. Follow posts along the first ridge system west of Swift Creek to 4100 feet for an overnight base camp on snow. Follow the ridge that trends slightly to the west. Intersect Monitor Ridge (7600 feet) 800 feet below the summit. The true summit is 0.3 mile west along the crater rim.

Cautions: The summit is laced with heavy cornices; do not venture out without a proper belay. Glissade slopes cautiously, looking for rocks and holes. Any sane person would not want to do this trip in late season, when blowing pumice is brutal. Volcanic dust is oppressive to eyes, especially with contact lenses, but ski goggles may help to protect them. Since the water is full of pumice, melting snow for water is better, or carry a competent and powerful water filter. Call the Mount Saint Helens National Volcanic Monument for information (see Appendix D).

Permits: A climbing permit is required year-round to hike above 4800 feet on Mount Saint Helens. During the summer and fall, fees are charged and climbing is limited to 100 people per day. Permits are free off-season. Get your permit at Jack's Restaurant and Store on SR 503, 23 miles east of Woodland. For more information on advance reservations or unreserved permits, call the Mount Saint Helens climbing information line (see Appendix D).

BOULDER PEAK, EVERETT PEAK, AND MOUNT APPLETON

Elevations: 5604 ft (1709 m), 5187 ft (1581 m), 6030 ft (1838 m)

Difficulty: S5/T4

Distance: 19 miles

Elevation gain: 5800 feet

Trip time: 2 days

Time to summit: 4 hours from Boulder Lake to Boulder; 2 hours from Boulder Lake to Everett; 3 hours from Everett to Appleton

Best time of year: June to October

Maps: USGS Bogachiel Peak, Mount Carrie; Custom Correct Seven Lakes Basin-Hoh

Contact: Olympic National Park

GPS WAYPOINT ROUTE
1. Appleton Pass Trail: 2100 ft (10U 448415mE 5313841mN)
2. Boulder Lake: 3.4 miles, 4350 ft (10U 444062mE 5313936mN)
3. Boulder summit: 4.5 miles, 5604 ft (10U 443540mE 5313238mN)
4. Everett summit: 5.7 miles, 5187 ft (10U 445023mE 5312467mN)
5. Appleton summit: 7 miles, 6030 ft (10U 445359mE 5310844mN)

Boulder Peak, Everett Peak, and Mount Appleton are modest peaks that form the high ridge from Boulder Lake on the north to Appleton Pass on the south. One of the most popular trails in the Olympic National Park, the Appleton Pass Trail climbs to green meadows sprinkled with flowers, with views of the High Divide and Mount Carrie.

This sector on the northern end of the park makes for a fine 2-day trip with high wandering and a picturesque overnight camp at pretty Boulder Lake. Any of the peaks can be done separately, but because of their proximity to each other, these triplets make for a superb mini-outing. Located at the start of the trip is the famous Olympic Hot Springs. The soothing hot mineral water is a welcome respite for sore muscles before or after the scramble (or both!).

Trailhead Directions: Drive US 101 west from Port Angeles 9 miles to where the highway crosses the Elwha River. Turn left (south) on the Olympic Hot Springs Road along the upper Elwha River and drive 10.5 paved miles.

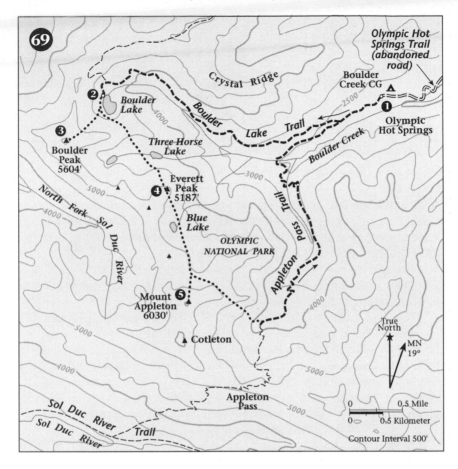

Just past the ranger station, turn right onto Boulder Creek Road. Park at the end of the road at the start of the Olympic Hot Springs Trail. (120 miles, 3 hours from Bainbridge Island)

Standard Route:

Day 1: Start at 2100 feet and hike 2.2 miles on an abandoned road to Boulder Creek Campground. Hike on the Appleton Pass Trail for 0.7 mile, and then take the right fork, Boulder Lake Trail, 2.7 miles to Boulder Lake (4350 feet). Set up camp at Boulder Lake, and then scramble steep heather and easy rock slopes to Boulder Peak just southwest of the lake. Return to camp that afternoon.

Day 2: From the camp at Boulder Lake, head southeast on a good climber's trail toward the ridge running east from Boulder Peak, crossing the saddle at about 4800 feet. Descend to the stream connecting upper and lower Three Horse Lake. Continue south up the eastern side of the creek that drains the northwest slopes of Everett Peak. Ascend to the saddle, from which you can see Blue Lake. Drop the overnight packs, turn left (east) and scramble easily to Everett Peak.

From the saddle, descend to Blue Lake, circle around on the left (east), and continue south up a flat ridge to the next basin containing a small lake. Travel

Appleton Pass (Photo by Mike Torok)

south around the lake, and then up into a cirque under the north face of Appleton. Continue nearly to the headwall of the cirque. Turn southeast (left) and ascend a snow finger (rock or scree in late season) to a saddle at about 5900 feet. Scramble left from the saddle to the summit.

Descend open slopes east from the saddle down to the south fork of Boulder Creek, and pick up the Appleton Pass Trail at 4000 feet. Follow the trail back to Boulder Creek Campground and the cars.

Note that because this trip is all off trail after Boulder Lake, routefinding skills are required. The trip is strenuous due to the need to carry overnight packs cross-country. However, a carryover is recommended, because returning from Appleton to Boulder Lake would necessitate a reclimb of most of Everett and Boulder.

Alternate Route: If the party has the energy, from Appleton scramble "Cotleton," the informal name of its slightly higher twin a short distance south. From there, a decent way trail leads down to Appleton Pass Trail.

70 MOUNT ANGELES

Elevation: 6454 ft (1968 m)

Difficulty: S1/T3

Distance: 6 miles

Elevation gain: 1800 ft

Trip time: 5 hours

Time to summit: 3 hours

Best time of year: May to October

Maps: USGS Mount Angeles; Custom Correct Hurricane Ridge

Contact: Olympic National Park

Special considerations: Loose rock in gullies, helmets advised

GPS WAYPOINT ROUTE
1. Hurricane Ridge–Klahhane Ridge trailhead: 5300 ft (10U 463150mE 5312889mN)

2. Junction: 2.6 miles, 5200 ft (10U 465004mE 5314974mN)
3. Mount Angeles summit: 3 miles, 6454 ft (10U 465242mE 5315684mN)

Situated at the northern edge of Olympic National Park, Mount Angeles floats above the city of Port Angeles and the waters of the Pacific Ocean. The summit offers a range of vision deep into the Olympic Mountains and across the Straits of San Juan de Fuca to the ice-capped peaks of Canada.

Located only 8 miles from tidewater and next to the visitors center at Hurricane Ridge, the lower trail provides a popular destination for day hikers who want a closer look at the face of the ridge. Hurricane Ridge itself is a favorite destination in the summer for casual tourists as well as hikers and scramblers because of its unique position at the northern portal of the Olympic Mountains.

Mount Angeles has several summits, of which the westernmost is the highest. This is a craggy peak with many routes to the top, but none of them is a walk-up. Moreover the rock is seriously loose in the big gullies. The easiest paths are scrambles, but only if you are a competent route finder through difficult terrain.

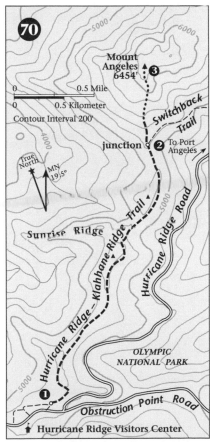

Trailhead Directions: Take a car ferry from Seattle to Bainbridge Island. (Alternatively, drive through Tacoma over the Tacoma Narrows Bridge.) Drive north on SR 305, and then north on SR 3. Cross the Hood Canal Bridge, and drive west on SR 104 and then on US 101 to Port Angeles. In town, follow the signs to Hurricane Ridge in Olympic National Park. From the park entrance toll booth, drive 9.6 miles on a paved road past Heart of the Hills Campground to the Hurricane Ridge Visitors Center parking lot, and locate Hurricane Ridge–Klahhane Ridge Trail. (110 miles, 2.75 hours from Bainbridge Island)

Standard Route: From the Hurricane Ridge–Klahhane Ridge trailhead at 5200 feet, hike 2.6 miles east through open meadowland. Turn left at a junction (5200 feet) onto a way trail that goes up toward the western slopes of the summit block. Make a level traverse nearly around the northwest corner about 300 feet below the summit. Ascend one of several dirt ravines to a short rock scramble near the summit.

Alternate Routes: From the western slope, 300 feet below the summit, look upslope and see a pair of obvious rock gullies that start on either side of a large boulder, just above an open scree slope. Pick either gully (left is fine) and scramble up to the notch in the summit ridge just south of, and 150 feet below, the summit. From the notch, turn left and go north to a 15-foot face. Climb the face and traverse left of it to make a long step into a gully. Or, bypass the face, either to its left or right, and climb up behind it. Continue up the summit ridge along the path of least resistance. This route is class 3 and therefore more advanced than a typical scramble. It is exposed in spots, but the rock is solid.

The trip is shorter when you start at the Switchback Trail. The parking area for the Switchback trailhead is beyond the Heart of the Hills Campground, but before the visitors center.

Mount Angeles couloir (Photo by Jason Griffith)

71 BAILEY RANGE TRAVERSE

Cat Peak, Mount Carrie, Stephen Peak, Mount Ferry, Mount Barnes, Mount Queets, Mount Noyes, Mount Seattle

Elevations: 5940 ft (1810 m), 6995 ft (2132 m), 6430 ft (1959 m), 6157 ft (1876 m), 5993 ft (1827 m), 6480 ft (1975 m), 6100 ft (1859 m), 6246 ft (1904 m)

Difficulty: S5/T5

Distance: 64 miles one way

Elevation gain: 17,000 ft

Trip time: 6 days, plus 1 day for car shuttle

Best time of year: July to September

Maps: USGS Bogachiel Peak, Mount Carrie, Mount Christie, Mount Hoquiam, Hurricane Hill, Mount Queets; Custom Correct Seven Lakes Basin-Hoh, Elwha Valley, Quinault-Colonel Bob

Contact: Olympic National Park

Special considerations: Crampons, ice axes, and helmets advised; difficult stream crossing

GPS WAYPOINT ROUTE

1. Cat summit: 13 miles, 5940 ft (10U 449280mE 5305221mN)
2. Carrie summit: 15 miles, 6995 ft (10U 451583mE 5304544mN)
3. Cream Lake: 18 miles, 4237 ft (10U 455094mE 5300805mN)
4. Stephen summit: 19 miles, 6430 ft (10U 455555mE 5301827mN)
5. Ferry summit: 22 miles, 6157 ft (10U 457595mE 5298791mN)
6. Barnes summit: 29 miles, 5993 ft (10U 456951mE 5292247mN)
7. Dodwell Rixon Pass: 27 miles, 4800 ft (10U 455667mE 5292333mN)
8. Queets summit: 33 miles, 6480 ft (10U 455505mE 5289852mN)
9. Noyes summit: 48 miles, 6100 ft (10U 455494mE 5287349mN)
10. Elwha River crossing: 40 miles, 2600 ft (10U 457608mE 5289083mN)
11. Low Divide: 46 miles, 3600 ft (10U 458158mE 5285521mN)
12. Seattle summit: 47 miles, 6246 ft (10U 456769mE 5286374mN)

Named for William E. Bailey, proprietor of the *Seattle Press*, the Bailey Range is a spiraling chain of peaks paralleling the upper Hoh River at the perimeter of Mount Olympus. The Bailey Range contains multiple summits averaging 6500 feet in elevation with 6995-foot Mount Carrie being the highest.

The Bailey Range traverse is a high and remote cross-country trek of unique and matchless beauty—it is truly one of the finest high traverses in Washington. At almost all points, the succession of views far down to the forests of the Hoh Valley is echoed by the profile of snowcapped Mount Olympus. This stately mountain and its attendant peaks form an immediate picture that follows you throughout the traverse in a glorious, continuous panorama.

All of the peaks described here are optional side trips. Other subsidiary peaks could be added to the scrambles listed, but this description is not intended to exhaust all the possibilities. Instead, it includes the major peaks and should satisfy all but the most compulsive peakbagger.

The Bailey Range traverse is a physically and mentally demanding trip. Substantial scrambling skills are necessary to plan, execute, and enjoy this trip and to reach the end unscathed. The party must be comfortable with rock, snow, and occasional ice travel, display competent routefinding, and exhibit stamina carrying a full pack. The path is largely off trail and the fact that it is 6 days long adds to the physical and mental demands. There are

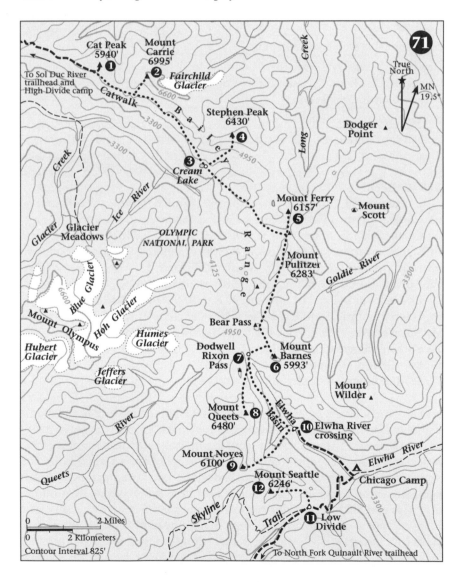

steep sections with exposure on some of the peaks, on the Catwalk near Cat Peak, and even on sections of narrow way trails for which the footing may seem delicate or dangerous. Crampons and ice axes may be needed for various snowfields including the Elwha Snow Finger, which may contain deep moats, holes, and thin snow bridges. Consider the Bailey Range traverse carefully, but if you have the desire and fortitude, this journey will be one that you will cherish for a lifetime.

Trailhead Directions: Drive US 101 west from Lake Crescent. Just past Fairholm at the western end of the lake, turn left on the Sol Duc River Road, signed "Sol Duc Hot Springs." Go past the Sol Duc Hot Springs Resort and Campground. At 14.2 miles reach the end of the road and the Sol Duc River trailhead. (104 miles, 2.5 hours from Bainbridge Island)

For the car shuttle, drive US 101 north from Aberdeen to Lake Quinault and get off on the South Shore Road. Drive 13 miles to an intersection. Turn left, cross the Quinault River, bear right on the North Fork Quinault Road and drive 3.5 miles to its end. Allow 1 day for the car shuttle trip. (142 miles, 3 hours from Bainbridge Island)

Standard Route:

Day 1: From the end of the Sol Duc River Road at 2000 feet, take the Sol Duc River Trail to Heart Lake at 8 miles, and camp near the High Divide at 8.5 miles.

Day 2: From camp, gain the 5100-foot crest of the High Divide and take the left fork at the trail junction. The spur trail of the High Divide Trail runs the ridge 3 miles east to a dead end on the side of Cat Peak. First scramble 200 feet up to the ridge top, on a steep way trail, and have a look at the Catwalk, immediately to the east. Drop packs for a scramble to the top of Cat Peak, back to the northwest. Scramble up past the 5600-foot false summit and then traverse on broken boulders to the true summit (1 hour from the packs). Retrieve packs, return to the abandoned trail, and continue on the steep, narrow Catwalk. There are plenty of good handholds and footholds, so use them freely.

The defined trail ends at the beginning of the Catwalk. To continue on the off-trail portion, traverse across the south slope of Mount Carrie using what is now a well-established way trail the entire way. It is easier to see the tread when going eastward. Drop packs along the way and scramble up the open slopes to the summit of Carrie.

Find excellent campsites midway between Carrie and Stephen in a hillside meadow near an enduring stream. There are also flat campsites 30 minutes past the Catwalk about 400 feet above the trail on the shoulder of Mount Carrie. A camp can also be established at Cream Lake.

Day 3: From Cream Lake, work easterly up through broken forest into the wide open spaces of upper Cream Lake basin. For Stephen Peak, drop the packs and ascend northerly up steep heather slopes to the ridge crest southeast of the summit. Contour northwest and climb up the narrow ridge on the northeast end of the summit (3 hours from the packs).

Retrieve the packs and continue south into the narrow valley just west of Mount Ferry. Scramble up and east between Mount Ferry and Point 6283 (Pulitzer). Continue up to the high plateau just south of the summit of Ferry.

Mount Pulitzer from the Bailey Range traverse (Photo by Dale Flynn)

Campsites are available, if you look around. Stroll to the nearby summit at your leisure. The eastern pinnacle is supposedly the highest.

Day 4: From camp, traverse south for 4 miles in high, open bench lands to Bear Pass. When coming from the north, avoid cliff bands on the steep slopes south of Bear Pass by staying high and following the ridgeline southeast toward Mount Barnes. Then walk easily down to Dodwell Rixon Pass. Along the way, drop the packs and do a short scramble up Barnes from its southwest corner.

Near Dodwell Rixon Pass (4800 feet), several campsites are possible. There is an excellent campsite at a nice lake 300 yards west of and 100 feet above the pass. To scramble Mount Queets from the pass, do an ascending traverse southwest and upward for 200 vertical feet. Traverse south on the eastern side of the ridge for 1 mile at the 5100 to 5300 foot level using benches, steep heather, rock and scree, and small ridge notches. Pass just below a major false summit buttress (Point 5819) and ascend scree and rock fields, then steep heather and small rock outcroppings to the summit ridge. Continue south on the ridge for 0.5 mile, easily bypassing several pinnacles and permanent snowfields. The actual summit is rather flat and humble, with a bit of rock sticking up (3 hours from the pass).

From the summit, it is possible to drop directly down to the Elwha Snow Finger at the "Big Snow Hump," but it is rather steep near the bottom of the descent. Otherwise, descend the scramble route and return to camp at Dodwell Rixon Pass.

Day 5: From Dodwell Rixon Pass, the Elwha Snow Finger descends at a moderate angle southeast to the upper Elwha River. Avalanches from Queets, Meany, Barnes, and Noyes pour tons of snow and debris into the narrow canyon, creating a very long and durable snow finger. Hazards of moats and melt holes exist, especially along the edges and where the stream runs under the snow, and the hazards may continue for quite a distance.

Descend the snow finger and cross to the southwest side of the river at about 3200 feet, about 1 mile below the "Big Snow Hump." Down below, the river drops into a steep, narrow gorge. A faint climber's trail, probably flagged, goes up a brushy slope to the right, crosses a ridge, and then emerges in the open meadows of Elwha Basin. Descend open slopes to the river.

For a scramble of Mount Noyes, drop the packs before crossing the river. Head southwest up the open valley toward the peak. Scramble up the steep, loose east skyline (3 hours from the packs).

Retrieve the packs, cross the river (hopefully on a nice, big log bridge), and immediately pick up the maintained trail, which descends to Chicago Camp in the Elwha River valley below. Take the right fork and continue up the valley for 3 miles to the Low Divide and established campsites.

For a scramble of Mount Seattle, walk to and directly behind the Low Divide Ranger Station. Then, ascend through open forest for 400 vertical feet, bearing slightly north. Traverse northwest, and then drop 100 feet to cross a creek bed in a major, straight, open drainage. Ascend west up the creek or follow way trails on the creek's north side to a large snow basin. Scramble snowfields and rock benches southward and then westward to the summit ridge. The south peak of Seattle lies slightly above. There is some good rock on the ridge top, and Seattle is, overall, an interesting and aesthetic scramble over a variety of terrain (3 hours from Low Divide).

Day 6: From the Low Divide, hike 16 miles down the North Fork Quinault River Trail to end your Bailey Range outing at the North Fork Ranger Station. If the party has time and energy, an alternative exit route is via the Skyline Trail, a high, scenic trail that traverses a number of pretty alpine basins. This route, which has a few scrambling sections of its own, meets up with the North Fork Quinault River Trail 24 miles from Low Divide.

72 MOUNT TOWNSEND

Elevation: 6280 ft (1914 m)

Difficulty: S2/T1

Distance: 8 miles

Elevation gain: 3200

Trip time: 7 hours

Time to summit: 4 hours

Best time of year: May to October

Maps: USGS Mount Townsend; Custom Correct Buckhorn Wilderness

Contact: Olympic National Park

GPS WAYPOINT ROUTE
1. Mount Townsend trailhead: 3400 ft (10U 497418mE 5300121mN)
2. Camp Windy: 2.3 miles, 5200 ft (10U 495783mE 5300279mN)
3. Summit ridge: 3.3 miles, 5900 ft (10U 495532mE 5300830mN)
4. Townsend summit: 4 miles, 6280 ft (10U 495654mE 5301372mN)

Mount Townsend is embraced as a winter and spring scramble because it has easy access and a trail that runs across the summit crest. As a northeastern corner post of the Olympic Mountains, Mount Townsend is well situated to provide a stunning outlook toward the entire Cascade Range, from the peaks in Canada to the three master volcanoes of Washington State: Mount Baker, Glacier Peak, and Mount Rainier. The shimmering ribbon of Puget Sound snakes through the hills and islands of the coast. The grillwork of Port Angeles, Bellingham to the north, and ports south along the mainland, interrupt the ice-clad spires of the Cascades.

Although the elevation of Townsend is not great by usual standards, the feeling of this easily accessible summit is of high, windswept tundra and alpine appeal. In May the snow level is significantly higher and the roads significantly clearer at this elevation than in the Cascade region. The south peak is 6280 feet, while the north peak is 6212 feet but seems higher. The summits are so evenly matched and close to each other that most scramblers travel to both. Soak up the view east over the waters to the Cascades and west over the rolling meadow ridges to the Olympics. The rugged peaks to the south are Mount Constance and farther away, The Brothers.

Trailhead Directions: Drive US 101 to 0.9 mile south of the Quilcene

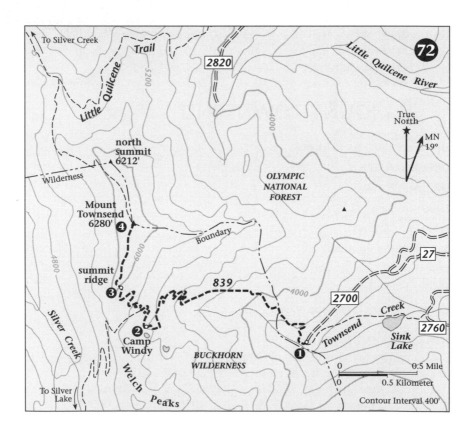

Mount Townsend (Photo by Jason Griffith)

Ranger Station, and then head west on Penny Creek Road. At 1.4 miles go left on Big Quilcene River Road, which becomes FS Road 27. At 13.4 miles pass up FS Road 2760, the lower of the two starts. At about 14 miles, find a sign that says "14 miles to 101." At this switchback there is also a sign "Mt Townsend Trail 1 mile." Continue left on FS Road 2700 for 2 miles to Mount Townsend Trail 839. (100 miles, 2.5 hours from Seattle)

Standard Route: From the Mount Townsend trailhead, ascend steadily in timber for 0.5 mile, and then through open steeper slopes up to Camp Windy (5200 feet). At 2.5 miles is a junction. Take the right fork heading upslope. Attain the summit ridge at 3.3 miles (5900 feet). Follow the crest, passing 100 feet below the first summit at 3.8 miles, and continue to the most northerly part of the ridge and the second summit.

From the south summit a trail connects with the Little Quilcene Trail, which leads west to Silver Creek and east to FS Road 2820. Do both summits, as they are almost the same in height, although the south peak is reported to be the highest.

Alternate Route: Townsend can also be approached from the Little Quilcene Trail via FS Road 2820.

73 MOUNT ELK LICK AND MOUNT LACROSSE

Elevations: 6517 ft (1987 m), 6417 ft (1956 m)	

Difficulty: S5/T5

Distance: 32 miles

Elevation gain: 6500 ft

Trip time: 3 days

Time to summit: 7 hours to Elk Lick summit; 4 hours from Elk Lick to LaCrosse

Best time of year: July to September

Maps: USGS The Brothers, Mount Steel; Custom Correct The Brothers-Mount Anderson

Contact: Olympic National Park

Special considerations: Beware of moderate rock fall. As of August 2000, the High Dose Bridge beyond Dose Forks on the West Fork Dosewallips Trail is out, making the Standard Route impassable. Use the Alternate Route to LaCrosse Pass and call Olympic National Park's Wilderness Information Center for current conditions (see Appendix D).

GPS WAYPOINT ROUTE
1. Dosewallips River trailhead: 1600 ft (10U 487629mE 5286909mN)
2. Junction: 9.4 miles, 3640 ft (10U 476481mE 5283212mN)
3. LaCrosse Pass: 13 miles, 5600 ft (10U 478291mE 5281214mN)
4. Elk Lick summit: 15 miles, 6517 ft (10U 480743mE 5281518mN)
5. LaCrosse summit: 18 miles, 6417 ft (10U 476674mE 5281101mN)

Situated on the Duckabush River–West Fork Dosewallips River divide, Elk Lick and LaCrosse are the high limits that make up the cleft of scenic and enchanting LaCrosse Pass. Deep in the interior of the Olympic National Park, this territory is more isolated and less frequented than other, outlying regions. But the mountain couple are deserving of the push, not only due to the remote nature of their location, but also for their terrain and vegetation, which are as pretty, wild, and untouched as any in the Olympics. A case in point, Elk Lick's original first ascent register from 1971 is still on the summit, with an average of one visit per year.

The first part of the trip follows the West Fork Dosewallips River Trail to Mount Anderson and the Anderson Glacier, one of the largest glaciers in the eastern Olympics. Along the way is Honeymoon Meadows, named by a Seattle couple celebrating their nuptials, who have long since celebrated their golden wedding anniversary. This is a renowned haven for wildflowers that stand out dramatically against the rugged background. Continuing on into the high country gives an even better perspective of Mounts Anderson, Henderson, Stone, and Steel. After camping at serene and heavenly LaCrosse

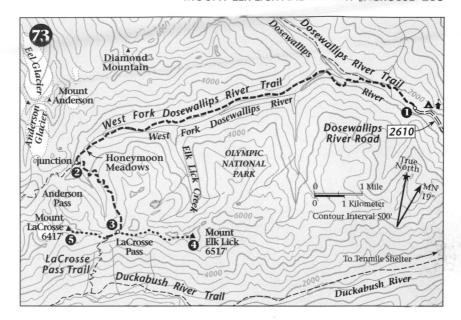

Pass, the distant duo of Elk Lick and LaCrosse can be combined for an athletic and lengthy summit day.

Trailhead Directions: Take the Seattle ferry to Bainbridge Island. Continue on SR 305 to SR 3. Go north on SR 3 and cross the Hood Canal Bridge. Continue 9 miles past the western end of the bridge and take US 101 south to Quilcene. Continue 11 miles to Brinnon. Alternatively, drive I-5 to Olympia and Exit 104, and then follow US 101 to just north of Brinnon.

Turn west on the Dosewallips River Road (FS Road 2610), reaching the end of pavement in 4.7 miles, the Elkhorn Campground junction at 10.7 miles, Constance Creek at 13.5 miles, and the road end at 15 miles. The Dosewallips River Trail begins behind the Dosewallips Campground and Ranger Station. (90 miles, 2.5 hours from Bainbridge Island)

Standard Route:

Day 1: From the trailhead at 1600 feet, hike the Dosewallips River Trail and at 1.4 miles, take the West Fork Dosewallips River Trail. Descend to campsites at 5 miles, and then climb again to Diamond Meadow (2700 feet). The trail crosses the river and begins a steady ascent. At 8.6 miles the valley opens into the broad, flat expanse of Honeymoon Meadows (3600 feet). At 9.4 miles, shortly after Honeymoon Meadows and before the trail ascends to Camp Siberia and Anderson Pass, take the left fork (east) leading to LaCrosse Pass. Continue hiking about 3 miles to LaCrosse Pass (5600 feet).

Campsites can be found just past the switchbacks near the pass in a basin about 50 feet above the trail. Water can be a problem in late season, but snow usually stays late in the basin nearby. Two campsites on the trail near the pass are not as desirable since they are located on sloping terrain.

Day 2: On summit day, prepare to scramble Elk Lick first. From camp head toward the saddle at 5880 feet, and then contour on the ridge for 0.3

Elk Lick (Photo by John Roper)

mile until a meadow just before another saddle at 5680 feet. If approaching from LaCrosse Pass, contour at 5500 feet, side-hilling the ridge for 0.6 mile to the meadow before the saddle at 5680 feet. Drop to 5100 feet in the meadow and contour through trees and meadows to a point below a rock face on a sub-ridge (a rock face can be seen before descending). Then traverse into the large flat meadow at 5200 feet.

From the meadow, head up the slope toward the right side of the saddle, at a bearing of 35 degrees, to 50 feet below a rock face. Then go left through a thin band of trees to a gully. Follow the gullies to the ridge but trend to the right. Follow the ridge toward the summit through tight-packed trees. At about 100 feet below the summit, contour to a rock face at the summit block and then scramble the rock along the edge of the trees for 20 feet before scrambling to the summit. Note that the trip to Elk Lick takes about 7 hours and it is much longer than it appears.

For LaCrosse, continue over LaCrosse Pass and toward the Duckabush River to the third switchback 140 feet below the pass. Leave the trail to gain the ridge. Follow the ridge to where it steepens to gain a false summit. At this point, descend 30 feet in a gully and go to a level point on the left ridge, traversing up an open slope left, below the false summit to a saddle. There are two bivy sites near the saddle. Do not ascend the scree up from the bivy sites, for this way is not a scramble. Contour for 40 feet along downsloping rock with treacherous loose pebbles, heading toward a 10-foot chimney covered with heather. Contouring on the downward sloping rocks is dicey, and the scrambler must learn to clean off and find or kick steps. This area may be somewhat more than a scramble, but with patience and good balance, the way is straightforward.

Ascend the chimney and contour up the slope to the ridge. Follow steep heather to the summit. Use an ice ax for balance on the perches. (Climb day combined: 7 miles, 2800 feet, 11 hours)

Day 3: Return via West Fork Dosewallips River Trail to the cars. If a car shuttle has been arranged, walk along the Duckabush River Trail to the alternative terminus.

Alternate Route: LaCrosse Pass can be approached from the Duckabush River Trail and the LaCross Pass Trail. Drive US 101 for 2.2 miles north of Hoodsport to 0.2 mile past the Duckabush River Bridge. At milepost 310, turn west on the Duckabush River Road, which at 3.7 miles becomes FS Road 2510. At 6 miles past the horse corral, turn right on FS Road 011, and drive 0.1 mile to Duckabush River Trail 803.

For Elk Lick, leave the Duckabush River Trail 3 miles above Tenmile Shelter (2100 feet). This is about 0.1 mile above the point where Crazy Creek joins the opposite side of the river but before another stream crossing. A camp can be made in the vicinity. Obtain water before leaving the trail. Climb north into steep forest, keeping to the right of the stream. Continue climbing north past timberline (5000 feet) to about 5500 feet. From this point, ascend a ridge northwest to about 6000 feet and scramble a steep snow chute, or in later season a gully. Continue up the east shoulder to the summit. This route takes 7 hours from Tenmile Shelter.

74 THE BROTHERS

Elevation: 6866 ft (2093 m)	
Difficulty: S5/T4	
Distance: 14 miles	
Elevation gain: 6200 ft	
Trip time: 13 hours; 1-2 days	
Time to summit: 8 hours	
Best time of year: May to October	
Maps: USGS The Brothers; Custom Correct The Brothers-Mount Anderson	
Contact: Olympic National Park	
Special considerations: Helmets necessary	

GPS WAYPOINT ROUTE
1. Lena Lake trailhead: 680 ft (10U 488768mE 5271625mN)
2. Lena Lake: 3 miles, 1960 ft (10U 487802mE 5273423mN)
3. Lena Forks Camp: 6 miles, 3100 ft (10U 490600mE 5276323mN)
4. The Brothers summit: 7 miles, 6866 ft (10U 489541mE 5277716mN)

A principal landmark of the western horizon from Seattle, the double summits of The Brothers fork into the blood red summer sun as it sets. The north peak is a climb, whereas the higher south peak is a scramble. The Brothers are situated in the Hamma Hamma River drainage on the eastern side of the Olympic Mountains. But only the very summit is in Olympic National Park; the eastern footings are within The Brothers Wilderness. Although Lena Lake on the approach to the mountain should have been a logical inclusion into The Brothers Wilderness in 1984, it was omitted because of a proposed hydroelectric project.

This area is heavily used by fishermen and hikers, but is commendable for exploration by scramblers who enjoy pristine, rushing waters in the deep shade of old growth forest. Part of the scramble to The Brothers passes under a steep narrow gully called the "Hourglass," which collects falling rocks and avalanche debris from the entire upper south slope. But most of the route travels a broad moderate slope. The trip is a 1-day strenuous venture, or a 2-day, more leisurely jaunt. It is also remarkable for the reverse perspective eastward toward the Seattle skyline, with the expanse of the Cascades from Baker to Rainier framing the picture.

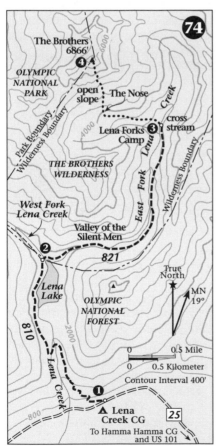

Trailhead Directions: Take the Seattle ferry to Bainbridge Island. Drive north on SR 305, and then on SR 3. Cross the Hood Canal Bridge, and drive west on SR 104 and then south on US 101. About 24 miles south of Brinnon, and before Eldon, turn right on FS Road 25 to Hamma Hamma Campground. Alternatively, drive through Tacoma over the Tacoma Narrows Bridge. Drive US 101 north past Hoodsport, cross the Hamma Hamma River Bridge, and 0.5-mile beyond Waketickeh Creek turn left on FS Road 24 and right on FS Road 2480 to the campground. Then drive on FS 25 Road for 8 miles to Lena Lake Trail 810. (80 miles, 2 hours from Bainbridge Island)

Standard Route: Begin at the Lena Lake trailhead (680 feet) and take Lena Lake Trail 810 up to and around Lena Lake. Note that the Lena Lake Trail is open to bicycles. Cross West Fork Lena Creek and continue up East Fork Lena Creek through the Valley of the Silent Men on Trail 821.

On the approach to The Brothers (Photo by Susan Alford)

At 6 miles, reach the Lena Forks Camp at the final creek crossing and the end of the established trail (3100 feet).

Follow a way trail along the left fork of the creek roughly northwest until reaching a small meadow. Cross the meadow and ascend west across "The Nose," a tree-covered ridge, to a gully that is ordinarily free of snow. Scramble up the gully on the left. In the second meadow at a gigantic boulder (5000 feet) go east, following rock ledges and scrambling on loose scree to an open, rocky slope. Climb north about 200 yards, then bear left into the upper couloir to about 6000 feet where the slope opens up. Look for a notch before the saddle is reached, with the summit to the right. Pass through the notch and scramble the last 200 feet through some loose rock to the summit, mainly on a boot trail.

75 MOUNT ELLINOR

Elevation: 5944 ft (1812 m)	
Difficulty: S1/T2	
Distance: 6 miles	
Elevation gain: 3200 ft	
Trip time: 5 hours	
Time to summit: 3 hours	
Best time of year: May to October	
Maps: USGS Mount Skokomish; Custom Correct Mount Skokomish-Lake Cushman	
Contact: Olympic National Forest, Hood Canal Ranger District	
Special considerations: Cliffs may be encountered on the route down.	

GPS WAYPOINT ROUTE

1. Lower Mount Ellinor trailhead: 2600 ft (10U 482619mE 5261278mN)
2. Upper Mount Ellinor trailhead: 1.7 miles, 3600 ft (10U 480974mE 5261512mN)

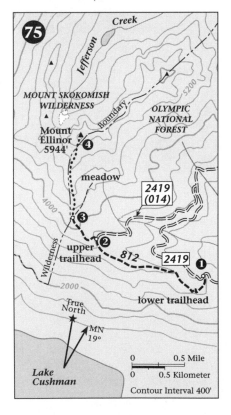

3. Meadow junction: 2 miles, 4100 ft (10U 480586mE 5261751mN)
4. Ellinor summit: 3 miles, 5944 ft (10U 480476mE 5262958mN)

Mount Ellinor was an old favorite of early scramblers long before Seattle was a megalopolis and the Hood Canal was a shoreline of vacation homes. The summit is relatively unpretentious, but due to its location at the end of the Olympics, the outlook toward the east is divine. From the top of Mount Ellinor, Puget Sound is exposed from end to end, with Glacier Peak, and Mounts Rainier and Adams on the horizon. In the other direction, in the background are Mount Olympus, Mount Stone, and The Brothers, while in the foreground are the abrupt cliffs of Mount Washington. The Mount Skokomish Wilderness lies just to the west and north.

George Davidson, a surveyor of

Puget Sound, named the major peaks in this sector of the range. He drew upon the Fauntleroy family of his employer, calling the southernmost peak Ellinor for the youngest daughter, the double-summit peak for her brothers, and the highest point for Constance, her older sister.

Logging roads and a new trail constructed by the Olympia branch of The Mountaineers and the Olympic National Forest have significantly shortened and simplified the trip to Ellinor's summit, which is now in reach of even inexperienced scramblers. When snow covers the slopes and the roads are closed to most other areas, Ellinor provides a short but refreshing spring adventure. The payoff is the view of the surrounding peaks, with the detailed tableau of the Cascades rimming the eastern skyline.

Trailhead Directions: Drive US 101 along Hood Canal to the center of Hoodsport. Turn west and go 9 miles on the Lake Cushman Road to a junction. Turn right at 1.6 miles on FS Road 24, and then left on Big Creek Road (FS Road 2419). At 4.8 miles from FS Road 24, pass the lower trailhead that is used when the road is blocked above. At 6.4 miles go left on FS Road 2419(014) another 0.7 mile to the end of the road and upper Mount Ellinor trailhead. (70 miles, 1.75 hour from Bainbridge Island)

Standard Route: The standard route begins at the lower Mount Ellinor trailhead at 2600 feet. Find the trail that climbs steeply up the nose of the ridge. At 1.7 miles, reach the upper Mount Ellinor trailhead. Continue upslope past a trail fork that leads right to a small meadow. The trail climbs steeply through meadows, forest, rockslides, scree slopes, and flower gardens. The tread is sometimes hard to find. Gain 1100 feet in 1.5 miles to reach the summit block. The final 50 feet consists of a rock scramble.

Return on the trail, or if the slopes are covered with snow, enjoy miniglissades. But be careful: the cliffs can suddenly appear on the way down.

Alternate Route: If early in the year before the road is open, leave the car at the first crossing of Big Creek at 3.6 miles (2200 feet) and hike up through a logged-over area to the hogback ridge. Climb to the ridge's junction with the Mount Ellinor Trail at just under 4000 feet.

Mount Ellinor (Photo by John Roper)

Appendix A:
Scramble Statistics

Scramble	Elevation	Difficulty	Season*	Miles	Gain (feet)	Days
Abernathy	8321	S5/T4	L	10	5200	1
Adams	12,276	S5/T4	M	12	6800	1
Alta	6250	S4/T1	E	12	4000	1
Angeles	6454	S1/T3	M	6	1800	1
Bailey Range Traverse	6995	S5/T5	M	68	17,000	6
Baring	6125	S4/T5	M	9	4000	1
Big Craggy and West Craggy	8470	S4/T4	L	9	5600	2
Bill, Bean, and Volcanic Neck	6917	S4/T5	M	11	4900	1
Boulder, Everett, and Appleton	6030	S5/T4	M	19	5800	2
Brothers	6866	S5/T4	E	14	6200	2
Carne	7085	S2/T1	M	8	3600	1
Cashmere	8501	S5/T3	M	17	5700	1
Chiwawa	8459	S5/T5	M	18	5700	2
Church	6315	S3/T5	M	9	4100	1
Colchuck	8705	S5/T5	E	13	5100	1
Curtis Gilbert	8184	S4/T4	M	18	4500	2
Daniel	7960	S5/T4	M	16	5200	2
Del Campo	6610	S4/T5	M	12	4500	1
Dirtyface	6240	S5/T4	E	13	6300	1
Dragontail	8840	S5/T5	M	14	5600	1
Echo and Observation	8364	S4/T4	M	11	3800	1
Elk Lick and LaCrosse	6517	S5/T5	M	32	6500	3

Ellinor	5944	S1/T2	E	6	3200	1
Enchantment	8520	S5/T2	L	24	7500	2
Entiat Crest	8590	S5/T5	M	42	14,000	5
Esmeralda	6765	S3/T3	M	8	3000	1
Fay, Pleasant, and Hessong	6492	S2/T2	L	6	3000	1
First Mother and Castle	6480	S2/T3	L	5	2400	1
Fortress and Buck	8674	S5/T5	L	40	10,900	4
Gilbert	8023	S4/T4	L	14	4600	2
Goat Island	7288	S3/T3	M	12	4000	1
Governors Ridge and Barrier	6620	S4/T5	M	11	3800	1
Granite and Trico	7144	S4/T3	L	19	4400	1
Grindstone	7533	S5/T3	M	10	5100	1
Hadley	7515	S5/T4	L	14	4700	1
Hannegan	6187	S2/T1	E	10	3100	1
Hibox	6560	S4/T4	M	10	3900	1
Hock	7750	S5/T4	M	18	4500	1
Hoodoo	8464	S3/T3	L	11	4500	1
Index	5979	S5/T4	M	8	4100	1
Ingalls South	7640	S4/T3	L	11	3600	1
Kaleetan	6259	S4/T4	M	12	4000	1
Kendall	5784	S2/T2	M	10	2800	1
Koppen and Iron	6519	S4/T2	E	14	5000	2
Labyrinth	6376	S1/T2	L	7	2700	1
Little Annapurna	8440	S4/T1	L	16	5500	2
Mastiff and Howard	7063	S5/T3	M	13	5500	1
Maude and Seven Fingered Jack	9082	S5/T4	L	14	6900	3
Monument and Lake	8592	S5/T4	M	33	10,400	3
Naches and Yakima	6452	S1/T4	L	5	1600	1

Scramble	Elevation	Difficulty	Season*	Miles	Gain (feet)	Days
North Gardner and Gardner	8956	S5/T4	E	27	8100	3
Osceola, Lago, and Carru	8745	S5/T4	M	40	11,500	4
Palisades and Marcus	7070	S3/T3	M	9	3400	1
Pass Butte and Lost Peak	8464	S5/T2	M	42	14,200	3
Pilchuck	5324	S2/T3	E	10	2900	1
Ptarmigan	8614	S4/T1	E	38	7200	3
Pugh	7224	S5/T1	M	11	5500	1
Red	5890	S3/T3	M	10	2900	1
Remmel	8685	S4/T1	M	32	5400	3
Robinson	8726	S5/T5	L	14	6500	2
Roosevelt	5835	S4/T5	M	14	3500	1
Ruby	7408	S5/T2	M	7	5600	1
Saint Helens	8365	S5/T4	E	12	5700	1
Sawtooth Ridge	8795	S5/T3	E	41	17,800	5
Silver	5605	S3/T3	E	9	3800	1
Skookum and Jolly	6443	S4/T2	M	9	2400	1
Snoqualmie and Guye	6278	S3/T3	E	7	4200	1
Snowking	7433	S5/T4	M	11	6500	2
Sperry and Vesper	6214	S5/T4	M	9	5800	1
Tatoosh Range Traverse	6562	S5/T5	M	10	5000	1
Three Fingers	6854	S4/T5	L	15	4200	1
Townsend	6280	S2/T1	E	8	3200	1
Wedge	6885	S2/T2	E	5	2600	1
Wow	6040	S4/T3	E	9	4400	1
Yellow Aster Butte	6241	S1/T1	L	8	2800	1

*Seasons are E=early (May to June), M=middle (July to August), and L=late (September to October)

Appendix B:
Scramble by Season

EARLY SEASON (MAY TO JUNE)
Alta
Brothers
Colchuck
Dirtyface
Ellinor
Hannegan
Koppen and Iron
North Gardner and Gardner
Pilchuck
Ptarmigan
Saint Helens
Sawtooth Ridge
Silver
Snoqualmie and Guye
Townsend
Wedge
Wow

MID-SEASON (JULY TO AUGUST)
Adams
Angeles
Bailey Range Traverse
Baring
Bill, Bean, and Volcanic Neck
Boulder, Everett, and Appleton
Carne
Cashmere
Curtis Gilbert
Daniel
Del Campo
Dragontail
Echo and Observation
Elk Lick and LaCrosse
Entiat Crest
Esmeralda
Goat Island
Governors Ridge and Barrier
Grindstone
Hibox
Hock
Index
Kaleetan
Kendall
Mastiff and Howard
Monument and Lake
Osceola, Lago, and Carru
Palisades and Marcus
Pass Butte and Lost Peak
Pugh
Red
Remmel
Roosevelt
Ruby
Skookum and Jolly
Snowking
Sperry and Vesper
Tatoosh Range Traverse

LATE SEASON (SEPTEMBER TO OCTOBER)
Abernathy
Big Craggy and West Craggy
Chiwawa
Church
Enchantment
Fay, Pleasant, and Hessong
First Mother and Castle
Fortress and Buck
Gilbert
Granite and Trico
Hadley
Hoodoo
Ingalls South
Labyrinth
Little Annapurna
Maude and Seven Fingered Jack
Naches and Yakima
Robinson
Three Fingers
Yellow Aster Butte

Appendix C:
Equipment Lists

ALL TRIPS
The Ten Essentials
Map
Compass
Headlamp with spare bulbs
 and batteries
Extra food
Extra clothing

Sunglasses
First-aid supplies
Pocket knife
Matches in waterproof container
 or lighter
Fire starter

Other Essentials
Water and water bottles
 with purification system
Altimeter
Watch

Emergency shelter
Sealable plastic bags to carry out
 toilet paper and trash

Clothing
Boots
Socks, inner liner and outer
Long underwear
Synthetic pants or shorts
Wind parka
Rain parka

Synthetic hat
Sun hat or visor
Gloves
Wind/rain pants
Gaiters (short or long)
Sweatband or bandanna

Equipment and Supplies
Food
Pack
Ice Ax
Sunscreen and lip protection

Toilet paper
Insect repellent
Whistle
Moleskin

Optional Equipment and Supplies
Camera and film
Binoculars

Energy bars and sports drink
Insulated seat pad

GEAR FOR SELECTED SCRAMBLES
Helmet
Crampons
Carabiners
Light climbing rope or hand line

Prusik slings for hand line
Goggles
Snowshoes

GEAR FOR OVERNIGHT TRIPS
Sleeping bag and stuff sack
Sleeping pad
Tent or bivy sack
Ground cloth
Water container
Stove, fuel, and accessories

Spoon and cup
Pots and cleaning pad
Toiletries
Camp footwear or waterproof socks
Garbage bags for boots and pack cover

Appendix D:
Contact Information

AVALANCHE HAZARD AND SNOW INFORMATION

Mount Hood/South Washington	503-326-2400
National Weather Service Forecast	206-526-6087
Northwest Weather and Avalanche Center	206-526-6677
	www.nwac.noaa.gov
Recreation Information Center	206-470-4060
Road Information	206-455-7900
Sno-Park Information	206-586-0185
State Department of Natural Resources	360-902-1650
State Department of Wildlife	360-902-2200
State Parks and Recreation	1-800-233-0321
U.S. Bureau of Land Management	509-536-1200
U.S. Geological Survey	509-353-2524

NATIONAL PARK SERVICE

Mount Rainier National Park
Park Headquarters Communications Center
Tahoma Woods, Star Route
Ashford, WA 98304
360-569-2211, ext. 3314
www.nps.gov/mora/

North Cascades National Park
North Cascades National Park Service Complex
Park Headquarters
2105 Highway 20
Sedro Woolley, WA 98284
360-856-5700
www.nps.gov/noca/

Ross Lake National Recreation Area
7280 Ranger Station Road
Marblemount, WA 98267
360-873-4500
www.nps.gov/rola/

Olympic National Park
Wilderness Information Center
3002 Mount Angeles Road
Port Angeles, WA 98362
360-565-3100
360-565-3131 (recorded message)
www.nps.gov/olym/

U.S. FOREST SERVICE

Gifford Pinchot National Forest
www.fs.fed.us/gpnf/

Mount Adams Ranger District
2455 Highway 141
Trout Lake, WA 98650-9724
509-395-3400

Mount Saint Helens National Volcanic Monument
42218 Northeast Yale Bridge Road
Amboy, WA 98601-9715
360-247-3900 (office)
360-247-3903 (recorded message)
360-247-3961 (climbing)

Mount Baker–Snoqualmie National Forest
www.fs.fed.us/r6/mbs/

Darrington Ranger Station
1405 Emmens Street
Darrington, WA 98241
360-436-1155

Mount Baker Ranger Station
2105 State Route 20
Sedro Woolley, WA 98284
360-856-5700

North Bend Office
42404 SE North Bend Way
North Bend, WA 98405
425-888-1421

Skykomish Ranger Station
74920 Northeast Stevens Pass Highway
Skykomish, WA 98288
360-677-2414

Okanogan National Forest
www.fs.fed.us/r6/okanogan/

Methow Valley Ranger District
P.O. Box 188
502 Glover Street
Twisp, WA 98856
509-997-2131

Olympic National Forest
www.fs.fed.us/r6/olympic/

Hood Canal Ranger District
Hoodsport Office
P.O. Box 68
150 N Lake Cushman Road
Hoodsport, WA 98548
360-877-5254

Wenatchee National Forest
www.fs.fed.us/r6/wenatchee/

Cle Elum Ranger District
803 West Second Street
Cle Elum, WA 98922
509-674-4411

Entiat Ranger District
P.O. Box 476
2108 Entiat Way
Entiat, WA 98822
509-784-1511

Lake Wenatchee Ranger District
22976 State Highway 207
Leavenworth, WA 98826
509-763-3103

Leavenworth Ranger District
600 Sherbourne Street
Leavenworth, WA 98826
509-548-6977

Naches Ranger District
10061 Highway 12
Naches, WA 98937
509-653-2205

PRIVATE ORGANIZATIONS
Washington Trails Association
206-625-1367
www.wta.org

Index

A

Abernathy Peak   87–88
Adams, Mount   216–219
age   10, 15
alpine climb   13
Alta Mountain   174–175
altimeter   23, 27
Angeles, Mount   224–226
Appleton, Mount 222–224
avalanche 30, 34, 41

B

Bailey Range Traverse   227–231
Baring Mountain   117–119
Barnes, Mount   230
Barrier Peak   207–208
Bean Peak   188–190
belay   13
Big Craggy Peak   73–75
Bigelow, Mount   95, 96
Bill Peak   188–190
bivouac   26, 29–30, 31, 39
boots   26, 35
Boulder Peak   222–224
Brothers, The   237–239
brush   25, 27
Buck Mountain   97–100
Buttermilk Ridge   94, 95–96

C

camping   38–39
Cardinal Peak   110
Carne Mountain   112–114
Carrie, Mount   229
Carru, Mount   64–67
Cashmere Mountain   145–147
Castle Peak   193–195
Cat Peak   229

Cheops   94, 96
Chiwawa Mountain   101–103
Church Mountain   45–47
Chutla Peak   211
class   13, 40
climate   13–14
climbing protection   10, 40
clothing   25–26
Colchuck Peak   150–153
compass   23, 26
conditioning   16–17, 28
conservation   10, 37, 40
contact information   43, 247–249
convergence zones   13
Cooney   95, 96
Courtney   94, 95
crampons   27
Curtis Gilbert, Mount   214–216

D

danger   15, 28, 32–35
Daniel, Mount   138–140
dehydration   28, 36
Del Campo Peak   132–135
Denman Peak   210
difficulty   40–41
Dirtyface Peak   123–125
distance   41
Dragontail Peak   153–155

E

Eagle Peak   211
Echo Rock   198–200
elevation   40, 43
elevation gain   41
Elk Lick, Mount   234–237
Ellinor, Mount   240–241
Emerald Peak   110

emergency 26, 30–32
Enchantment Peak 156–158
Entiat Crest 107–112
equipment 26–28, 246
Esmeralda Peaks 186–187
Everett Peak 222–224

F
Fay Peak 195–198
Ferry, Mount 229–230
first aid 26, 30
mountain-oriented first aid 30–31
First Mother Mountain 193–195
Fortress Mountain 97–100
Gardner Mountain 56–58
gender 16
giardia 36

G
Gilbert Mountain 84–86
Global Positioning System (GPS)
    23, 32, 43
Goat Island Mountain 203–205
Governors Ridge 207–208
GPS waypoint route 23, 43
Granite Mountain 140–143
Grindstone Mountain 143–144
Guye Peak 167–169

H
Hadley Peak 51–53
hand line 27
handhold 18, 33
Hannegan Peak 49–51
hazards 28, 30, 32–36, 44
health 11, 17
heat exhaustion 32–33
Hessong Rock 195–198
Hibox Mountain 176–177
Hock Mountain 58–60
Hoodoo Peak 89–90
Howard, Mount 121–123
human-waste disposal 38
hypothermia 25, 30, 32

I
ice ax 18, 27
Index, Mount 115–117
Ingalls South Peak 183–185
insects 35–36
Iron Peak 191–192

J
Jolly Mountain 181–183
judgment 15, 28, 29

K
Kaleetan Peak 162–164
Kendall Peak 172–173
Koppen Mountain 191–192

L
LaCrosse, Mount 234–237
Labyrinth Mountain 119–121
Lago, Mount 64–67
Lake Mountain 79–80
land management 11, 21, 20, 37
Lane Peak 210
leadership 15, 30, 39
Leave No Trace 39
lightning 33
Little Annapurna 158–161
Lost Peak 76–79
lost, if you are 31–32

M
maps 22–23, 25, 26, 43
using contours 21–22, 25, 31
Marcus Peak 201–203
Martin Peak 94–96
Mastiff, Mount 121–123
Monument Peak 79–81
Mount Maude 104–107
Mountaineers, The 12, 14

N
Naches Peak 205–206
navigation 21–23, 31
North Gardner Mountain 56–58

Northwest Forest Pass   21
Noyes, Mount   231
nutrition   28

O
Observation Rock   198–200
Osceola Peak   64–67
Oval Peak   94, 96

P
Palisades, The   201–203
Pass Butte   76–79
permits   20–21
Pilchuck, Mount   126–128
Pinnacle Mountain   110, 112
Pinnacle Peak   210
Pleasant, Mount   195–198
Plummer Peak   210
Ptarmigan Peak   68–70
Pugh, Mount   130–132
Pulitzer, Mount   229

Q
Queets, Mount   230

R
Red Mountain   170–171
Remmel Mountain   71–73
rescue   29, 31, 32
rest step   18
risk   15, 28
Robinson Mountain   82–83
rock fall   18, 33
Roosevelt, Mount   165–167
routefinding   24–25, 28, 34
Ruby Mountain   53–55

S
safety   28–32, 44
Saint Helens, Mount   219–221
Saska Peak   110
Sawtooth Ridge   91–96
scrambling
    areas   40

benefits   11, 16
computers and   11, 22
definition   10, 13
difficulty   13, 40–41
skills   15, 17–19, 34
Seattle, Mount   231
self–arrest   18, 27
Seven Fingered Jack   104–107
Silver Peak   178–180
Skookum, Mount   181–183
Snoqualmie Mountain   167–169
Snowking Mountain   60–63
speed of travel   22, 29
Sperry Peak   135–137
standard route   43
Star Peak   94, 96
Stephen Peak   229
stream crossings   27, 34–35

T
Tatoosh Range Traverse   209–211
Ten Essentials   26, 29, 246
Three Fingers South Peak   128–130
time of year   41, 245
time to summit 41
Townsend, Mount   231–233
trailhead directions 43
Trico Mountain   140–143
trip planning   20–21
trip time   41
turnaround time   29

U
UTM grid   23

V
Vesper Peak   135–137
Volcanic Neck   188–190

W
Wahpenayo Peak   211
Washington Trails Association   21
water purification   27–28, 36
weather 13–14, 32–33

Wedge Mountain   147–150
West Craggy Peak   73–75
wilderness areas   20, 40
wilderness ethics   37–40
wildlife   35
Wow, Mount   212–213

Y
Yakima Peak   205–206
Yellow Aster Butte   47–49

About the Author

Peggy Goldman is an avid outdoorswoman and accomplished climber and scrambler who has years of experience backpacking, scrambling, and climbing throughout Washington State. She has been a member of The Mountaineers Club for more than ten years, has served on the Alpine Scrambling Committee, and has been a Scrambling Leader since 1994. Goldman has extensive experience with map and compass and GPS use. For over twenty years she was a staff physician in the Department of Emergency Medical Services at Swedish Medical Center in Seattle. She is presently a medical consultant and writer

Photo by John Roper

THE MOUNTAINEERS, founded in 1906, is a nonprofit outdoor activity and conservation club, whose mission is "to explore, study, preserve, and enjoy the natural beauty of the outdoors...." Based in Seattle, Washington, the club is now the third-largest such organization in the United States, with 15,000 members and five branches throughout Washington State.

The Mountaineers sponsors both classes and year-round outdoor activities in the Pacific Northwest, which include hiking, mountain climbing, ski-touring, snowshoeing, bicycling, camping, kayaking and canoeing, nature study, sailing, and adventure travel. The club's conservation division supports environmental causes through educational activities, sponsoring legislation, and presenting informational programs. All club activities are led by skilled, experienced volunteers, who are dedicated to promoting safe and responsible enjoyment and preservation of the outdoors.

If you would like to participate in these organized outdoor activities or the club's programs, consider a membership in The Mountaineers. For information and an application, write or call The Mountaineers, Club Headquarters, 300 Third Avenue West, Seattle, WA 98119; 206-284-6310.

The Mountaineers Books, an active, nonprofit publishing program of the club, produces guidebooks, instructional texts, historical works, natural history guides, and works on environmental conservation. All books produced by The Mountaineers Books fulfill the club's mission.

Send or call for our catalog of more than 500 outdoor titles:

The Mountaineers Books
1001 SW Klickitat Way, Suite 201
Seattle, WA 98134
800-553-4453
mbooks@mountaineers.org
www.mountaineersbooks.org

Other titles you may enjoy from The Mountaineers Books:

BACKPACKER'S EVERYDAY WISDOM: 1001 Expert Tips for Hikers,
Karen Berger
Expert tips and tricks for hikers and backpackers selected from one of the
most popular *BACKPACKER* magazine columns.

EXPLORING WASHINGTON'S WILD AREAS: A Guide for Hikers,
Backpackers, Climber, X-C Skiers & Paddlers, 2nd Edition, *Marge and*
Ted Mueller
A guide to the undisturbed trails of Washington's federally preserved
backcountry, featuring 55 wildernesses and roadless areas and over 1000
mapped trails.

HIKING WASHINGTON'S GEOLOGY, *Scott Babcock and Bob Carson*
Explores the geologic history of Washington's dramatic landscape. Four to
thirteen hikes are listed for each of eight different regions exemplifying the
major events that have shaped the area.

100 HIKES IN™ SERIES: The most comprehensive and useful guides to
hiking regions across the United States. These are our fully detailed, best-
selling hiking guides with complete descriptions, maps, and photos. Chock-
full of trail data, including access, mileage, elevation, hiking time, and the
best season to go; safety tips; and wilderness etiquette.
    100 CLASSIC HIKES IN™ WASHINGTON, *Ira Spring and Harvey Manning*
    100 HIKES IN™ WASHINGTON'S NORTH CASCADES NATIONAL
       PARK REGION, 3rd Edition, *Ira Spring and Harvey Manning*
    100 HIKES IN™ WASHINGTON'S SOUTH CASCADES & OLYMPICS,
       3rd Edition, *Ira Spring and Harvey Manning*
    50 HIKES IN™ MOUNT RAINIER NATIONAL PARK, 4th Edition, *Ira Spring*
       and Harvey Manning
    100 HIKES IN™ WASHINGTON'S ALPINE LAKES, 3rd Edition, *Vicky Spring,*
       Ira Spring, and Harvey Manning
    100 HIKES IN™ WASHINGTON'S GLACIER PEAK REGION: The North
       Cascades, 4th Edition, *Ira Spring and Harvey Manning*

LEAVE NO TRACE: A Guide to the New Wilderness Etiquette, 2nd
Edition, *Annette McGivney*
A guide to realistic and doable practices for moving gently through the
land. Based on the Leave No Trace ethic and techniques as developed by
the National Outdoor Leadership School.